Lecture Notes in Computer Science 6529

Commenced Publication in 1973
Founding and Former Series Editors:
Gerhard Goos, Juris Hartmanis, and Jan van Leeuwen

Francisco V. Cipolla Ficarra
Carlos de Castro Lozano   Emma Nicol
Andreas Kratky   Miguel Cipolla-Ficarra (Eds.)

Human-Computer Interaction, Tourism and Cultural Heritage

First International Workshop, HCITOCH 2010
Brescello, Italy, September 7-8, 2010
Revised Selected Papers

 Springer

Volume Editors

Francisco V. Cipolla Ficarra
HCI Lab., Via Pascoli, S. 15 - CP 7, 24121 Bergamo, Italy
E-mail: ficarra@alaipo.com

Carlos de Castro Lozano
EATCO Research Group, Universitiy of Cordoba, Campus Rabanales
14071 Cordoba, Spain
E-mail: malcaloc@uco.es

Emma Nicol
University of Strathclyde, Computer and Information Sciences
Livingstone Tower, 26 Richmond st., Glasgow G1 1XH, UK
E-mail: emma.nicol@cis.strath.ac.uk

Andreas Kratky
University of Southern California, Interactive Media Division
School of Cinematic Arts
900 West 34th Street, SCA 201, Los Angeles, CA 90089-2211, USA
E-mail: akratky@cinema.usc.edu

Miguel Cipolla-Ficarra
HCI Lab., Via Pascoli, S. 15 - CP 7, 24121 Bergamo, Italy
E-mail: ficarra@ainci.com

ISSN 0302-9743   e-ISSN 0302-9743
ISBN 978-3-642-18347-8   e-ISBN 978-3-642-18348-5
DOI 10.1007/978-3-642-18348-5
Springer Heidelberg Dordrecht London New York

Library of Congress Control Number: 2010942521

CR Subject Classification (1998): H.4, H.5, C.2, H.3, I.2, D.2

LNCS Sublibrary: SL 3 – Information Systems and Application, incl. Internet/Web
and HCI

Typesetting: Camera-ready by author, data conversion by Scientific Publishing Services, Chennai, India

Printed on acid-free paper

Springer is part of Springer Science+Business Media (www.springer.com)

Preface

One of the key elements in the evolution of humankind has been creativity. Creativity is a term that is associated with the originality of solutions in the face of some given problems, which have led the scientific community to accumulate a series of discoveries and inventions along time that have revolutionized the daily coexistence of human beings.

New technologies offer us a series of instruments to develop the potential of human beings with the goal of increasing the quality of life of millions of users of interactive systems in our global village. The relationship between the triad computer science, quality design and communicability has proven very productive in the new millennium.

In the current era of qualitative communication, the present virtual space is intended to be a meeting point of all those who freely wish to boost and perfect the set of strategies and techniques to improve the human–computer interaction, tourism and cultural heritage. The main goal is to facilitate communicability and make the fruition of the new technologies more pleasant.

Our effort focuses on finding the common denominator between the human–computer interaction, cultural heritage and the global village. That is, we address all those who are currently working to increase the quality of life of human beings through the new technologies and all their derivations, wanting to know the latest advances in the factual and formal science. This international workshop serves as a meeting point to boost the current and future lines of research of investigators belonging to universities, governmental bodies and enterprises and industries of the private sector.

The Program Committee of the workshop consisted of Albert, C. (Spain), Anderson, S. (USA), Balsamo, A. (USA), Bellandi, V. (Italy), Bleecker, J. (USA), Buzzi, M. (Italy), Cipolla-Ficarra, M. (Italy and Spain), Colorado-Castellary, A. (Spain), Crestani, F. (Switzerland), Cuevas-Aedo, I. (Spain), De Castro-Lozano, C. (Spain), Díaz-Pérez. P. (Spain), Dormido-Bencomo, S. (Spain), El Sadik, A. (Canada), Fogli, D. (Italy), Fotouhi, F. (USA), Garrido-Lora, M. (Spain), Griffith, S. (Jamaica), Grosky. W. (USA), Guarinos-Galán, V. (Spain), Guerrero-Ginel, J. (Spain), Hadad, G. (Argentina), Hourcade, J. (USA), Ilavarasan. V. (India), Kratky, A. (Germany), Lau, A. (Australia), Lau, F. (China), Levialdi-Ghiron, S. (Italy), Marcos, C. (Argentina), Moreno-Sánchez, I. (Spain), Možina, K. (Slovenia), Nicol, E. (UK), Pastor-Vargas, R. (Spain), Pérez-García, F. (Spain), Pérez-Jiménez, M. (Spain), Pestano-Rodríguez, J. (Spain), Pieters, W. (The Netherlands), Pino-Mejias, J. (Spain), Read, T. (Spain), Rodríguez-de la Heras, A. (Spain), Rubio-Royo, E. (Spain), Ruipérez, G. (Spain), Sainz de Abajo, B. (Spain), Salvendy, G. (USA), Sánchez-Bonilla, M. (Spain), Sánchez-Montoya, R. (Spain), Silva-Salmerón, J. (Canada), Stanchev, P. (USA), Styliaras, G. (Greece), Tamai, T. (Japan), Torres-Gallardo, E. (Puerto Rico),

Väänänen-Vainio-Mattila, K. (Finland), Valeiras-Reina, G. (Spain), Veltman, K. (Canada), Zato-Recellado, J. (Spain), who supported the preparation of the workshop. I would like to thank all of the authors and speakers for their effort as well as the referees for their kind collaboration. Finally, a special thanks to Maria Ficarra (ALAIPO & AInCI), Anna Krammer, Ingrid Beyer and Alfred Hofmann (Springer), Brescello people and authorities (Giuseppe Vezzani and Andrea Setti), Gabriele Carpi (Pro Loco), Simone Mazotti, Valeria Taiani (Tourist Office), Virginio dall'Aglio (International Festival Film) and to all those who financially supported this international workshop.

September 2010   Francisco V.C. Ficarra

Acknowledgements

City Council of Brescello

Italian Tourism

Reggio nell'Emilia Province

Pro loco di Brescello

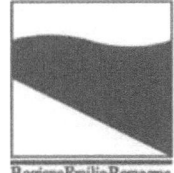

Emilia Romagna Region

Festival Film

Table of Contents

Re-thinking Reading in the Context of a New Wave of Electronic Reading Devices

Andreas Kratky

University of Southern California
Interactive Media Division
School of Cinematic Arts
900 West 34th Street, SCA 201
Los Angeles, CA 90089-2211
akratky@cinema.usc.edu

Abstract. We are currently witnessing a new wave of digital reading devices that will probably significantly change the way we read and publish. This is not the first digital revolution of aspects of cultural production and perception. This paper compares the previous digital revolutions of the music, film and publishing industries and attempts a prognosis of coming changes in the way we will work with digital texts. As a conclusion a new notion of interface design for the emerging reading ecology is proposed.

Keywords: Digital reading, Ubiquitous computing, Touch interfaces, Hypertext, Video game, Allegorical interface.

1 Introduction

With the introduction of the *iPad* by Apple Inc. in the United States and later in Europe we see not only an unexpectedly high amount of devices sold, there is also a wave of new tablet devices coming into the market from other companies. All these devices, including the *iPad*, are marketed as eBook readers and the expectation that they will revolutionize the reading and publishing landscape is widely held. By far not the first revolution of text as an essential component of human culture, it might be a revolution that will show lasting effects on how we read, write and share written knowledge. We witnessed similar revolutions induced by digital technologies in the music and in the film and television businesses that fundamentally transformed the nature of the two industries and the audience habits [1], [2], [3]. In both cases the combination of easy to use personal playback devices as well as content distribution enabled through the Internet changed how people consume music and films and how they conceive of ownership of the media they consume. These fundamental changes originated out of an amalgamation of accessible technology, appropriate interface designs and fashion. Bill Buxton gives a good analysis of the coinciding aspects in the success of the *iPod*, an earlier very successful music playback device [4]. We have a potentially similar situation currently in the field of digital reading devices in conjunction with emerging distribution platforms and there are indicators for a lasting transformation.

F.V. Cipolla Ficarra et al. (Eds.): HCITOCH 2010, LNCS 6529, pp. 1–11, 2011.
© Springer-Verlag Berlin Heidelberg 2011

This paper will attempt an analysis of the current situation and construct from a media-inherent perspective what kind of transformation we will likely have to expect in the way we perceive text and how we work with text in a developing network-supported personal reading ecology. While the reception and distribution of digital texts is rather well established and accepted in the academic context [5] and in general information oriented reading, in literary reading there are so far no comparable standards or practices in existence. But it is the area of leisure and entertainment reading which very likely will be most affected by the recent wave of e-reading devices and the emerging digital distribution formats. For the purpose of our analysis we will briefly review the previous revolutions of reading, and in comparison with the changes in the music and film industry highlight the particular characteristics of literary reading that resisted so far a general acceptance and widespread distribution of digital reading. The paper will conclude with the formulation of a conceptual approach to rethink the interface design of digital texts as a literary category.

2   Digital Revolutions of Cultural Practices

2.1   Reshaping the Music and Film Industries

In order to understand the emerging transformation of the reading process through digital technologies better, it is helpful to firstly analyze the aspects of the two previous transformations that formed the digital music revolution and – in a slightly different form – the digital film revolution. Secondly it is necessary to compare the current situation with the earlier developments in the area of digital text distribution. The transformation that is termed the 'digital music revolution' is the fruit of several fundamentally technological aspects lining up in a way that was favorable to create a lasting transformation in the consumer habits as well as in business practices. The main components that led to the revolution that we generally see as marked by the personal music player *iPod*, which was released by Apple Inc. in 2001, were an increasing bandwidth of the internet, the miniaturization of digital electronic devices, and the development of efficient, high quality compression algorithms as they became available with the MP3 format. The extra ingredient that made the *iPod* extremely successful was a very well targeted marketing campaign that gave this device a strong aspect of fashion and desirability. At this point a vivid sharing culture of music recordings on compact cassette existed already enabled by the *Walkman*, one of the first portable personal music players released by Sony in 1979 [6]. The habit of creating mix-tapes with personal selections of music tracks and an underground circulation of pirated tapes etc. existed already in the 1980s and 1990s, but in large the audience was still depending on the music industry to publish recordings. This changed with the distribution of music tracks on a global scale over the Internet through applications like *Napster* (1999) and later, in January 2001, *iTunes*. The logical complement to the digital distribution was a digital playback device, which came in October 2001 with the *iPod*, which was not the first device, but the most successful.

The digital revolution of the film industry started later than the one in the music area and originated from a slightly different situation. The traditional organization in a tiered exploitation structure with intermediary distributors as well as the selling and rental business of video tapes and DVDs is impacted by it, because more and more platforms and opportunities exist that allow the audience to view and share films and video clips online [7]. Here the digital format also triggered a much higher participation on the side of the audience through digital video and sharing platforms like *Youtube*, which was introduced in 2005 [8]. There is no one particular device that can be identified as the turning point, but in 2006 a new version of the *iPod* was released that allowed video playback on the portable device.

The most significant aspect in the success of these digital revolutions is the seamless integration of music listening, sharing, and managing into the every day structure. The combination of software and devices fulfilled what Mark Weiser termed *ubiquitous computing*: "The most profound technologies are those that disappear. They weave themselves into the fabric of everyday life until they are indistinguishable from it." [9] It is in this sense a usability aspect that was fueling this success. As Nicolas Negroponte predicted 1995 in his book "Being Digital" it is the moment when digital devices become delicate, smart, and flexible enough to adopt the qualities that the book and fine paper had since a long time [10] that digital media will become part of our being. Paired with good product design these requirements are almost met, the small personal digital devices such as cell phones and probably in the near future also e-readers have the status of fashion objects that are sometimes treated almost as jewelry. These devices will allow the digital book to come close to the user, to be read in bed, and to accompany him on his travels.

2.2   Reshaping Reading: Hypertext

The currently proclaimed revolution of reading is not the first digital revolution that happened to text as a medium. A very important transformation in the past was the introduction of hypertext. As a reaction to computers becoming more powerful and more available the concept of hypertext was seen as the inherently digital form of how we perceive texts in the new medium: "new possibilities emerge for extending the traditional notion of 'flat' text files by allowing more complex organizations of the material. Mechanisms are being devised which allow direct machine supported references from one textual chunk to another; new interfaces provide the user with the ability to interact directly with these chunks and to establish new relationships between them." [11] This passage published as an introduction to the medium of hypertext gives several insights into the characteristics of this new medium and how it restructures the reader's perception of text in the digital format. The main characteristic is the existence of references between texts called *hyperlink* and paradigmatically implemented in the navigation structure of the World Wide Web interface. A related aspect to the systems of links is the notion of reading as an interaction with the text, deliberately selecting and following links that the text offers. While reading was traditionally conceived of as the linear decoding of one text as provided by an author, hypertext introduces the notion of non-linearity and an amalgamation of multiple texts into a single reading process [12]. Hypertext therefore constituted a restructuring of the reading process, which is inherent to the implementation and architecture of the medium that delivers this new form of text. This system, though, is not necessarily an appropriate medium to deliver texts that were not conceived for this architecture. Around the development of hypertext and its establishment as a new form of text arose an extensive debate whether hypertext is a satisfactory replacement for earlier forms of text or whether it is a technological impasse that is harmful to the established forms of culture. While it is not the purpose of this paper to trace this discussion, it is worthwhile to revisit some of the arguments for and against hypertext in order to differentiate the revolution of reading attributed to hypertext from the currently emerging revolution attributed mainly to miniaturized personal reading devices and new distribution channels. This will allow us to elaborate some of the perceived problems of hypertext and understand why it did not end up replacing older forms of textuality.

The fragmentation that hypertext structures impose on the text and its embedding into a large set of linked text-elements external to the original text were constituting the core aspect of the new technology as well as the main point of criticism. Often termed the phenomenon of being 'lost in hyperspace' the criticism held that readers are challenged to actively choose from the offered links and explore those while still following the argument of the original text. As Zellweger [13] argues, the difficulty of negotiating several layers of text concurrently is an extra burden on the reader, an obstacle in the way of understanding, and a source of disorientation [14]. From this structure of richly interlinked text fragments also stems another criticism, which contends that hypertext is not a suitable text form for all kinds of textual information: For example the classical structure of arguments is not suitably supported by a hypertext system, which does not provide author control over how text fragments are accessed by the reader. Arguments rely on sequential structures like causal or temporal chains and pieces of information build upon previous information and therefore do not work well in a structure where this succession cannot be controlled. Thus in order to make an argument that is effective in hypertext authors needs to reshape the structure of their argument [15]. A third important point of criticism was the volatility and perceived instability of hypertexts. While the classical printed text source is stable and once printed, it remains in its form – no matter when it is accessed it will always be the same. The electronic hypertext from its architecture is flexible and can be in a "continuous process of construction, deconstruction, and reconstruction" [16]. This characteristic was equally seen as the end of a reliable text source and a responsible author as it was hailed as a new achievement of flexibility and dynamism.

The direction of this criticism indicates that the hypertext revolution was playing out mostly on a content level, and was not restricted to the level of delivery formats and devices.

2.3   Comparing the Revolutions

The characteristics of the transformations induced by the digital reshaping of the music and film industries were significantly different that those addressed by hypertext. While the first were aligned with new models of distribution using the improved bandwidth of the Internet and modern forms of online business transactions, the latter were mainly concerned with a shift in the perceptual and content structure of text. For the consumption of music as well as moving images it was possible to develop technological frameworks that make use of the distribution and delivery possibilities offered by contemporary online services in conjunction with small personal devices enabling consumption in flexible, mobile settings, and still deliver the content in a perceptual form more or less identical to the traditional form of delivery. Small adjustments for screen sizes or processing requirements (compression) had to be made, but on a perceptual level the music or the moving images still reach the consumer as they always did no matter if their delivery is digital or not. Of course it was a shock to listen to a disembodied voice coming from a machine when the first mechanical recordings were presented in the 1870s [17] but after people had gotten used to this kind of technical voice – the way it came out of the *Walkman* or *iPod* was still perceptually the same format. This was true also for the moving image: The very beginning was a very small image in Edison's *Kinetoscope*, watched through a peephole with a later series of adjustments to growing screen sizes. The step back to a miniature screen in personal video devices such as the *iPod* with video function or the small formats of online streaming video was not a fundamental change in the perceptual format of the moving image experience.

So far only for text it was not easily possible to come up with a seamless technology that could successfully compete with the established technology of the book. The energy required to power a display, the size of a display necessary to show meaningful amounts of content, the inability to match the ease of access and lightness of a book, all these obstacles delayed the kind of personal digital reading revolution that happened earlier in the other fields.

The main delivery formats for hypertexts were in the early stage CD-Rom media and later, with the proposal of the World Wide Web as a hypertext project in 1990, online delivery via the Internet [18]. Despite the WWW there is still tremendous expectation for the growth potential of the CD-Rom as the publishing medium of the future [19], [20]. Publishers obviously prefer the CD-Rom to the online delivery since as an encapsulated unit that can be individually sold in a way very similar to books it keeps the traditional business strategies intact. Even though these were new and revolutionary delivery formats they did not start as pervasive a transformation as was expected.

With the market launch of devices like the *Reader* from Sony or the *Kindle* from Amazon this situation began to change. Finally devices with long lasting batteries and a reading experience that could up to a certain extend compete with the book or deliver an acceptable alternative. The new generation of reading devices now comes with a fashion aspect, online distribution through dedicated stores, and efficient marketing so that we might see a noticeable shift over to digital reading in the near future.

3   The Reading to Come

3.1   Previous Obstacles in the Way of Digital Reading

One of the main questions is what do we have to expect from this shift and what will this future reading be like? For the first time after two decades of literary reading on decline the statistical report of the National Endowment for the Arts issued in 2009 indicated a rise in literary reading in the United States [21]. Earlier NEA diagnosed the steady decline of reading due to a society more and more permeated by electronic communication and entertainment technologies. The reports did not make the claim that these technologies were the cause for the decline but showed enough correlation to suggest this hypothesis [22], [23]. The latest report from 2009 shows an inversion of this trend, indicating that there is interest in literary reading and from these findings we can conclude that a successful combination of contemporary communication and entertainment technologies and literary reading can potentially trigger an even stronger renaissance of reading. While in the field that we earlier referred to as 'information oriented reading' usage patterns for electronic access and distribution of texts are established, mostly the fields of newspaper and magazine reading as well as literary reading will be impacted by the emerging transformations.

For our focus on the field of literary reading in this paper it will be necessary to question why this field did not go similar changes as information oriented reading in the earlier described transformations. The hypertext format was also used for the production of literary texts. Not only were there efforts to bring existing works into the new digital format, but also original productions for the hypertext format. The most ambitious effort in making existing texts available in a digital format is probably the Project Gutenberg, which started in 1971 and had a significant growth in 2002, claiming 30,000 items in the collection in 2009 (http://www.gutenberg.org). Other efforts besides those of commercial publishers such as Voyager's Enhanced Books in this direction are the Internet Archive (http://www.archive.org), founded in 1996, and Google Books (http://books.google.com), which started in 2004. The production of literary hypertexts was more of a specialty for a limited audience. CD-Rom Publications like Michael Joyce's "afternoon, a story" or Shelley Jackson's "Patchwork Girl" were often quoted by the hypertext research community but were published and distributed only by a specialized hypertext publisher. Expected to be the beginning of a new kind of textuality [12], digital reading did so far not make it into a general cultural practice with a significant established audience. The efforts on the side of lot of the publishers who were aiming to follow the revolution towards the eBook decreased and finally efforts to produce CD-Roms were abandoned in the mid to late 1990s [24]. We can identify several aspects that are responsible for the lack of broad success of this medium. The discomfort of having to read on a computer, be it desktop or laptop computer with a heavy power supply versus a book that is independent, flexible and light is evident and will be remedied by current and future digital reading devices. The new devices make electronic reading more seamless and even go beyond the book in the sense that a single reader can store a large amount of books and thus reduces the weight of carrying several books in comparison with the printed book. Another point of criticism is the inferiority in speed and accuracy and an increased eye-fatigue that was generally attributed to reading on the computer screen [25]. The current screen technologies such as e-ink or high quality high-resolution displays in the new reader devices are set to remedy this aspect as well. While these basic technological aspects are very likely to disappear with the new devices, there are more aspects that cannot simply addressed by technological refinement and require deeper analysis.

An important aspect that distinguishes the reading in a book from the reading on an electronic device is the haptic experience of the reading process itself. Not only convenience of carrying but also our interaction with the text as a material artefact is an important aspect of the reading experience. The organization of the text on the page, its connection with the reading surface as well as the placement in the context of the entire text have an impact on the reading and the process of the construction of meaning. The possibility of being "physically and phenomenologically (and literally) in touch with the material substrate of the text" is perceived important for our cognitive processing of the text as well as the immersive experience of the content [26]. These issues are a combination of interface design and aspects of hardware technology. Thus with the new hardware developments likely to be able to support novel interfaces strategies to improve on the previous situation, we have to reframe this discussion in the context of interface design.

3.2 Interfaces for Reading

While the notion of interface and questions of effective design have received significant attention and research in the realm of task oriented computer applications, in the realm of the arts our understanding of interface is still in the process of formation and will require very focused research in order to deliver compelling solutions to the emerging field of electronic literary reading. As Siegfried Zielinski expresses in his preliminary sketch for a short organon for the artistic interface: "Art which is expressed via media is becoming more and more the art of the interface. Theory of media seems to become theory of the interface." [27]

In terms of usability the new reading devices are promising a simpler and more seamless reading experience that older laptop or desktop computer-based systems. The dedicated e-reader devices such as the *Kindle* are not conceived as multi purpose devices and therefore have rather reduced and simplified interfaces custom tailored to facilitate reading. Reading in this understanding consists of managing digital copies of books, turning pages, marking pages – all basic functions of the navigation in text organized in successive pages. The *iPad* in comparison provides more general computing functions than the basic set of reading functions available on the *Kindle* and therefore has more complicated interfaces for different applications. It generated considerable excitement about the touch-screen interface but a lot of the early *apps* that became available soon after the launch of the device had consistency issues as well as some usability issues in terms of font sizes required to read versus font sizes required to be touched. In the reading applications both devices were found to be sticking very strongly to the print metaphor of turning successive pages and inherently linear access [28], [29]. The relative simplicity and specialization of these devices alleviates a lot of the burden of interface design that needed to harmonize a universal machine and its input devices with specialized applications. The so far most successful and still widely used method of harmonizing the technological machine with the user's mental concepts of specific tasks is the Graphical User Interface (GUI) and the Desktop Metaphor. The Desktop Metaphor was a strategy to map the familiar actions carried out in an office environment to the file management tasks necessary for the operation of a personal computer. This strategy was intended to make the operation of the computer easier for users by providing a familiar mental model for the operation of the machine. It was invented in 1970 and began to become widely popular in 1984.

For digital reading devices we can argue that such metaphors are not necessary because the complexity of operation is reduced enough to not require such conceptual support, and more importantly we argue that the use of metaphors or representations in the interface design should not support the operation of an anyways simple device but it should support the content of the text that is being read on the device. Page turning animations as part of the interface design referencing the printed book may be able to avoid the feeling of being lost in the jump from one page to another because the animation allows the eye to follow the displacement rather than jumping without mediation from one item to another. Nevertheless this creates a hybridized approach between the printed book and the digital device. Emulating the book as a metaphor to make the operation of digital texts easier is based on the same idea as implementing the desktop metaphor and makes references to other, historic media formats. It remains extraneous to the actual text and the construction of meaning from this text.

3.3 Towards an Allegorical Interface

A similar critical position has been developed by Espen Aarseth who distinguishes reading situations which require so called 'trivial' effort such as page turning etc. to experience the content of the text from what he calls *ergodic* literature, where "non-trivial effort is required to allow the reader to traverse the text" [30]. This distinction is useful to construct a notion of interfaces that work not as a metaphor for the device in which a certain experience is delivered but realize a form that is inherently supporting the experience, i.e. the content of the text. We would like to call this type of interface *allegorical interface*. Allegory is a literary figure that expresses meaning in a way that is not formulated literally in the text. It uses language, images or other kinds of representation to express its meaning [31]. An allegorical interface constitutes a figurative or symbolic representation of one or more core aspects of the text that is experienced through this interface. As an interface for a dynamic medium the notion of allegory encompasses besides the visual and textual also procedural allegories, which we can conceive of as functional mechanisms consisting of a series of actions that the reader goes through while reading the text that express a certain aspect of the content. The approach of integrating the navigational mechanism and the interface design into the structure of the text experience is a goal that has been pursued in a similar way in the field of video games. This approach is often formulated with the idea of simulation as its core and developed in opposition to narrative and representation. Simulation is conceived of as a mimetic likeness, a functional model that shares behavioral aspects of the situation to be expressed [32].

Our concept of the allegorical interface does not follow this strong opposition and rather focuses on the aspect of representation as a more abstract structural form that becomes part of the structure of the reading process. The reading process can be divided into two parts, the visual scanning and decoding of the signs, which is strongly dependent on the materiality and layout of the sign material, and the construction of meaning, which uses an ongoing process of constructing hypotheses and verifying them based on the sign material in correspondence with internal knowledge [33]. The structural form of the text and the reader's working through this structure is an existential part of the reading process, which is dependent on the medium in which the text is delivered and that has to be considered in its creative and expressive values accordingly. The term allegory of course has a long history and a broad range of connotations, we are focusing here on the more literal sense of 'figurative speaking', which can, as Fineman elaborates, be seen as part of any literary structure [34]. The simulation approach as well as the concept of the allegorical interface are not mutually exclusive and can coexist as different attempts of re-formulating the reading experience in the framework of digital media. While the simulation approach does not focus actually on the reading process per se but the simulating action, the allegorical interface stands more closely in the literary context. But nevertheless it does not deliver the text as it was classically delivered in the printed book. Every translation of content from one medium into another necessitates changes in the structure and the form of experience of this content. In a by now classic way we have observed this in the process of adapting novels to the film medium [35] and in a similar way adaptation processes will be necessary here, too. It is impossible to think that we can deliver the same experience quality as in the printed book in digital reading devices, even though some of the implementations of page turning and page marking in current reading interfaces might suggest that.

4 Conclusions and Future Research

We are currently in a situation where the field of reading on digital devices is at the beginning of a most likely fundamental restructuring process. We have to see how the introduction of touch sensitive devices that in an unprecedented way allow for very intuitive and immersive interaction strategies such as direct manipulation [36] will reshape the kinds of applications we see in this field. The development of interfaces that make use of the quality of 'quasi-tangible' interactions is promising and seems apt to deliver at least part of the material and haptic qualities of the reading process. There are so far not many examples in existence that have been created for the specific affordances of these devices and we are still in an early state of the interface design in this field. To shape the future development it will be necessary to evaluate existing approaches in the field of digital literature and analyze them in respect to possible lessons to learn. In particular the field of DVD-Rom publications provides examples that are fruitful study objects despite the fact that the DVD-Rom never reached larger market penetration and audiences. On the other hand it will be necessary to develop experimental implementation of the concept of allegorical interfaces for digital texts that will allow us to refine this concept and further to develop formal evaluation criteria.

The metrics for the evaluation of interface designs for artistic applications are very different from those that have been elaborated for task-oriented interfaces. While it is possible to extract quality criteria such as speed and precision to evaluate task oriented interfaces in respect to the task they are intended to support, formulating corresponding criteria for the literary and artistic realm will require further research. In the hypertext research field some work has been done in this direction which will be a fruitful resource [36], [37]. By nature of its concept allegorical interfaces are specifically created for one particular application and they have a probably low reusability factor. While it is common to create interface targeted for only on application in the field of task oriented applications, this will constitute a shift in the way the current publishing methods of digital texts work. Since interfaces so far have been created for the reading device and not for a specific text it is common practice to reuse these interfaces. The fact, though, that more and more publications appear as *apps*, as applications in their own right, rather than as content modules that are accessed through standardized reading software such as the eBook Reader, suggest that this transition is already underway.

References

1. Haring, B.: Beyond the Charts: MP3 and the Digital Music Revolution. JM Northern Media (2000)
2. Peitz, M., Waelbroeck, P.: An Economist's Guide to Digital Music. CESifo Economic Studies 51(2-3), 359–428 (2005)
3. Buxton, B.: Sketching User Experiences: Getting the Design Right and the Right Design. Morgan Kaufman Publishers, San Francisco (2007)
4. Greenblatt, A.: Television's Future. CQ Researcher, 17, 145–168, (2007) from CQ Researcher,
   http://library.cqpress.com/cqresearcher/cqresrre2007021600 (retrieved June 7, 2010)
5. Willinsky, J.: The Nine Flavours of Open Access Scholarly Publishing. J. Postgrad. Med. 49, 263–267 (2003)
6. Sony History: Mr. Morita, I would Like a Walkman,
   http://www.sony.net/Fun/SH/1-18/h4.html (retrieved June 7 2010)
7. Zhu, K.: Internet-based Distribution of Digital Videos: The Economic Impacts of Digitization on the Motion Picture Industry. Electronic Markets 11(4), 273–280 (2001)
8. Jenkins, H.: Quentin Tarantion's Star Wars? Digital Cinema, Media Convergence, and Participatory Culture. In: Thornburn, D., Jenkins, H. (eds.) Rethinking Media Change: The Aesthetics of Transition, pp. 281–312. MIT Press, Cambridge Massachusetts (2003)
9. Weiser, M.: The Computer for the 21st Century. ACM SIGMOBILE Mobile Computing and Communications Review 3, 3–11 (1999)
10. Negroponte, N.: Being Digital. A. Knopf, 71 (1995)
11. Conklin, J.: Hypertext: An Introduction and Survey. Computer 20(9), 17–41 (1987)
12. Dalgaard, R.: Hypertext and the Scholarly Archive: Intertexts, Paratexts and Metatexts at Work. In: Proceedings of the 12th ACM Conference on Hypertext and Hypermedia, pp. 175–184 (2001)
13. Bernstein, M., et al.: Structure, Navigation, and Hypertext: The Status of the Navigation Problem. In: Proceedings of the 3rd ACM Conference on Hypertext and Hypermedia, pp. 363–366 (1991)
14. Carter, L.M.: Arguments in Hypertext: A Rhetorical Approach. In: Proceedings of the 11th ACM Conference on Hypertext and Hypermedia, pp. 85–91 (2000)
15. Botafogo, R.A., Shneiderman, B.: Identifying Aggregates in Hypertext Structures. In: Proceedings of the 3rd ACM Conference on Hypertext and Hypermedia, pp. 363–366 (1991)
16. Bernstein, M., et al.: Architectures for Volatile Hypertext. In: Proceedings of the 3rd ACM Conference on Hypertext and Hypermedia, pp. 243–260 (1991)
17. Picker, J.M.: Victorian Soundscapes. Oxford University Press, New York (2003)
18. Berners-Lee, T., Cailliau, R.: WorldWideWeb: Proposal for a hypertexts Project (1990),
    http://w3.org/Proposal.html (retrieved June 16, 2010)
19. ZKM | Center for Art and Media: Artinact 1. Cantz Verlag, Ostfildern (1994)
20. Hauffe, H.: Die elektronische Revolution und ihre Auswirkungen auf Verlage und Bibliotheken. In: Bollmann, S. (ed.) Kursbuch Neue Medien. Bollmann Verlag, Mannheim (1995)
21. Office of Research & Analysis, National Endowment for the Arts: Reading on the Rise (2009)
22. Office of Research & Analysis, National Endowment for the Arts: Reading at Risk (2004)
23. Office of Research & Analysis, National Endowment for the Arts: To Read or not to Read (2007)

24. Jacsó, P.: Who is doing what in the CD-ROM Publishing Realm? Computers in Libraries, 55–56 (1996)
25. Dillon, A., McKnight, C., Richardson, J.: Reading from Paper versus Reading from Screen. The Computer Journal 31(5), 457–464 (1988)
26. Mangen, A.: Hypertext Fiction Reading: Haptics and Immersion. Journal of Research in Reading 31(4), 404–419 (2008)
27. Röller, N., Zielinski, S.: On the Difficulty to Think Twofold in One. In: Diebner, H., Druckrey, T., Weibel, P. (eds.) Sciences of the Interface, Genista, Tübingen, pp. 282–291 (2001)
28. Nielsen, J.: iPad Usability: First Findings From User Testing, http://www.useit.com/alertbox/ipad.html (retrieved June 17, 2010)
29. Nielsen, J.: Kindle 2 Usability review (2009), http://www.useit.com/alertbox/kindle-usability-review.htm (retrieved June 17, 2010)
30. Aarseth, E.: Cybertext. Johns Hopkins University Press, Baltimore (1997)
31. Allegory. Encyclopædia Britannica, from Encyclopædia Britannica, http://www.britannica.com/EBchecked/topic/16078/allegory (retrieved June 17, 2010)
32. Frasca, G.: Simulation versus Narrative. In: Wolf, M.J.P., Perron, B. (eds.) The Video Game Theory Reader, pp. 221–235. Routledge, New York (2003)
33. Gross, S.: Lese-Zeichen. Wissenschaftliche Buchgesellschaft, Darmstadt (1994)
34. Fineman, J.: The Structure of Allegorical Desire, October 12, pp. 46–66 (1980)
35. Chatman, S.: What Novels Can Do That Films Can't (And Vice Versa). Critical Inquiry 7(1), 121–140 (1980)
36. Shneideman, B.: Designing the User Interface. Addison-Wesley, Reading (1998)
37. Golovchinsky, G., Marshall, C.C.: Hypertext Interaction Revisited. In: Proceedings of the 11th ACM Conference on Hypertext and Hypermedia, pp. 171–179 (2000)
38. Carassai, M.: From Machinic Intelligence to Digital Narrative Subjectivity: Electronic Literature and Intermediation as "form of life Modification". In: Proceedings of the Digital Arts and Culture Conference (2009)

Electronic Commerce "in the dark"

Maria Claudia Buzzi[1], Marina Buzzi[1], Barbara Leporini[2], and Caterina Senette[1]

[1] IIT – CNR, via Moruzzi, 1 – 56124 Pisa, Italy
[2] ISTI - CNR, via Moruzzi, 1 – 56124 Pisa, Italy
{Claudia.Buzzi,Marina.Buzzi,Caterina.Senette}@iit.cnr.it,
Barbara.Leporini@iit.cnr.it

Abstract. The widespread diffusion of electronic commerce offers a great opportunity for blind people. We describe the results of an electronic survey carried out with 22 blind and 22 sighted users in order to understand the difficulties and obstacles they experience shopping on-line, and solicit their expectations and suggestions for making the interaction simpler and more satisfying. Results show that blind users shop on-line much less than their sighted counterparts, since they encounter more difficulties not only when making a purchase, but even in the navigation phase preceding the commercial transaction. Complex layouts and unstructured content can prevent an e-transaction from being successfully completed. Furthermore, security, privacy and trustiness, common concerns for all consumers, also impact on the fear of buying via Internet for the visually impaired. Poor usability leads to a potential loss of revenue for on-line companies and a lost opportunity to increase a blind person's independence. Providing simpler, more understandable UIs would benefit all users and fuel the expansion of electronic commerce.

Keywords: eCommerce, Blind, Accessibility, Usability, Screen reader.

1 Introduction

Electronic commerce (eCommerce) websites are steadily multiplying, attracting more and more visitors and consumers. User experience depends on many features such as website structure, navigation and retrieval times, transaction efficiency and security, reliability of delivery services, etc. Specifically, User Interface (UI) usability and consumer trust are key factors in the diffusion of eCommerce and on-line transactions.

eCommerce services are particularly interesting for blind persons, who may have mobility problems and often cannot shop on their own. Blind users generally access Internet services using a screen reader and a voice synthesizer. The screen reader is an assistive technology that interprets and announces screen content to the user. Mixing text and structure (links, tables, headings), a screen reader makes it difficult to interact with websites that have complex layout and dynamic content (such as popular eCommerce and auction Web sites). In addition, to perceive page content aurally, visually impaired people usually interact via keyboard since vocal commands are subject to error and difficult to manage. Designing for blind users requires special consideration for three subsystems -- the perceptual, motor and cognitive -- of the

F.V. Cipolla Ficarra et al. (Eds.): HCITOCH 2010, LNCS 6529, pp. 12–22, 2011.
© Springer-Verlag Berlin Heidelberg 2011

"Human Processor" [4]. Furthermore, lack of vision may lead to creation of a mental scheme of a website that differs greatly from the reality.

The screen reader reads and interprets a webpage by announcing its content sequentially, from the first (URL and title of the page) to the last word, losing formatting and other visual cues. Menus, navigation bar, and banner are repeated on every page, making navigation of content time-consuming, and interaction difficult and frustrating. As a consequence, blind users often stop the screen reading at the beginning, and prefer to navigate by Tab Key from link to link, or explore content row by row via arrow keys.

Interaction via screen reader involves several issues:

1. Information overload, if content is not appropriately designed and structured.
2. Lack of interface overview. Blind persons do not perceive the overall structure of the interface, and may navigate for a long time without finding relevant content.
3. Lack of context. When navigating via Tab and arrow keys the user can access only small portions of text and may lose the overall context of the page; thus it may be necessary to reiterate the reading process.
4. Additional cognitive effort is required to interpret and separate webpage content from other elements. The screen reader announces the most important interface elements such as links, images and window objects as they appear in the code. These elements are important for figuring out the page structure, but can create problems. For instance, if the table's content is organized in columns, the screen reader (which reads by rows) announces the page contents out of order, and the information becomes confusing or misleading for the user.
5. Difficulty understanding UI elements. Links, content, and button labels should be context-independent and self-explanatory.
6. Difficulty working with form control elements, dynamic content and widgets, if the screen reader is not able to deal with these elements and transfer information to the users.
7. A blind person is unable to access multimedia content; equivalent alternative descriptions should be provided, otherwise the user may miss important content.

In [3] an example of interaction via screen reader to carry out a commercial transaction with a popular eCommerce website (eBay) is shown and obstacles are discussed in detail.

We think that eCommerce services could be particularly interesting for blind people, who have mobility problems and often depend on others for buying goods and services. In this paper we investigate the usability and perception of trustworthiness of on-line services involving commercial transactions by both blind and sighted individuals, to identify differences and similarities.

To evaluate the use of eCommerce by blind users, we designed an on-line survey for both sighted and blind users in order to compare behaviours and characteristics, and to analyze eventual differences. We also prepared a downloadable version for blind persons who are only familiar with text editors (such as Microsoft Word).

The paper is organized thus: Section 2 presents related works, Section 3 describes the survey, highlighting features and design. In Section 4 we discuss the results and lastly, present our conclusions.

2 Related Work

By simplifying processes and services, computers and the Internet enable new, more efficient ways of working and living. However, an important question is related to user satisfaction, and his/her trust in on-line services. Since user acceptance plays a fundamental role in the widespread adoption of eCommerce services, usability and security are crucial aspects when designing both the application and its user interfaces.

The nature of eCommerce applications poses serious privacy and security issues. The impossibility of physically examining products before payment, the safety of the online transaction, communication (and preservation) of sensitive data (credit card numbers and consumer personal data) feeds customers doubts and fears [5, 8, 10, 17]. Electronic fraud can harm unskilled users, create fear, and induce people to limit the use of eCommerce services.

Intangibility is a harmful factor for the growth of the eCommerce market. By conducting a user test with a large sample of skilled undergraduate business students, Featherman and Wells [9] investigated perceived consumer risks (i.e. Performance, Financial, Privacy, Time, Social, Psychological, Mental Intangibility) of on-line transactions. A classic face-to-face transaction offers a degree of physical tangibility (goods, paper receipt, bag) while eCommerce services only rely on virtual cues. It is crucial to create ways to make e-services more "tangible". Providing consumers with creative visualizations and tangible evidence of service states may contribute to creating a strong mental model of the e-service, allowing the user better control and thus more confidence [9]. Pinhanez proposes a framework for understanding and dealing with problems when developing e-service applications. Starting with basic characteristics of services (customer-as-input, heterogeneity, simultaneity, perishability, coproduction, and intangibility) he derived several fundamental issues for designing and evaluating the UIs of on-line services [15].

Many user studies suggest that totally blind users encounter more difficulty than people with other sensorial disabilities (such as low vision, motor or hearing impairments) when executing specific tasks [6, 12, 14]. Petrie et al. [14] presented the results of accessibility testing of 100 websites with users who had visual, motor and perceptual disabilities, showing that websites that are accessible for differently-abled users can also be visually pleasing. Specifically, 100 websites spread out over five sectors were tested with automated verification and user testing, involving 51 differently-abled users, including 10 who were totally blind. Results showed a mean task success rate of 76% that fell to 53% if considering only the totally blind (the lowest score of all user categories). Likewise, regarding user satisfaction, the authors recorded that blind users encountered more difficulty than other differently-abled users (4.2 on a 1-7 Likert scale, the lowest score of all the user categories). Researchers at Manchester Metropolitan University [6] highlighted issues of non-visual access by studying a sample of blind and visually-impaired users. Visually-impaired users searching the Web for a specific piece of information took on average 2.5 times longer than sighted users. The efficiency gap was further quantified by Ivory et al. [12]; when blind subjects executed a set of tasks, they took twice as long as sighted users to explore search results and three times as long to explore the corresponding web pages.

eCommerce systems pose new design challenges, since user interfaces are complex, and contain many elements, dynamic contents, and security features (secure http sessions). Stenitzer et al. [16] carried out several user tests of eCommerce Web sites with older adults (between 50 and 72 years), visually impaired and blind persons, noting usability problems that ranged from an unpleasant experience (difficult, frustrating) to insurmountable accessibility barriers. Petrie and al. [13] investigate conformance of a set of eCommerce and financial websites to "accessibility logos", verifying that the level of conformance to the Web Content Accessibility Guidelines (WCAG) version 1.0 was overestimated in 30% of the analyzed sites.

Accessibility allows users to explore web page content, while usability provides online users with simple, efficient, and satisfying navigation and interaction. Navigation is vital for people with special needs, and especially for blind people, since it is crucial for them to be aware of their current location on the webpage and how to return to the beginning, or how to reach a certain point in the material [7].

Organizing a page in logical sections enhances the navigation experience of a blind user in two ways: it provides a page overview and permits the user to jump from section to section. Specifically, heading levels can improve navigation since screen readers have special commands for moving from one heading to another. Brudvik et al. [1] present an interesting study on how sighted users associate headings with a web page, observing very different results depending on factors such as whether the page has a hierarchic structure, how users identify sections, etc. Furthermore, authors applied techniques of information retrieval, developing a system for automatically inferring from the context (font, size, color, etc.) whether a phrase "works semantically" as a heading, and dynamically adds the heading level using Javascript. The system called HeadingHunter was evaluated using human-labeled headings gathered from the study and showed high precision (0.92 with 1 the max).

Most common website usability factors involve meeting business objectives while providing a satisfying user experience. Therefore, accessibility and usability should be seen as a challenge to designers and implementers rather than a constraint. To share best practices in designing for blind people, in [11] authors describe their experience developing the online shop of the Royal National Institute of Blind People (RNIB), which enhances user experience by means of a natural language interface.

Customers' lack of trust is one of the main barriers to the development of eCommerce [5, 8, 10]. This is more relevant for blind users who must interact via screen reader with a further degree of difficulty and additional effort, compared to sighted users. The perception of trust of blind persons, when performing an online transaction, is discussed in [2]. Since they are unable to interpret visual clues, it is crucial to provide blind people with security information (technical features, trusted provider, privacy policy etc.) that can be explored early in the interaction via screen reader. Furthermore structuring contents, using hidden labels for improving user orientation (between list of products), providing accessible tables, and communicating dynamic changes of the UIs may provide more control over interaction in the commercial session [2], [3].

3   The Survey

To understand whether eCommerce is considered an "important" means of achieving independence, we decided to compare results from sighted and visually-impaired users. Indeed, reasons for using eCommerce could be different for the two user categories. For sighted users it can save time, offering a wider choice of products at a better price. For people with disabilities, eCommerce could also be a "very useful" (or innovative) tool for achieving more independence. For this reason, both sighted and visually-impaired users were asked to fill out the same questionnaire.

To satisfy different needs and user skills, the survey was created in two formats: 1) MS word document (questions with multiple sequential labelled answers) and 2) Web page, to complete on-line. The design of the survey, especially for the web form, had to respond to usability and accessibility recommendations since a gap in terms of accessibility might compromise the number and quality of (blind) user answers.

At present, several open source or commercial platforms allow easy creation of a quite personalized survey, but frequently these software programs emphasize visual appearance without providing accessibility for blind users. Various solutions were tested before creating the final on-line questionnaire, since we found that interaction with a screen reader was not easy. Generally, interaction with an electronic survey is similar to filling in a web form: blind people who perform a basic web navigation with no knowledge of advanced screen reader commands have problems using combo boxes, check boxes and radio buttons, especially since there is no easy way to move rapidly from one to another without special commands. To improve the survey's usability we added an HTML heading tag to each question to enable users to identify each question by moving from one heading to the next (or previous).

Of the different solutions, we chose Google Docs (http://docs.google.com/), the only platform offering fewer interaction difficulties (via screen reader), and with the additional goal of learning how this kind of software, nowadays very popular, could become a real work tool for blind people. The survey, physically stored in a Google server, was proposed to potential participants selected from institutional associations for the blind (that were involved in our previous studies), and contacted via open mailing lists of visually-impaired communities.

Buying a product is very different from navigation and search: it requires users hav clear and complete feedback on correctness of the commercial transaction. To learn what kind of feedback people need vs what they actually receive, we structured the questionnaire with multi-choice questions (with potential drawbacks) and text boxes for free description of difficulties experienced by users. We organized the questionnaire in sections (invisible to the user), each one aiming to investigate one user feature: characterization of the sample relative to genre, age and Internet knowledge; purchasing habits; knowledge and use of eCommerce; problems or general perception of user trust in economic transactions. Another optional section (only for visually-impaired users) concerned assistive technologies. Last, the final section of the survey investigates the degree of difficulty experienced by users when filling out the questionnaire, in order to understand potential limits or misunderstandings and be able to correctly interpret user answers. A pilot test was performed with two users (one blind) to verify the questionnaire's usability (comprehension, clarity, navigation via screen reader, etc.) and refine the questions.

4   Discussion

In this section we describe the results of the survey. To simplify reading, we discuss results first for the blind and then sighted users, also highlighting differences and similarities between the two samples.

4.1   Visually-Impaired Sample

We received a total of 22 questionnaires from visually impaired persons: 12 from the on-line survey and 10 in the Word version. The sample comprised 23% females and 77% males: 82% were totally blind and 18% visually impaired. The sample age is shown in Fig 1.

Regarding Internet and Web knowledge, the skill levels in the sample consisted of 59% intermediate, 9% novice and 32% expert.

A total of 77% of the sample uses the Jaws screen reader (88% of whom utilize v 10.0 or later). It is notable that 64% of the sample uses the screen reader only in basic interaction mode, without taking advantage of its advanced commands. The remaining 23% uses other screen readers such as Supernova and NVDA and/or magnifiers.

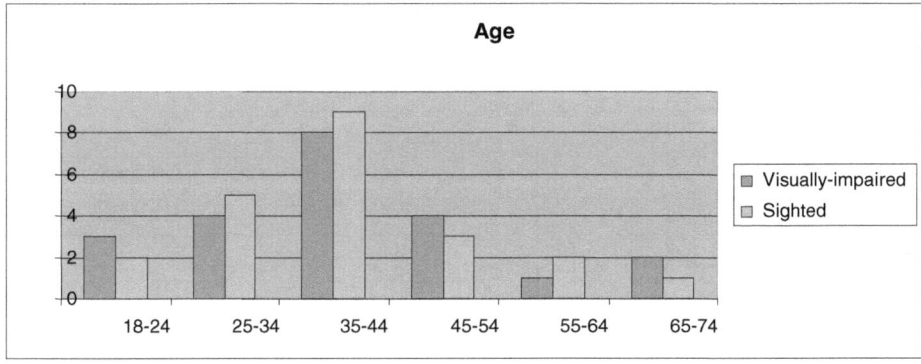

Fig. 1. Age of the sample of visually-impaired persons participating in the survey compared with sighted users

Concerning habits in buying goods, 32% of users buy basic necessities by themselves and 59% buy other items (electronic devices, clothes, household appliances, etc.). It is notable that only 14% of the sample performs online shopping habitually. However, 86% of users find information and evaluations before buying an expensive item, using mainly Internet sources (product info and user evaluations) and asking friends (64% and 59% respectively). Furthermore, 82% of the sample report needing the help of a sighted person to carry out commercial transactions (involving money and sensitive data).

Regarding eCommerce use, seven people from the sample had never performed online shopping, six rarely and only eight often or always, as shown in Fig. 2. However, almost all are familiar with popular eCommerce websites, such as eBay, Amazon, airlines, railways, travelling/holiday services, etc.

For seven blind users who have never performed online shopping, the main obstacle to using eCommerce sites is the low perception of security and trustiness of the site (and its economic transactions) (six of seven users), and the perception that buying on-line is too difficult or not useful (three users).

Concerning the kind of goods purchased, 50% of the sample purchased electronic devices and 41% flights/train tickets. Besides, 50% of the sample declared they would buy basic necessities (such as food or wine), if interaction was simpler.

Difficulties encountered by online buyers (or users who had attempted to buy) are shown in Fig. 3: 64% had navigation problems while 45% thought they did not received adequate information in both search and product evaluation phases; only 8 users of 22 felt that the economic transaction was not secure. Figure 3 clearly shows that difficulties for the blind are mainly concentrated in the UI. One-third of the sample was unable to overcome this barrier, so this is a lost opportunity for the blind and a potential loss of revenue for companies.

Some responders mentioned difficulty solving a captcha, required by some eCommerce Websites to complete the purchase. Although alternative audio versions are available for visual captchas, a different language and poor rendering of the synthesized voice may impact the blind user tremendously, making this step very hard.

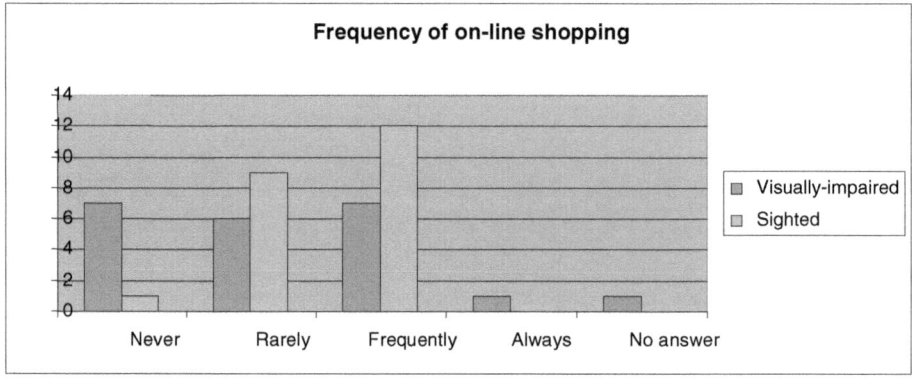

Fig. 2. Number of people who had experienced on-line shopping

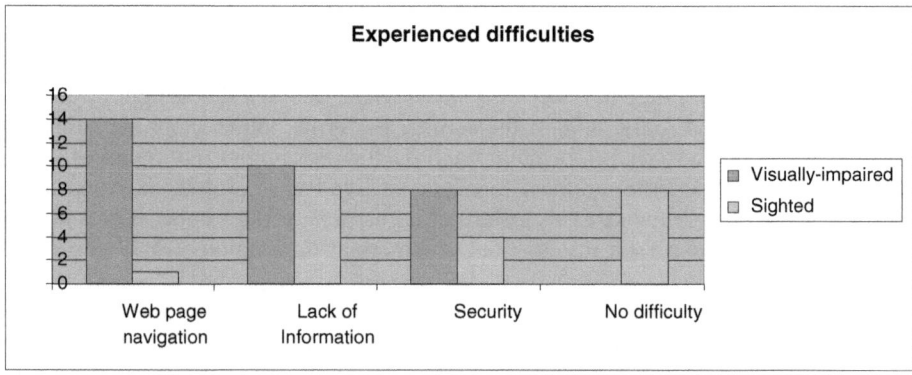

Fig. 3. Difficulties encountered by both samples

Regarding the usefulness/convenience of purchasing on-line, 77% believe it is or will be very useful (40%) and 68% agree that eCommerce will have a great (positive) influence on their quality of life (see Fig. 4).

4.2   Sighted Persons Sample

For sighted users we experienced no problem involving a large number of people to better simulate the average user. However, we decided to balance the number of sighted/blind users to compare two samples of the same cardinality. Twenty-two sighted persons filled out the survey on-line: 64% of the sample was female and 36% male, with age distribution as shown in Fig. 1.

Regarding Internet and Web knowledge, 55% of users declared themselves to be intermediate, 9% novice and 36% expert.

Concerning habits in buying goods, of the sighted users, 77% purchase basic necessities by themselves and 77% buy other more expensive goods. Only 23% habitually perform online shopping. Of sighted users, 73% get information before purchasing an expensive item (of these, 86% via Internet and 68% from friends). It is notable that 59% of sighted responders often ask for help from other more skilled persons. Since difficulties are experienced not only by the visually-impaired but also by unskilled users, more usable UI are needed.

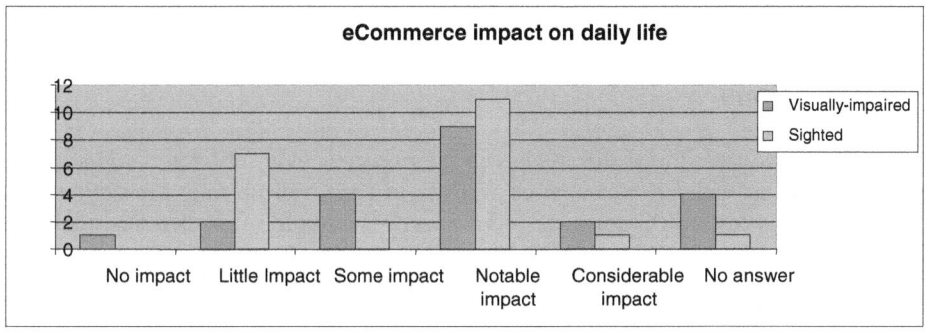

Fig. 4. eCommerce impact on life of blind and sighted persons

Regarding eCommerce use, as shown in Fig. 2, only 1 user in 22 never shopped online, while 55% did it often or always and 41% rarely.

Figure 2 shows the lower utilization of eCommerce services by blind compared to sighted users, due to greater difficulties experienced: 7 of 22 visually impaired users never purchased anything online, although almost all the sample agrees that it would have a positive impact on their lives (Fig. 4). Popular eCommerce sites such as Ebay, Amazon, and travelling/holiday online services (such as Expedia, e-Dreams, etc.) are visited by 91% of the sample. The only users who do not use eCommerce services declared lack of security and trust perception (both in terms of website reputation and security of economic online transaction) to be the main causes for diffidence and fear of using this intangible and virtual service.

Concerning the kind of goods purchased, 41% bought electronic devices, 95% traveling (plan/train) tickets, 45% books/CDs, and 27% clothes. Furthermore, 15 of 22 users declared that they would like to purchase different types of goods, especially basic necessities (9 users) and clothes (5 users), if interaction was simpler.

Difficulties encountered by online buyers are shown in Fig. 3, where 36% of the sample do not encounter any problems, but the same percentage experience difficulty with the degree of quality and quantity of product information, both when searching and carrying out the economic transaction. Ten of 22 users experienced transactions concluded incorrectly, and 50% of them also specified (as free comment) that operations are too long and very complex. The relative numbers of people are shown in Fig. 3.

Lastly, **regarding the usefulness/convenience of purchasing on-line,** 91% of sighted responders believe that eCommerce would be useful or very useful (54%) and 64% think that on-line purchases would have great impact on their everyday life. The importance of the latter percentage must be considered, since it is not easy for people who already experience difficulty in everyday situations to have much confidence and hope in a potential tool for achieving greater autonomy. Figure 4 shows the major impact of eCommerce on the lives of visually-impaired persons. This highlights the need for simple and efficient ways to enable their independence.

Regarding the survey platform, of the 12 blind users using the online version, 8 refer that they had no difficulty and only 2 users encountered some difficulty. This suggests that Google Docs, appropriately customized, could be a good tool for creating on-line surveys accessible via screen reader.

5 Conclusions

In this paper we investigate differences in the experiences of blind and sighted users when interacting with an eCommerce website to carry out on-line transactions. We performed a survey on eCommerce services with a sample of 44 persons, including equal numbers of blind and sighted individuals.

Results of the survey showed that difficulties also exist for sighted users, although the blind experience greater (sometimes insurmountable) obstacles that require the assistance of others to successfully complete an online transaction. Specifically, blind users encounter greater difficulty not only when making an on-line purchase but also in the navigation phase (when searching and choosing between products), even before carrying out the commercial transaction. This explains the lower utilization of eCommerce services by blind compared to sighted users according to the survey results.

However, even unskilled sighted users experience difficulty interacting with complex eCommerce applications. The exchange of sensitive data such as credit card numbers and personal info in online transactions is a critical factor: it is notable that many sighted users often ask for help from more skilled friends, to complete this critical phase of the online purchase. This denotes that clear and simple UIs are needed by all. A sighted user complained that the notion of registration in order to enable the initial transaction is a difficult concept to understand for an unskilled person. When buying in a shop, no personal information is required -- only a credit card or cash is needed. Supplying additional information as required in a virtual space may not be intuitive.

Survey results also suggest that potential users are missing out on services and this has a negative impact on their lives as well as on eCommerce providers, losing potential customers. More natural UIs should be designed to allow rapid and satisfying interaction and to reassure users about the safety of eCommerce services.

Our survey is a preliminary step in a study aimed at improving interaction via screen reader when shopping online. This improvement would have great impact on the autonomy of blind users who often depend on other people for everyday purchases. In future studies, we plan to define guidelines for making eCommerce websites more usable for blind people, in order to reduce usability problems and offer more control of on-line transactions. The survey sheds light on some obstacles experienced by a blind person when performing eCommerce transactions and is the basis for formulating design criteria for creating a simple, efficient and satisfactory access when interacting via screen reader. Last, we plan to apply these criteria to the user interface of a popular eCommerce site, and perform a user-test with totally blind users to verify the real impact of the proposed guidelines.

References

1. Brudvik, J.T., Bigham, J.P., Cavander, A.C., Ladner, R.E.: Hunting for headings: sighted labeling vs. automatic classification of headings. In: Proc. 10th International ACM SIGACCESS conference on Computers and Accessibility, pp. 201–208 (2008)
2. Buzzi, M.C., Buzzi, M., Leporini, B., Akhter, F.: User Trust of eCommerce Services: perception via screen reader. In: Proceedings of 3rd International Conference on New Trends in Information and Service Science (NISS 2009), pp. 1166–1171 (2009)
3. Buzzi, M.C., Buzzi, M., Leporini, B., Akhter, F.: Usability and Accessibility of eBay by Screen Reader. In: Holzinger, A., Miesenberger, K. (eds.) USAB 2009. LNCS, vol. 5889, pp. 500–510. Springer, Heidelberg (2009)
4. Card, S.K., Moran, A., Newell, T.P.: The Psychology of Human-Computer Interaction. Lawrence Erlbaum Associates Inc., New Jersey (1983)
5. Chong, B., Yang, Z., Wong, M.: Asymmetrical impact of trustworthiness attributes on trust, perceived value and purchase intention: a conceptual framework for cross-cultural study on consumer perception of online auction. In: Proc. 5th International Conference on Electronic Commerce, pp. 213–219. ACM, New York (2003)
6. Craven, J., Brophy, P.: Non-visual access to the digital library: the use of digital library interfaces by blind and visually impaired people. Technical report, Manchester: Centre for Research in Library and Information Management - CERLIM (2003), http://www.cerlim.ac.uk/pubs/index.php
7. Debevc, M., Verlic, M., Kosec, P., Stjepanovic, Z.: How Can HCI Factors Improve Accessibility of m-Learning for Persons with Special Needs? In: Stephanidis, C. (ed.) HCI 2007. LNCS, vol. 4556, pp. 539–548. Springer, Heidelberg (2007)
8. Egger, F.N.: Trust me, I'm an online vendor: towards a model of trust for e-commerce system design. In: CHI 2000 extended abstracts on Human factors in computing systems, pp. 101–102. ACM, New York (2000)

9. Featherman, M.S., Wells, J.D.: The Intangibility of e-Services: Effects on Perceived Risk and Acceptance. The DATA BASE for Advances in Information Systems 41(2), 110–131 (2010)
10. Friedman, B., Khan Jr., P.H., Howe, D.C.: Trust online. Communications of the ACM 43(12), 34–40 (2000)
11. Gladstone, K., Rundle, C., Alexander, T.: Accessibility and Usability of eCommerce Systems. In: Miesenberger, K., Klaus, J., Zagler, W.L. (eds.) ICCHP 2002. LNCS, vol. 2398, pp. 11–18. Springer, Heidelberg (2002)
12. Ivory, M.Y., Yu, S., Gronemyer, K.: Search result exploration: a preliminary study of blind and sighted users' decision making and performance. In: Extended abstracts of CHI 2004, pp. 453–456 (2004)
13. Petrie, H., Badani, A., Bhalla, A.: Sex, lies and Web accessibility: the use of accessibility logos and statements on e-commerce and financial websites. In: Proc. Accessible Design in the Digital World Conference (2005),
    http://publ.bcs.boxuk.net/upload/pdf/ewic_ad05_s5paper2.pdf
14. Petrie, H., Hamilton, F., King, N.: Tension, what tension?: Website accessibility and visual design. In: Proc. 2004 International Cross-disciplinary Workshop on Web Accessibility (W4A), pp. 13–18 (2004)
15. Pinhanez, C.: A Service Science Perspective for Interfaces of Online Service Applications. In: Proceedings of IHC 2008, pp. 11–20 (2008)
16. Stenitzer, M., Putzhuber, M., Nemecek, S., Büchler, F.: Accessible Online Shops for the Older Generation and People with Disabilities. In: Miesenberger, K., Klaus, J., Zagler, W.L., Karshmer, A.I. (eds.) ICCHP 2008. LNCS, vol. 5105, pp. 462–465. Springer, Heidelberg (2008)
17. Ye, Q., Li, Y., Kiang, M., Wu, W.: The Impact of Seller Reputation on the Performance of online sales: evidence from TaoBao buy-it-now (BIN) data. In: ACM SIGMIS Database archive, vol. 40(1), pp. 12–19. ACM, New York (2009)

The Leap of a Provincial SME into the Global Market Using E-commerce: The Success of Adequate Planning

Beatriz Sainz de Abajo[1], Enrique García Salcines[2], F. Javier Burón Fernández[2], Miguel López Coronado[1], and Carlos de Castro Lozano[2]

[1] Telecommunications Technical School (ETSIT), University of Valladolid, Campus Miguel, Delibes, Paseo de Belén nº 15, 47011 Valladolid, Spain
{beasai,miglop}@tel.uva.es
[2] EATCO Research Group, University of Cordoba,
Edificio Leonardo da Vinci, Campus de Rabanales, 14071 Córdoba, Spain
{egsalcines,jburon,malcaloc}@uco.es

Abstract. The leap into the global market is not easy when it involves a provincial family business. This article demonstrates how adequate planning is fundamental in a small and medium-sized enterprise (SME) with the tight budget they have available to them, in order to be able to differentiate themselves in a highly competitive market, taking into accounts the benefits and risks involved. The Information Technology (IT) tools put in place will give the necessary support and allow for the possibility of increasing and improving the infrastructure as the company requires. An adequate strategy for the future to increases sales would be e-marketing techniques as well as the current promotions which contribute to diffusing the brand.

Keywords: Commercial strategy, e-commerce, Small and Medium Enterprise (SME), success, Enterprise Resource Planning (ERP).

1 Introduction

Small and medium-sized enterprises (SMEs) are companies normally directed at niche markets where the competition still does not have a huge presence in the Internet [1-2]. Technological improvements and advances in electronic commerce have incentivized many of these companies to make a change of strategy, in order to improve profit margins by making the jump into the global market, which allows them unlimited geographical access and improved competitivity, without an excessive risk of investment, if we compare it with the capital lay-out involved in the expansion of the physical business [3].

Research has shown that SMEs are rapidly adopting e-commerce and Internet [4-10]. The Website may be valuable to SMEs and to exporters in particular [11-12].

But electronic commerce not only signifies buying things through the web, it also gives the possibility of establishing a stable line of commerce using electronic means, including all the legal problems involved, which are outside the electronic environment. The success of an Internet business depends on many factors and the beginnings tend to be complicated without a good strategy.

F.V. Cipolla Ficarra et al. (Eds.): HCITOCH 2010, LNCS 6529, pp. 23–32, 2011.
© Springer-Verlag Berlin Heidelberg 2011

Amongst the most important goals at the time of planning, we must take into account how important it is that the consumer can find easily the product, its price and the whereabouts of the seller.

Information search is a critical stage in the Internet purchase process [13] hence good positioning in the Internet and an adequate strategy are the best ways of ensuring customer loyalty. Customer Relationship Management (CRM) is an integral component of a business strategy for on-line service providers [14]. For the company, the interactivity offered by the Web and improvement in customer service in turn improves the bond of trust so necessary to improve the positioning of the small business.

The SMEs are especially vulnerable to failure with e-commerce as a consequence of poor management coming from inadequate knowledge and the employment of the wrong marketing strategy. Given that the SME, on most occasions, does not have available sufficient funds to carry out adequate strategic planning which would guarantee success it is advisable to turn to a third party to carry out the appropriate planning. This is where we come in. Putting in place an electronic commerce solution requires exhaustive analysis, a complete business plan, the right definition of the product and the client, and obviously providing the SME with the appropriate system. Carrying out a methodological study of the company, its clients and it competitors is vital, in order to define a strategy and objectives to be achieved in the digital business.

The case which presents itself is that of a provincial distribution company which initially dedicates itself to the distribution of pharmaceutical products and which, through the setting up of e-commerce, has greatly diversified its offer, the number of clients and better management.

The most important practical contribution of the paper is that it provides practitioners with a tool to systematically plan.

Good strategic planning guarantees a higher success rate in this type of business. It is important that the organizational characteristics are taken into account when planning, implementing and monitoring strategies in an uncertain business milieu [15-16]. Equally the IT tools put in place in the SME for the development of e-commerce are detailed, given the needs and the budget of the same, because one of the major concerns of senior management in this endeavor is the cost of adopting Web services [17]. In the future the possibility will exist to increase and improve the infrastructure as the company requires (such as the integration of the two major platforms of the video company: the virtual and the physical businesses). A growing body of literature suggests that greater benefits of e-business will be obtained when e-business is integrated throughout a supply chain [18]. The deficiencies which show up during the set up will be solved as the budget of the company grows, in line with the profit which e-commerce can generate. Our provincial company will gain experience and knowledge in e-commerce in a number of steps.

The purpose of proper planning involves identifying existing problems and raises a number of initiatives to improve the internal management of orders, work to facilitate trade and increase customer base and sales volume of our case study.

2   Case Study

The case study is centred on a distribution company for pharmaceuticals which has a stable customer base and concentrates its efforts on maintaining said base. The company personnel is made up of 15 employees, 8 of whom are mobile sales representatives. The remainder work in the company headquarters, in an industrial estate, from where the distribution takes place.

Before e-commerce was implemented, the sales representatives visited the customers to find out what they needed, relative to the purchase of new products. At the end of the day they sent the order by fax to the headquarters, indicating the products sold to each client. Two problems arose from this procedure:

- Those products in stock at the beginning of the day might not still be there by the end. This brought about complaints from the customers, relating to the delay in receiving the products bought.
- The sales representatives were not always familiar with the conditions associated with each customer which brought about complaints from those customers, imbalances and the necessary readjustments to the invoices. Given that the customers normally pay at a later stage by bank draft once the goods have been received, each customer has different invoicing conditions according to the volume of the products bought.

For management purposes, before the implementation of e-commerce, the pharmaceutical products distribution company put in place the Enterprise Resource Planning (ERP) SAGE Line 100 to carry out a centralized management of the business. The implementation raised a series of problems with respect to its functionality:

- The configuration and parametrization of the ERP was not carried out correctly, which did not allow the company to make the most of the functionality of the software in an efficient way, relative to the application of discounts for customers and stock control.
- The server where the ERP was lodged was constantly crashing, causing problems related to the availability of the service and the changing of the information in the database as a consequence of the poor configuration carried out when the server was installed.

3   Phases of the Project

A two-phase plan was carried out, each phase separated by a break of two years. Phase I comprised all the work involved with stabilization, configuration and improving the existing ERP. Phase II corresponded with the implementation of the new e-commerce platform allowing access to the global market which improved the distribution and the final profits. In the first phase the objectives to be achieved were as follows:

- New implementation and configuration of the server in which the internal management tools of the business were lodged, in order to stabilize the service.
- Improvement of the functional efficiency of the ERP SAGE Line with relation to the needs of the company.

In the second phase, once the management system has been stabilized and was functioning correctly, we focused on improving the strategy of the customer orders which came in by fax at the end of the day. Therefore in this phase:

- We developed an authentic e-commerce linked to the ERP database in real time, where the sales rep is able to put in the orders knowing what stock actually exists in the warehouse at that moment in time.
- We improved the account handling of the sales representatives by providing them with the promotions and discounts which apply to each customer at the present moment.

3.1 Phase I: Stabilization of the ERP

The first problem which the distribution company for pharmaceuticals wants to confront is the stabilization of its ERP which was not appropriately configured nor used. In addition to this and as a consequence of the poor functioning of the old server, the database was corrupted. Therefore during the first phase an HP ML 350 server was installed in which the ERP was reinstalled and an Uninterruptible Power Supply (UPS) was purchased to protect the server from isolated power problems. This point was critical for the client, given that the headquarters was based in an industrial estate where the electricity network caused various problems. The infrastructure set up on a descriptive level is shown in the following diagram:

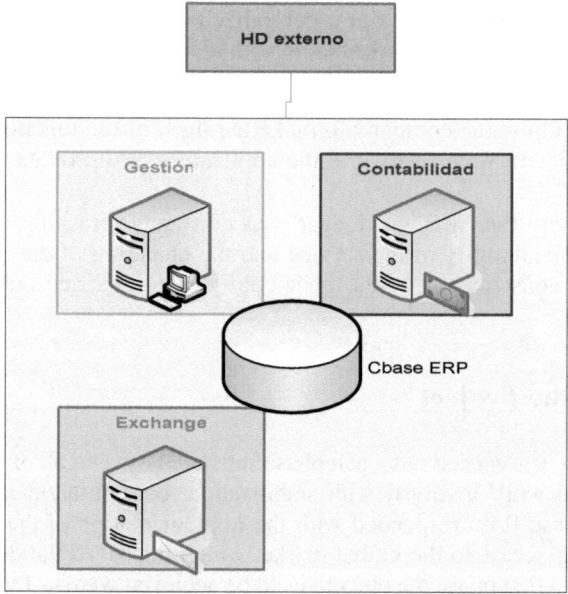

Fig. 1. Infrastructure in phase I

This infrastructure is integrated by an HP ML 350 server with operating system Windows Small Business Server 2003; Windows Firewall; Microsoft Exchange Server mail server; ERP 100 line from SAGE; CBase Access database; data storage in Redundant Array of Inexpensive Disks (RAID) 1.

The choice of the 'Small business' operating system was due to the fact that this version of the server is only valid for 75 client access licenses, sufficient for the company. The advantage of this one is that it includes the mail server of Microsoft Exchange and turns out to be more economical than a conventional 2003 Server.

Increasing the number of licenses of that the ERP already had was not necessary and the work was orientated more towards consultancy and the parametrization of the ERP. These activities were centred on the following aspects:

- Discounts. Each type of business generally works with discounts which depend on the client and the volume to be invoiced. To manage this, the ERP´s own triggers were used. These hard-coded triggers are programmed in the ERP and are launched when a series of predefined conditions are met: for example, it is configured that those products sold to the chemist X must always be offered with a discount of 3% on the usual price.
- Gifts. In addition to discounting, this is standard practice. In the ERP, the parametrization is set up in such a way that a certain line of products has a 100% discount applied to it. In the same way as with discounting, gifts are applied per customer.
- Risk control (scoring). The ERP is configured in such a way that it automatically carries out risk control related to non-payment. Risk control is carried out in conjunction with an external company. The idea is to detect customers who have failed to make payments in order to block any further sales.

The distribution company for pharmaceuticals does not carry out monetary management tasks. They only need to install licenses of accounting and management. The database set up in this company is the default data base of this type of ERP: CBase, owner of SAGE, which has two principal limitations: it has a maximum storage of 1.5 Gb and it does not have a search engine in the server, which makes the searches very slow.

There are two hard disks in RAID 1 in the server. An exact copy (mirror) of all the information is created, which exponentially increases the reliability compared to just one disk. The read rate is more or less doubled, given that two different pieces of information in two different disks can be read simultaneously.

The hard disk is divided into three partitions or Windows units. Unit C houses the operating system, unit D the information, and E is used to store the backups. Copies of each of the units C, D and E are made daily and with the same frequency this backup information is exported to an external hard disk via Universal Serial Bus (USB). This external disk is replaced weekly, so that if a disaster occurs the range of the possible loss would be a maximum of one week.

One of management screens of the ERP looks like this:

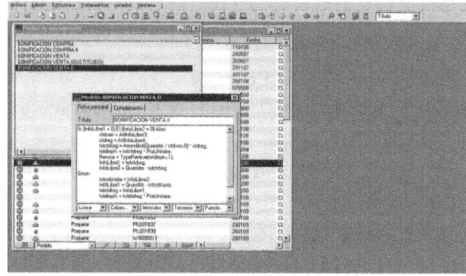

Fig. 2. The ERP management software online

3.2   Phase II: E-commerce Platform for Sales Representatives

The objective carried out in this phase is to create an e-commerce platform which makes the daily work of the company´s sales representatives easier, such as consistency of stock management.

Given that the budget of the distribution company is limited, a solution had to be proposed based on one single server, the same which houses the ERP, which acts as a Web and mail server, creating a Web interface accessible to the sales representatives from their mobile devices, with authentication using a login and password. In this way the sales representative is only able to access the information relating to his customers. This matching between sales rep and customers is first defined in the client file.

The sales rep out in the field is able to consult and show the sales catalogue, access the available invoicing information (old invoices, prices, etc.) and look his client files, as can be seen in the following:

EMPRESA

REGISTRO

PEDIDOS

El Artículo tiene los siguientes precios por categorías tarifarias :

El Artículo no tiene condicionante:

ORTOPEDIA
PUBI: 0,75

FARMACIA
PUBI: 0,75

El Artículo tiene las siguientes bonificaciones :

Ámbito	Título	CVENDIDA1	VENTASC1	CVENDIDA2	VENTASC2
1	BONIFICACION VENTA	0	1	0	0

Volver

gestión de vendedores

Fig. 3. Using the commercial Web interface

One of the advantages provided by the ERP is that the sales people can control the management of discounts and gifts for the customer, as the following demonstrates:

Fig. 4. Online access the Web interface to manage and register discounts and presents

Once the order has been made, the sales representative must be able to leave a written document confirming the order with the customer. To avoid burdening the sales rep with a portable printer, a 'virtual printer' is created. Instead of printing off the document it is sent as a fax to the customer, using the fax number which appears in the customer file.

Payments are made later off-line, generally in the form of a bank draft a few days after. The fact that delayed payment is allowed or not depends upon the reliability of the customers. What generally happens is that existing customers use this form of payment. New customers only have available the pre-payment method (the product only leaves the warehouse once the transfer has been received). This casuistry is also parametrized in the ERP.

A bespoke Web interface has been designed in .NET for the distribution company which consists of a simple and functional platform adequate for displaying it in the mobile devices of the sales representatives (mini portable computers of 7") which come with a USB modem for connecting to the Internet. The possibility is being looked at of replacing the mini computers with PDAs. The implementation of this is quite possible and would only require the redesigning of the screens of the Web interface to allow them to be displayed in PDA format. This Web interface accesses directly the database of the ERP. In this way the coherence and the consistency of the information is assured.

The sales representatives use the mail server mounted on the server using a Web to Outlook access (OWA: Outlook Web Access) and in this way are able to access their electronic mail and register daily in Outlook Calendar their visits to customers. These calendars are shared amongst the sales reps and the main office so that a control of the visits can be carried out. It is, in short, the beginning of CRM.

Globally, the infrastructure of the business looks like this:

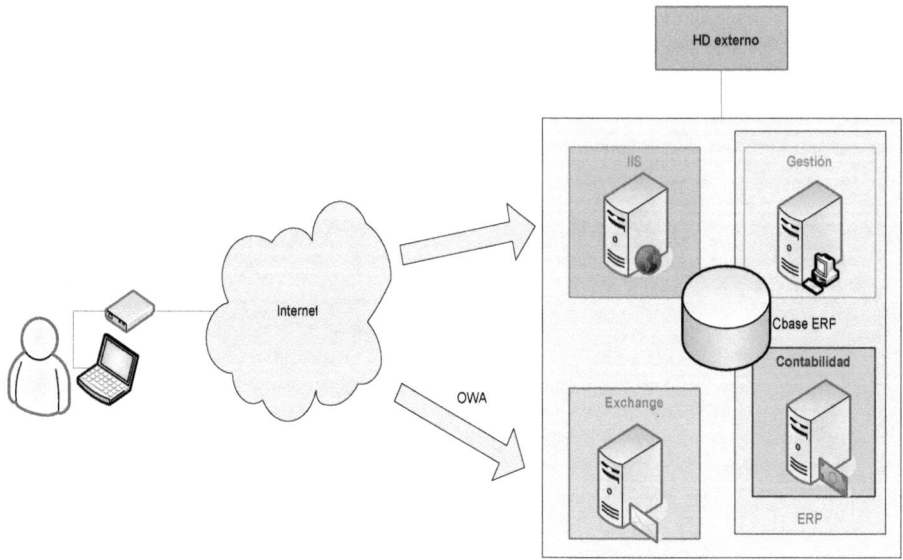

Fig. 5. Entire infrastructure of the network

The additional infrastructure in the second phase consists of an HP ML 350 Server with Windows Firewall and Web Server (Internet Information Server: IIS) and a communications infrastructure (with Signal Swing + Internet Firewall and Internet networks working in parallel: ADSL or Cable).

The total cost of both phases of the project as well as the follow-on support is about 12.000 €. The infrastructure improves the integration of the virtual and physical businesses. When the ERP starts to become scarce, the company could think about the possibility of migrating to SQL. Put into practice e-marketing, as well as improving the marketing practices already in place.

4 Future Works

The following iniciatives are planned:

- Instructing the customers in how to use e-commerce to make orders. This would require a slight adaptation of the system for use by the end customer, given that it has only been configured to support sales made by the representatives.
- Integrate the current Web interface with a CRM application, substituting the actual procedures related to the follow-up of the activity of the sales reps using the OWA. The point would be to try and obtain and analyze the information relative to this data in a more optimized and efficient way.
- Attracting new customers through a major investment destined specifically at improving positioning in search engines.

5 Conclusions

The advent and remarkable development of digital technologies and e-commerce have had profound effects on the world economy. New technologies are affecting almost every aspect of business processes and every industry, dramatically enhancing productivity of the world economy. E-commerce sales have grown at a vigorous pace for nearly 10 years and the tempo will remain very strong.

SMEs have an important role in the economy of our country, making up 99% of the fabric of Spanish business. They are companies normally directed at niche markets where the competition still does not have a huge presence in the Internet. Therefore good strategic planning can guarantee a higher rate of success in these types of organizations. Often the sector of small- and medium-sized business lacks sufficient resources to carry out this strategic planning. Therefore good strategic planning can guarantee a higher rate of success in these types of organizations.

The needs of the small business (where the management of the physical business is carried out independently of the virtual business) are different from those of larger businesses, which are conscious of the importance of carrying out a centralized management of the virtual and physical aspects of the company, in order to achieve efficient logistical control of the provision of products sold through the different distribution channels.

The lack of experience in ICT of SMEs working on small budgets makes them especially vulnerable. In the same way, lack of knowledge of the competition and an inadequate strategic approach can contribute to the failure. It is for this reason that this type of local SME, as in this case study, must rely on the appropriate advice of companies or consultants. It will be these companies who carry out the correct planning that the experience and knowledge of the sector has given them, because the setting up of e-commerce requires an exhaustive analysis and a definition of the best strategy and objectives. In this way the SME will be provided with the most suitable infrastructure to take them into digital commerce according to the costing forecast, which is a determining factor which must be taken into account. The reinvestment of the profits obtained will provide the SME with better technology and the integration of the virtual and physical sides of the company, in the same way as putting into effect the e-marketing strategies which have demonstrated through existing literature their effectiveness.

Acknowledgments. Thanks to ALCA T.I.C. of the group ALCA (http://www. grupoalca.net/) for providing the data of one company that gives support to, and whose data had not been possible to study this case.

References

1. Saee, J., Benli, F.: The role of marketing knowledge for Australian ICT based entrepreneurs in terms of their internationalization strategy. In: Proceedings of the 8th European Conference on Knowledge Management, vol. 1-2, pp. 829–834 (2007)
2. Nooteboom, B.: Innovation and diffusion in small firms - Theory and evidence. Small Business Economics 6(5), 327–347 (1994)

3. Knight, G.A., Kim, D.: International business competence and the contemporary firm. Journal of International Business Studies 40(2), 255–273 (2009)
4. Stiller, A.D.: What should university courses teach graduates so they can be successful - E-business analysis for SMEs. Issues and Trends of Information Technology Management in Contemporary Organizations 1(2), 398–401 (2002)
5. Dholakia, R.R., Kshetri, N.: Factors impacting the adoption of the Internet among SMEs. Small Business Economics 23(4), 311–322 (2004)
6. Lee, R.P., Grewal, R.: Strategic responses to new technologies and their impact on firm performance. Journal of Marketing 68(4), 157–171 (2004)
7. Mehrtens, J., Cragg, P.B., Mills, A.M.: A model of Internet adoption by SMEs. Information & Management 39(3), 165–176 (2001)
8. Raymond, L.: Determinants of Web site implementation in small businesses. Internet Research-Electronic Networking Applications and Policy 11(5), 411–422 (2001)
9. Sadowski, B.M., Maitland, C., van Dongen, J.: Strategic use of the Internet by small- and medium-sized companies: an exploratory study. Information Economics and Policy 14(1), 75–93 (2002)
10. Grandon, E.E., Pearson, J.M.: Electronic commerce adoption: an empirical study of small and medium US businesses. Information & Management 42(1), 197–216 (2004)
11. Houghton, K.A., Winklhofer, H.: The effect of website and E-commerce adoption on the relationship between SMEs and their export intermediaries. International Small Business Journal 22(4), 369–388 (2004)
12. Merono-Cerdan, A.L., Soto-Acosta, P.: External Web content and its influence on organizational performance. European Journal of Information Systems 16(1), 66–80 (2007)
13. Su, B.C.: Characteristics of consumer search on-line: How much do we search? International Journal of Electronic Commerce 13(1), 109–129 (2008)
14. Massad, N., Heckman, R., Crowston, K.: Customer satisfaction with electronic service encounters. International Journal of Electronic Commerce 10(4), 73–104 (2006)
15. Jauhola, E.: ARCTIC PERFORMANCE MANAGEMENT - A case analysis on management and performance measurement practices in North-Russian SMEs. In: Accounting and Performance Management Perspectives in Business and Public Sector Organizations, Conference Proceedings,, pp. 152–164 (2005)
16. Burgess, S., Schauder, D.: Interacting with customers on the internet: Developing a model for small businesses Challenges of Information Technology Management in the 21st century, pp. 517–521 (2000)
17. Chen, A.N.K., Sen, S., Shao, B.B.M.: Strategies for effective Web services adoption for dynamic e-businesses. Decision Support Systems 42(2), 789–809 (2006)
18. Zheng, J.R., Bakker, E., Knight, L., Gilhespy, H., Harland, C., Walker, H.: A strategic case for e-adoption in healthcare supply chains. International Journal of Information Management 26(4), 290–301 (2006)

Improving User Experience by Taking Advance of Semantic Information of Microformats on Municipal Websites

Rocío Rodríguez[1], Pablo Vera[1], Elsa Estevez[2,5], Daniel Giulianelli[1],
León Welicki[3,4], and Artemisa Trigueros[1]

[1] National University of La Matanza
Department of Engineer and Technological Research
Buenos Aires, Argentina
rrodri@unlam.edu.ar,
pablovera@unlam.edu.ar,
dgiulian@unlam.edu.ar,
artemisa@unlam.edu.ar
[2] South National University
Department of Computer Science and Engineer
Buenos Aires, Argentina
ece@cs.uns.edu.ar
[3] Pontifical University of Salamanca
Madrid Campus, Spain
lwelicki@acm.org
[4] Microsoft Redmond
Washington, United States
[5] UNU-IIST Center for Electronic Governance
PO Box 3058, Macao SAR, China

Abstract. This research regards about the use of microformats as a tool to add semantic information to government web sites. The use of microformats allows the developer to add different resources such as maps, calendars, etc, in an easy way. The paper also shows a survey of the already existing microformats and which of them are useful to be applied to government web sites.

Keywords: Microformats, Web sites, Electronic Government.

1 Introduction

Government's web sites provide their citizens with useful information. They become a powerful information channel that allows the government delivering services, receiving opinions and broadcasting information to the people. However, this information is often, very difficult to find. The existing searchers are text based and literally searches where it is intended to find certain words according to the criteria of person who is performing the search. This way, citizens are not able to perform searches according to the meaning of the published contents. On the other hand, the information that is shown is simply textual. The citizen has the responsibility of making his own

F.V. Cipolla Ficarra et al. (Eds.): HCITOCH 2010, LNCS 6529, pp. 33–38, 2011.
© Springer-Verlag Berlin Heidelberg 2011

interpretation and give sense to this information and also, using it to his own good. These are some of the reasons why it is necessary to incorporate additional information to the web site's text; this information would provide a meaning and would allow that the text will be interpreted not only by people but also by computers in automatic way. This is just the goal of the Semantic Web [16] that allows incorporate metadata, adding information to texts presented in the web.

There are different technologies in order to add semantic information to a web site, for example OWL, RDF, Microformats, etc.

Microformats specially define standards to add semantic information to different domains; for example: persons and entities, addresses, reviews, etc. Their utilization goes beyond the addition of legible meaning by a computer. Through different plugins that are available in the browsers, microformats allow offering users with additional tools, improving their experience of navigation and use. For example, if a web page has an hCalendar microformat that allows the definition of events information, the user, with a plugin in his browser is able to detect that event and just with a simple click he can export the event to his own calendar in Outlook, Google calendar, etc.

Also, some search engines such as Google, take advantage of the information provided by microformats and RDF information, if they are present in the web sites, in order to improve the search results and also to show a more complete web site's information in the result's pages [8].

The pursued goals of this research are:

- Survey the existing microformats.
- Analyze the applicability of each one of the microformat to government's web sites.
- Classify the microformats. For example, one criteria would be the use. It must be able to differentiate those microformats used only in an internal way for example by searchers, from those microformats that allow to enhance the user experience interpreting the information by a browser's plugin.
- Analyze and compare the different browsers' current plugins.
- Propose an implementing methodology for the government's web site's microformats.
- Propose and develop improvements for the current plugins.
- Survey web sites that include this technology nowadays.

2 Microformats

The first step of the research was to analyze the different current plugins in order to determine those microformats that allow to show enriched information to the users and in which way they perform this task.

The following plugins corresponding to different browsers were analyzed:

- Oomph, for Internet Explorer [10]
- Operator, for Firefox [11]
- Microformats, for Chrome [12]

(A) Developed Microformats

According to these plugins possibilities, the mircroformats that bring additional information to the users are the following:

- **hCalendar:** it is used for calendars and events [2]. For example: a government's web site could inform moratoriums' expiration dates corresponding to different taxes using microformats. This way, the citizen would be able to know all these dates as events, and would be able too, to export them and add them directly to his schedule manager such as Outllook, Google Calendar, etc. Picture 1 shows an example of hCalendar with three events and the actions that can be performed with them using the Operator plugin of Firefox.

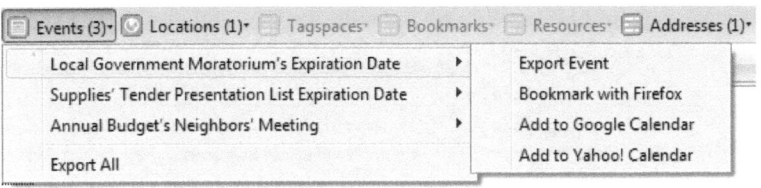

Fig. 1. An example of hCalendar with Operator

The event's information includes:

-    *Summary* – the text that the user is able to see as the event's identification.
-    *Location* – it can be optionally mentioned the location where the event is going to be performed.
-    *Beginning and end's date and time* – including the time zone where it is defined.
-    *Description* – text that explains the event's details.
-    *Tags* – other information.

- **hCard:** they are introducing cards [3], such as personal cards with an individual or organization's information. In it, all the contact data belonging to a particular person can be described, for example: name, telephone number, address, email address, web site, and also NIC names used in messenger, or the URL where his contact photograph is published. Picture 2 shows an example of iCard where three contacts are shown, and the possibilities for the user to export those contacts, for example to Yahoo, or to another file that can be read by any scheduler manager.

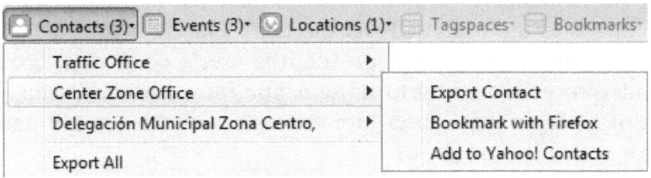

Fig. 2. Examples of hCard with Operator

This microformat could be used to load, for example, the telephone numbers, email addresses, etc. corresponding to different local government's areas. This way, citizens can get with only one click the telephone numbers and other contact data of the government's areas he is interested in, and also he can include them to his contacts.

- • **Geo:** This microformat provides geographic information that allows defining the location by the class Geo [1]. The use of this class allows defining the entity latitude and longitude. In an automatic way the user can search an address by using a geographic location program such as Google Maps. Picture 3 shows an example of the microformat Geo use where because of the latitude and longitude's incorporation, the plugin is able to locate this address in a map, for example Google Maps.

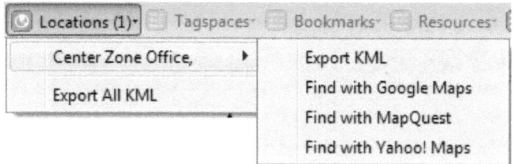

Fig. 3. Example of Geo with Operator

There also are other microformats, that although they don´t have a direct influence over the user interface, they allow adding semantic information to enhance the searches. One of the microformats established as standard that pursues this goal is: **rel-tag**. This microformat allows defining tags inside the web page that denotes key words that identify the page's content or a part of it [15]. The tags are similar to the meta keywords but the difference is that they can be seen as links in order to allow the user noticing the information that is related to the page but this information is not explicitly shown as it is in the meta keywords case.

The tags are specified in the following way:

<a href="http://direccion/tagname" rel="tag">tagname</a>

The URL must point to a page that contains this word definition. The URLs must have a uniform format where the name that is place behind the last bar represents the tag's name. The text of the link doesn´t define the tag but its URL. For example, if it is defined:

<a href="http://address/procedures" rel="tag">Places</a>

In this case the semantic information that is included in the tag shows that it concerns a procedure but, the user will see the text "Places". It must take special care when the tag's definition in order to prevent the user's confusion, because the computer would interpret it according to its semantic information. On the other hand, if the user lacks of a plugin that shows him the tag's value, he would understand it according to the text that the tag shows.

The tags can be used for the information search and also to perform contents' categorization inside the web site.

(B) Microformats that are actually in a Development Stage

There are other microformats that are in a maturation stage, and that they haven't been established as standards yet. However they can be useful to add information in order to improve the searches and the contents organization. Some of them are the following:

- **hReview:** its implementation can be interesting in the government web sites because they provide a notation to specify the product, event, service, etc. review [7]. This feature could be used, for example, to show web sites polls' results, enhancing the results value. It can be included to qualify the government's providers or the achievement of the government's goals.
- **rel="home":** the concept of this microformat, although it is very simple, can be a great help because it allows to define that a determined points to the web site's home page [13]. This microformat added to the plugin use, or much better, integrating them in the browsers in a future, will allow returning to the home page of the site which the user is navigating. If the browser provides a home button inside itself, it won´t be necessary to struggle against the different ways of returning to the home page that nowadays provide the different government web sites. For example: some of them uses a banner with a link to go home, other have a button in the main menu, etc. The implementation and standardization of this microformat would simplify the web site's navigation.
- **rel-payment:** this microformat allows specifying the different payments way of a product or service in the web [14]. It could be use, for example, to show the different ways to pay taxes, traffic fines, etc. This way, the user would be able to see the payment's options and to use a plugin that links him directly to a web site where the tax or fine is already selected and he can pay it very easily. This way of paying taxes or fines is more accessible to citizens that don't know how to use electronic payment.

There are other microformats that are in development stage and allow to add useful information to the context and that can be used in government's web sites:

- **hMedia:** for images, videos and audio [4].
- **hNews:** for the news[5].
- **hResume:** for government agents' curriculum vitae[6].

3 Conclusions and Future Works

Gradually the semantic web is being inserted and complements the current web sites adding them standardized information in order to be interpreted, not only by users but also by programs. The possibility for a software agent to be able to understand the information makes possible to create browsers' complements capable of exploiting this information providing the final user with more opportunities to take advantage of it.

Microformats are a quick and easy way of adding that semantic information to the current web sites, with defined standards focused in clear goals. Although nowadays there can be find some plugins for the most popular browsers, a lot of them are not very known and they already have limited functionalities. Therefore is it necessary, in the first place to raise users' consciousness about the microformats use and their benefits; in the second place the necessity of having better and richer plugins in order of using the information that they provide in a better way.

As future work the proposal is the creation of a plugin for Internet Explorer that allows a higher microformats' integration and a better use of them, always focused in the goal of enhancing the user's experience while he is navigating a web site.

References

1. Geo, microformats.org (2009), `http://microformats.org/wiki/geo`
2. Calendar, microformats.org (2009),
   `http://microformats.org/wiki/hcalendar`
3. Card, microformats.org (2010), `http://microformats.org/wiki/hcard`
4. Media, microformats.org (2010), `http://microformats.org/wiki/hmedia`
5. News, microformats.org (2010), `http://microformats.org/wiki/hnews`
6. Resume, microformats.org (2010), `http://microformats.org/wiki/hresume`
7. Review, microformats.org (2010), `http://microformats.org/wiki/hreview`
8. Goel, K., Ramanathan, V., Guha, Y., Hansson, O.: Introducing Rich Snippets.
   `http://googlewebmastercentral.blogspot.com/2009/05/`
   `introducing-rich-snippets.html`
9. Berriman, F., Cederholm, D., Çelik, T., Khare, R., King, R., Marks, K., Ward, B.: Micro-formats (2009), `http://microformats.org/`
10. Flynn, M.: Plugin Oomph para Internet Explorer (2009),
    `http://www.ieaddons.com/en/details/toolbars/`
    `Oomph_2_A_Microformats_Toolbar/`
11. Musings, M.: Plugin Operator para Firefox (2010),
    `https://addons.mozilla.org/es-ES/firefox/addon/4106`
12. Piasetzki, J.: Plugin para Google Chrome (2010),
    `https://chrome.google.com/extensions/detail/`
    `igipijakdobkinkdmiiadhghmbjhciol`
13. rel-home, microformats.org (2009),
    `http://microformats.org/wiki/rel-home`
14. rel-payment, microformats.org (2009),
    `http://microformats.org/wiki/rel-payment`
15. rel-tag, microformats.org (2009), `http://microformats.org/wiki/rel-tag`
16. W3C: Guía Breve de Web Semántica (2008),
    `http://www.w3c.es/Divulgacion/Guiasbreves/WebSemantica`

Human-Computer Interaction, Tourism and Cultural Heritage

Francisco V. Cipolla Ficarra[1,2]

HCI Lab. – F&F Multimedia Communic@tions Corp.
[1] ALAIPO: Asociación Latina de Interacción Persona-Ordenador
[2] AINCI: Asociación Internacional de la Comunicación Interactiva
Via Pascoli, S. 15 – CP 7, 24121 Bergamo, Italy
ficarra@alaipo.com

Abstract. We present a state of the art of the human-computer interaction aimed at tourism and cultural heritage in some cities of the European Mediterranean. In the work an analysis is made of the main problems deriving from training understood as business and which can derail the continuous growth of the HCI, the new technologies and tourism industry. Through a semiotic and epistemological study the current mistakes in the context of the interrelations of the formal and factual sciences will be detected and also the human factors that have an influence on the professionals devoted to the development of interactive systems in order to safeguard and boost cultural heritage.

Keywords: Human-Computer Interaction, Interactive Systems, Teaching, Human Factors, Semiotics, Cultural Heritage, Tourism.

1 Introduction

Tourism is an essential industry in many countries of southern Europe, taking the first places as a source of income for the GNP (gross national product) and the GNI (gross national income) in countries like France, Greece, Italy, Portugal and Spain. With the first off-line and on-line multimedia systems there was already some talk about virtual tourism. A virtual tourism where the visitor or user could navigate through the reconstructed ruins of a city swept away by an earthquake in antiquity or through the 3D works that were designed by Leonardo Da Vinci [1]. In the case of the great figures of universal history, many of them were used in each of the different stages that were overcome by the intersection of software and hardware. To the extent that we have Leonardo Da Vinci from the hypertextual system, going through the multimedia until reaching the hypermedia and the on-line interactive systems [2] [3] [4] (figure 1).

Along all this time, a kind of new language known as *interactive* has been created. In this sense, we have the educational aspect of the early multimedia systems aimed at cultural heritage [5] [6]. However, in the late nineties, the entertainment industry became the main economic engine of the multimedia sector in southern Europe [7]. Consequently, the merger of contents between interactive works of the cultural heritage and entertainment starts, until the off-line multimedia systems are sidelined because of the eruption of the Internet. In all this productive process, the provisions

F.V. Cipolla Ficarra et al. (Eds.): HCITOCH 2010, LNCS 6529, pp. 39–50, 2011.

Fig. 1. Leonardo Da Vinci –from floppy (hypertext) to CD-ROM (multimedia and hypermedia)

made by software engineering [8], for instance, are totally obsolete, because of endless human factors [9] [10] and globalization [11].

The theoretical solutions do not adjust quickly to the productive reality of the industry of the interactive systems on-line. The cost factor of transforming into digital support the cultural heritage, joined to the copyright policies are the main roadblock in Europe. For instance, in the sector of cartography stored in the state files of Italy, every local institution has its own rules for the artistic reproduction in the on-line and off-line interactive systems.

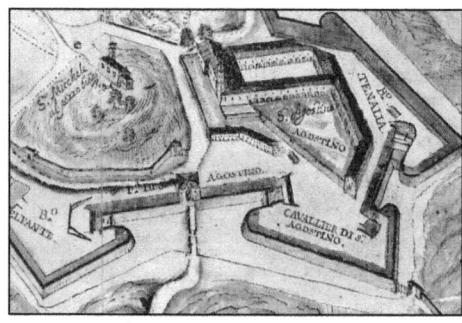

Fig. 2. Map of the upper city of Bergamo –17th century (area St. Augustine)

These state and public files can be cornerstones to boost the realization of endless interactive systems once their contents are stored in databases and their 2D images can be the source of a cultural revolution in the Internet. We can find some proof of this in the 2D and/or 3D scientific visualization that is made in many research labs in different nations of the world. However, in some cases, the human factor derived from the lack of a homogeneous and coherent policy in regard to the definition of cultural heritage prevents having homogeneity inside the borders of a single state, to the extent that the personal use of this heritage is consented or authorized for just one computer. Evidently, a heritage that has been the addition of all the inhabitants of a territory is ruled by a few, thus discouraging the access to it, even with educational and/or tourism ends.

The research work starts with an analysis of the expansion of the interactive systems and the importance of human-computer interaction. The phenomena which cause such confusion in the current research works in the HCI are studied. These phenomena derive from the poor use of the terms multidisciplinarity, interdisciplinarity, transdisciplinarity, etc. Besides, examples are presented of the human factors that, from the industrial, training and commercial sector of computer science and the universities may boost or diminish these confusions. Finally, the profile of the communicability analyst to eradicate these ambiguities and promote a correct design of the interactive systems is briefly presented.

2 Human-Computer Interaction and the Expansion of the Interactive Systems

Human-computer interaction is without any doubt one of the fields of scientific knowledge where the formal sciences and the factual sciences interact among themselves and which has yielded evidence in the last decades of an exponential growth [12] [13]. This is due to the expansion of the interactive systems and the momentum of the micro-computing devices also known as mobile computing. In the current work both notions are used as synonymous. Simultaneously, the international context, from the economic point of view, has boosted in the last five years the resources of the cultural and natural heritage in the world with the purpose of fostering local, national and international tourism. Consequently in the current environment there are three central axes which interact among themselves in a two-way fashion: the breakthroughs of computing and telecommunications, and in a special way, the software and the hardware, the users, grouped in relation to the competence and/or knowledge in the use of these new interactive technologies and the resources of the cultural and natural heritage, whose contents have started to be digitalized in off-line and on-line interactive systems since the 90s. Graphically:

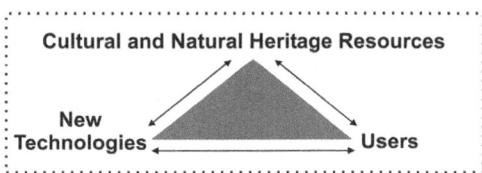

Fig. 3. Central axes for cultural and natural heritage promotion

If we analyze the literature concerning the forecasts about the future which were made in the late 90 and early 2000, we can see that many of the research goals have been achieved. This is due to the fact that this is a sector where the transdisciplinarity or multidisciplinarity of the sciences are respected in the realization of complex R+D projects aimed at the new interactive systems. In this case we have used three terms as if they were synonymous. However, they are not dependent on the country from which the works related to the human-computer-interaction are presented, for instance. Evidently you can find interdisciplinarity in the arts and in the humanistic studies. An example in the art and the design can be the approach of an interdisciplinary discourse in the convergence of the research in the arts, science, interactive technology. Now one has to be very cautious in the use of these notions, especially in certain educational areas such as the audiovisual, where some Catalan colleges have not distinguished these boundaries very clearly in the last two decades thus causing huge damage in their future professionals dedicated to the interactive design of tourist systems because to them the terms "transdisciplinarity", "interdisciplinarity", "multidisciplinarity", "multimedia", "hypermedia", "virtual reality", "computer art", etc. are simply synonymous. The purpose of this confusion is the educational mercantilism in certain masters or post-graduate courses, for instance.

While in the USA one can see a continuous tendency to adapt the university curricula related to the new technologies to the new realities deriving from the software and the hardware, for instance [15] [16] [17] [18]. In contrast to this cosmos, we have the European Union, whose member states have kept their competences in an autonomous way in each country, thus generating a kind of Babel Tower in these issues. Therefore, nobody should be surprised that a Portuguese PhD. in computing or multimedia can't have his titled homologated to the Italian, because previously he has to homologate the bachelor or engineer degree. That is, that a Portuguese, Spanish, French PhD has a lower category than an Italian graduate or engineer, for not having made his PhD or engineering studies in Italy. Besides, this entails that that person who should validate his title must visit the same academic units of the state to find that where the greatest number of taken subjects is recognized and so having to elaborate again a final project. Having obtained the title of graduate or engineer, he can just start the steps to homologate the PhD. Once the recognition of the PhD title is obtained, he/she must be qualified as a college professor, as it happens since the start of the new century in Spain, for instance.

In the qualification courses one can see how the examiners, those professors generated through the university reform of the new millennium, who have just a degree in computer science or systems engineering of 3 years, but who have got an automatic qualification prior to the reform, as it also happens in the rest of the Iberian Peninsula. Theoretically, the Bologna plan will solve these issues. However, today we can meet in Europe engineers or PhDs in nuclear energy as chiefs of several multimedia communication college labs, and even as university deans, who are not over 40 years old and have fewer than 5 scientific publications, when taking office. Others start to publish in magazines, conventions, etc., as if they were PhD. when in fact they are just graduates in maths, business, physics, chemistry, etc. but who direct doctor thesis.

The solution to many of the problems described which exist in this European educational context could be found if the most avant-garde models of the European education were imposed to the rest of the member countries. These are countries where the merit of the professionals is rewarded and not the parochialism defined by Saussure [19] or the college education understood as a statistical number or a low quality industry of training, where there is an interest to increase every year the profits won by the increase in the registration of students. In these environments, there is no publicity campaign which can hide the wild marketing made even in alleged public universities, within states that border with Saussure's homeland.

3   Educational and Industrial Sectors: Formation or Marketing Interrelations?

These are approaches based on the industrial sector of the tridimensional animation of the 80s, and which are automatically transferred to the educational environment in the

90s. All of this in the audiovisual and multimedia sectors. Although there was talk of different disciplines (graphic designers, computing, making of video, television, etc.) the aim was to differentiate the art from the computer technologies.

A rudimentary or archaic guideline which could work very well in the vertical and/or dictatorial structures of a pioneering European industrial sector, such as computer animation. That is to say that in the face of a technical problem, computer experts were required, for instance. Whereas when dealing with creative problems it was necessary to count on fine arts professionals, that is, a different kind of expertise. The team had to work between technicians and artists.

Later on these artists were called designers. The working premise was that the technicians had to understand the concerns and the difficulties of the creative artists and vice versa. In few words, a mix-up of terms and functions and professional roles unprecedented in the autonomic university educational sector in Barcelona in the 90s and which, oddly enough, is exported or fostered in our days in other countries which are on the border with Switzerland, for instance, in some faculties of training sciences in the Lombardy. In contrast to the Catalan case, in which at least there are specific disciplines, in the Lombardian context the anthropologists, on the basis of some notions by Jean Piaget [20] can spoil the notion of transdisciplinarity as stated by Piaget himself in 1970.

The purpose is building professor teams where the status or the elitism of the places where these university titles have been obtained prevails, enhancing the prestige of computing graduates and downgrading the titles of PhD but holding positions such as expert in the local chapters of HCI within prestigious international associations such as the Association for Computing Machinery –ACM, for example. At the same time, the very same graduates in philology, after hardly finishing those college studies, become experts or specialists in E-learning, multimedia communication, education technologies, emotive and cognitive systems, logical programming for computers, musical production technician, visual effects, etc.

These people without pedagogical and technological experience become even tutors or directors of postgraduate courses on-line to doctors, earning salaries which are tantamount to twice or three times more than the yearly average of the National Research Centre or Superior Council of a R+D European country. Obviously to this we can add the name of St. Augustine (for instance, a former convent turned into a faculty), we are in the face of an educational medieval stonewall, from which they pretend to obstruct the real goals of the Human-Computer Interaction in Europe. Schematically, both examples of obstruction in Southern Europe can be depicted in the following way:

A) **Computer Science + Artists + Others Disciplines** = Confusion Professional

B) **Inter, Multi, Trans ... disciplinarity + Cloning Professional (cut, copy & past)** = Pseudo Professional

Fig. 4. Central axes for cultural and natural heritage promotion

The consequences of these conceptual mistakes in the context of the multimedia interactive systems on-line and off-line can be seen in the way of making the transfer of technologies between the industrial sector and the educational sector in some countries of the EU. On the one hand we have the constant lack of experience, that is, the technical or practical aspect of the new professionals, and on the other hand inside the training sector there is the lack of knowledge of the real world, in our case inside the previously mentioned triad. Besides, not only the scientific growth and the quality of life of all the members of those societies is slowed down, but it is also remarkable that their inhabitants are very vulnerable to the hazards of globalization due to the scarce or poor training. We are in the face of one of the main problems of the convergences and/or divergences from the educational point of view.

4 Sciencies into HCI: Evolution of the Disciplinarity

Under the name of HCI, in many universities and faculties that were inaugurated in the 90s or early 21st century, even today, there is no correct definition of the functions of said HCI and the roles of the main components of the structure which regulate and guide the directions to be followed at present, immediate future and much less across time [16]. Basically, this is a mistake deriving from the fact that its directors, in an independent way, lack the knowledge or adequate training for a 360% vision, that is, from the point of view of the formal and factual sciences. The most striking example is the Human Computer Interaction where currently the virtual reality, the interactive language, the cognitive sciences, full-body interaction for children and youngsters, videogame design and development, artificial intelligence techniques, etc., are placed under it in certain audiovisual, multimedia and centres of Mediterranean Europe. Evidently, there is an overlapping of areas, and the originality of the projects is practically non-existent because of this lack of setting down the specific limits of the disciplines. The purpose of these imprecise boundaries is the wild marketing, which seeks to present pseudoinnovating contents to draw students to these classrooms. Consequently, it is very important to try to define accurately the three terms we are analyzing. In the scientific contexts of central Europe, the transdisciplinarity word is used in several ways. In the countries of Central and Northern Europe, the term usually refers to the converging ways of research. This definition collides with the understanding of transdisciplinarity as a principle of unity of knowledge beyond the disciplines [21]. Here it is very important to point out that many of these notions are presented by anthropologists who claim to be science philosophers and pedagogues. In the face of this reality, the discipline that can help us to understand and analyze the presented conceptual context is semiotics or semiology [19]. As for the principle of converging ways of research, the transdisciplinarity encompasses a family of methods to relate scientific knowledge, extra-scientific experience and the practice of problem solving [22]. In problem solving, during the so-called software quality age, when from the USA it was claimed that it was necessary to insert psychologists, anthropologists, etc., that is, transdisciplinarity in order to improve the final products.

Evidently, that was a solution that worked well in the USA with a horizontal vision of the labour, educational, R+D structures, etc., in contrast to the vertical structures where a technician or a graduate in humanity sciences has more power of decision than an engineer with a PhD, for instance. In this understanding transdisciplinary research is oriented towards the aspects of the real world, rather than to those which have only origin and relevance in the scientific debate. An issue of major importance in transdisciplinary research is to what extent you can achieve the convergence and integration of the different scientific perspectives in a common intersection area. This area is something very hard to reach in the European universities and industries and easier to achieve in the countries of the American continent. The reason are the strategies of college education followed in many places of the American continent, where a simple computing technician must also be acquainted with the main notions of social sciences. This common area of intersection is often used to distinguish between transdisciplinarity, interdisciplinarity and multidisciplinarity [23] [24].

The transdisciplinary research field is hard to structure as a result of these different and in some ways inconsistent concepts and terminologies. A transdisciplinary style of research can only emerge if the participation of the expert people interacts in the way of an open discussion and of dialogue, accepting every perspective as of equal importance and relating the different prospects among them. For instance, there are evaluation techniques of usability engineering such as simplified thinking aloud, participatory heuristic evaluation [25] [26] or within creative design brainstorming [27]. The joint work in an intradisciplinary way is difficult, because those who participate are often overloaded by the amount of information of daily praxis and by the incommensurability of the specialized languages in each one of the fields of experience. Here is one of the reasons why it is important to use the main notions of the hypertextual and hypermedia systems in order to avoid confusions and waste of money and time among the participants at the moment of designing, evaluating, producing services and interactive products. So become necessary people with moderation, mediation, association and transfer to begin and promote a constructive and permanent dialogue. Here come into play the skills of the psychologists, anthropologists, etc., who in Europe quickly lead those groups of professionals. However, these individuals do not have a deep knowledge of their own and a know-how in regard to the involved disciplines. The results from the technological point of view are very poor, and even from the social point of view, because usually the teams they lead fade away after a few months.

The production of knowledge in the transdisciplinary framework means the surpassing of the "basic knowledge and applied knowledge" antagonism, oriented to a dynamic circulation among the different levels of knowledge and outside the hierarchic structures, homogeneous and stable such as those of the traditional university. In many universities and faculties of recent construction this entails having to face pedagogues with a long tradition in university training and the anthropologists have merely political or power purposes, as if they were a kind of star enunciator and his points of view must prevail over the rest of the group. In his place, the production of knowledge under the paradigm of transdisciplinarity does not work according to the opposition "basic knowledge –applied knowledge", but within the framework of dynamic structures and heterogeneous and transitory groupings. Hence transdisciplinarity approaches problematic settings instead of epistemologically defined knowledge territories, for which it is necessary an integrating or converging approach of knowledge in order to work systematically. The serious mistake that is usually made by many pundits or pseudo experts inside this integrating context is that they can't tell a system from a structure.

5 Transdiciplinarity from Theorical and Computer Experiences

The South African mathematician Seymour Papert worked in the university of Geneva with Jean Piaget. Seymour Papert in the 60s went to the Massachusetts Institute of Technology to work with Marvin Minsky and the group that worked on artificial intelligence. Evidently, they were real professionals of the formal sciences and the factual sciences, among whom existed the daily praxis of transdisciplinarity in their work. An evidence of this is the LOGO language invented by Papert (derived from the functional programming language Lisp –LISt Processing) aimed at very young kids so that they started to interact with the computers from childhood [28]. That is, a context of work and interaction of theories and practice where it would be impossible to say that semiotics is an engineering, for instance. Jean Piaget and his working team presented a different approach of transdisciplinarity.

In Piaget's conception, transdisciplinarity is radically different from interdisciplinarity. Interdisciplinarity deals with the transfer of methods within disciplines. Now like multidisciplinarity, interdisciplinarity goes beyond the disciplines but its goals still remain within the framework of disciplinary research (for instance, in the figure 4, the "a" option is positive in regard to "b", because at least disciplines are mentioned. As the prefix "trans" shows, transdisciplinarity entails that which is at the same time among the disciplines, that is, through the different disciplines, and beyond each individual discipline [29]. Its goal is the understanding of the current world, for which each one of the imperatives is the unity of global knowledge. In the current era of communicability expansion, joined to the global village achieved through the internet and the mass media, the social sciences that interact with the formal sciences can be very important [29]. However, the label of specialist in new technologies and communicability can't, nor must be placed, or even worse, place itself for the simple fact of having university studies or technical knowledge in computing, or systems software, electronics, industrial engineering, etc. joined to a B.A. or master in geography, psychology, sociology, anthropology, etc.

That is, to eradicate that mercantilist purpose which is usually made from the private and/or public university educational institutions presenting pseudo-specialists at the summit of the pyramid of college knowledge or in the working context, within businesses, industries, etc., which are aimed more at the formal sciences than the social sciences. The Romanian author Basarab Eftimie Nicolescu claims from the formal sciences that transdisciplinarity is defined through three methodological postulates: complexity, the existence of reality levels, and the logic of the included intermediates [29]. The presence of different levels of reality, the space among the disciplines and beyond the disciplines is full of information. With the Internet this information grows second by second, and the human being must know how to seek and distinguish that which is true or real from that which is not. To that end he resorts to the knowledge of several disciplines. Now, the disciplinary research entails, at most, a single level of reality, although in most cases it only involves fragments from a level of reality. In contrast, transdisciplinarity implies the dynamic generated by the action of several levels of reality at the same time. The discovery of these dynamics necessarily goes through disciplinary knowledge. Transdisciplinarity, even if it is not a new discipline or superdiscipline, is fed by the disciplinary studies. Consequently, transdisciplinary knowledge clarifies disciplinary research in a novel and fruitful way. In this sense, transdisciplinary research and the disciplinary are not antagonistic but complementary to multidisciplinary research or interdisciplinary research. Transdisciplinarity is in any case radically different from multidisciplinarity and interdisciplinarity due to its goal, the understanding of the current world, which can't be reached in the plotting of the disciplinary studies. Here is the reason why certain analysis methodologies of the interactive systems, with their matching attributes of quality and metrics, have had a great success since the start, such as: MEHEM –Methodology for Heuristic Evaluation in Multimedia, MECEM –Metrics for the Communications Evaluation in Multimedia, and MEDIE –Method for a Evaluation of the Design in Industrial Ecommerce [30].

Lastly, the goal of interdisciplinarity and multidisciplinarity always remains in the context of disciplinary research. Now if transdisciplinarity is presented in a lax and confusing way with the interdisciplinarity and with the multidisciplinarity, that is, outside the real scientific sector, which doesn't seek profit and respecting the main principles of science. The same happens with the interdisciplinarity that is usually mistaken for multidisciplinarity, this is explained from the scientific point of view because to a great extent the three surpass the borders among the disciplines. From the point of view of the human factors, those who foster these distortions such as star enunciators in the Internet, who since the mid-nineties have been trying to generate authoritarian pyramids, occupying their summits, to the detriment of horizontality and democratization of the access to the Internet contents. This confusion is very harmful, because it hides the great potential of transdisciplinarity.

6   Communicability Analyst in Interactive Systems

The profile of the professional in the analysis of communicability for the interactive systems which is next presented has been mainly aimed at cultural and natural heritage. This is a new professional who intends to solve the great loopholes existing in the university and work training environment. This professional is the result of the intersection of the formal sciences and the factual sciences. Joining this result to a long experience in the realization of the off-line and on-line interactive systems leads to great success because of the high quality-low costs equation. Graphically:

After carrying out a heuristic study analyzing 40 university degree curricula related to tourism in the American and European continents, our expert in communicability needs to join the following fields of knowledge: tourism legislation, tourism geography and history of the local cultural and natural heritage, marketing of the touristic enterprises, planning and evaluation of touristic projects, information technology, and communication applied to tourism. These curricula have been randomly chosen from a listing of 120 university teaching centres aimed at tourism and cultural heritage. Besides, these experts may collaborate in the training of professionals capable of applying the methodology of scientific research, that is, to generate knowledge and development of products and touristic services which contribute to increase the social,

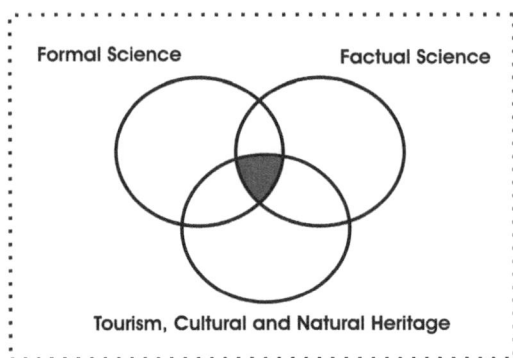

Fig. 5. Analysis of communicability for tourism, cultural and natural heritage –red area, field of knowledge

cultural and economic standard of living, with the help of the new technologies and in a special way with the multimedia interactive systems.

7 Conclusion

In the current work it has been made apparent that a humanistic training is not a warrant of quality in the production of interactive software, especially with the students trained in certain public and private colleges in Europe. The human factors that derive from these trainers and students in the humanities may distort and cause heavy losses in the industrial sector of the new technologies and human computer interaction. There are some who intend to turn the umbrella of the human-computer interaction into some kind of beach parasol, placing under it other areas of the dynamic and static means that have not had a great acceptance by the basis of the pyramid of the users, such as virtual reality, for instance. The reason is the mercantilist factor that surrounds the virtual reality under the terms "transdisciplinarity", "interdisciplinarity" and "multidisciplinarity". Evidently, in the past decades the solid theoretical training was important to reach important results from a practical point of view. This was the secret of the university professionals capable of doing a u-turn to find the best solution, in a record time and with low costs.

Today in some contexts of the audiovisual and/or computer science and college environment the learning of commercial programs prevails for the elaboration of interactive systems aimed at tourism, the cultural, natural heritage, etc., because the latter are "fashionable" contents. The risk of that mercantilism is that it prompts the umpteenth stop in the creativity and originality of the interactive systems, as happened in the late nineties with the off-line hypermedia. However, the development of the tourist industry and all the components that it entails, requires another kind of professional, capable of boosting, in an autonomous way and through the net the free access to the multimedia databases, where the dynamic and static data of the past and the present, of the local, national and international community are all stored. In the future works we will try to set up the guidelines to be followed by this new professional, on the basis of the intersection of the formal sciences and the factual sciences.

Acknowledgments

Thanks to Sara Diana (Auckland University), Simone Mazotti, Sonia Flores, Maria Ficarra (Alaipo & Ainci – Italy and Spain) and Carlos for their precious collaboration.

References

1. CD-ROM Il Codice Atlantico di Leonardo da Vinci: Atum Corporation, Tokyo (2006)
2. Flopyy Leonardo Drawings: Silbermann, Firenze (1994)
3. CD-ROM Leonardo Da Vinci Drawings: Silbermann, Firenze (1996)
4. CD-ROM Galleria d'arte Leonardo: Istituto Geografico De Agostini, Novara (2001)
5. Landaw, G.: Hypertext 3.0: Critical Theory and New Media in an Era of Globalization. The Johns Hopkins University Press, London (2006)
6. Cipolla-Ficarra, F.: Communicability design and evaluation in cultural and ecological multimedia systems. In: Proc. of the 1st ACM International Workshop on Communicability Design and Evaluation in Cultural and Ecological Multimedia System, pp. 1–8. ACM Press, New York (2008)
7. Lamborghini, B.: European Information Technology Observatory. EITO-EEIG, Frankfurt (2001)
8. Kructhten, P., Obbink, H., Stafford, J.: The Past, Present, and Future of Software Architecture. IEEE Software 23(2), 22–29 (2006)
9. Berenbach, B., Broy, M.: Professional and Ethical Dilemmas in Software Engineering. IEEE Software 42(2), 74–80 (2009)
10. Tudor, L.: Human Factors : Does Your Management Hear You? Interactions 1(1), 16–24 (1998)
11. Arora, A., Drev, M., Forman, C.: Economic and Business Dimensions: The Extent of Globalization of Software Innovation. Communications of the ACM 52(2), 20–22 (2009)
12. Erickson, T., McDonald, D.: HCI Remixed: Reflections on Works That Have Influenced the HCI Community. MIT Press, Massachussetts (2008)
13. Kortum, P.: HCI Beyond the GUI: Design for Haptic, Speech, Olfactory, and Other Nontraditional Interfaces. Morgan Kaufmann, Burlington (2008)
14. Baecker, R.: Themes in the Early History of HCI –Some Unanswered Questions. Interactions 15(2), 22–25 (2008)
15. Sung, K.: Computer Games and Traditional CS Courses. Communications of the ACM 52(12), 74–78 (2009)
16. Ritter, F., Freed, A., Haskett, O.: Discovering User Information Needs: The Case of University Department Web Sites. Interactions 12(5), 19–27 (2005)
17. Pyster, A., et al.: Master's Degrees in Software Engineering: An Analysis of 28 University Programs. IEEE Software 26(5), 94–101 (2009)
18. Litecky, C., et al.: Mining for Computing Jobs. IEEE Software 27(1), 78–85 (2010)
19. Nöth, W.: Handbook of Semiotics. Indiana University Press, Indianapolis (1995)
20. Wadsworth, B.: Piaget's Theory of Cognitive and Affective Development: Foundations of Constructivism. Allyn & Bacon, Boston (2004)
21. Repko, A.: Interdisciplinary Research: Process and Theory. Sage Publications, Thousand Oaks (2008)
22. Roughley, N.: Being Humans: Anthropological Universality and Particularity in Transdisciplinary Perspectives. Walter de Gruyter Publishing, Berlin (2000)

23. Klein, J.: Interdisciplinarity: History, Theory, and Practice. Wayne State University Press, Detroit (1991)
24. Grudin, J.: Is HCI Homeless? In Search of Inter-Disciplinary Status. Interactions 13(1), 54–59 (2006)
25. Muller, M., et al.: Participatory Heurristic Evaluation. Interactions 5(6), 59–66 (1998)
26. Carter, P.: Liberating Usability Testing. Interactions 14(2), 18–22 (2007)
27. Martin, R., Riel, J.: Designing Interactions at Work: Applying Design to Discussions, Meetings, and Relationships. Interactions 17(2), 16–19 (2010)
28. Piaget, J.: The Children Machine. Basic Books, New York (1993)
29. Paymal, N.: Pedagogia 3000. Brujas, Cordoba (2008)
30. Cipolla-Ficarra, F.: Quality and Communicability for Ineractive Hypermedia Systems: Concepts and Practices for Design. IGI Global, Hershey (2010)

Strategies for a Creative Future with Computer Science, Quality Design and Communicability

Francisco V. Cipolla Ficarra[1,2] and Maria Villarreal[3]

HCI Lab. – F&F Multimedia Communic@tions Corp.
[1] ALAIPO: Asociación Latina de Interacción Persona-Ordenador
[2] AINCI: Asociación Internacional de la Comunicación Interactiva
[3] Universidad Nacional de La Pampa
Via Pascoli, S. 15 – CP 7, 24121 Bergamo, Italy
ficarra@alaipo.com

Abstract. In the current work is presented the importance of the two-way triad between computer science, design and communicability. It is demonstrated how the principles of quality of software engineering are not universal since they are disappearing inside university training. Besides, a short analysis of the term "creativity" males apparent the existence of plagiarism as a human factor that damages the future of communicability applied to the on-line and off-line contents of the open software. A set of measures and guidelines are presented so that the triad works again correctly in the next years to foster the qualitative design of the interactive systems on-line and/or off-line.

Keywords: Creativity, Design, Quality, Computer Science, Hypermedia, Interface, Communicability, Education.

1 Introduction

Creativity applied to the new or latest technologies, according to the perspective from which it is watched by the user of the on-line and off-line interactive systems, is without any doubt any of the environments where the knowledge of the different disciplines converge [1] [2] [3]. Many of them are varied, in certain university centres, to try to find always solutions to the posed problems, such as the middle and long term tendencies in the scientific context, for instance [4] [5] [6]. The word creativity is the origin in many cases of those solutions that theoretically set research lines inside the technological breakthroughs [7] [8]. In the context of computer science there is an endless number of publications in specialized magazines of important associations such as ACM –Association for Computing Machinery and IEEE –Institute of Electrical and Electronic Engineers, just to mention two examples. The authors of the projects or presented research draw lines to be followed inside the context of the programming languages, the databases, telecommunications, safety of information, etc., or as it is our case, those called potential users. That is, an endless series of variables that aside from the creativity or originality of the solutions is opening the technological gap among the researchers, developers, etc. and the users. The former are placed at the summit of the pyramid, and the latter, at the feet.

F.V. Cipolla Ficarra et al. (Eds.): HCITOCH 2010, LNCS 6529, pp. 51–62, 2011.
© Springer-Verlag Berlin Heidelberg 2011

All of this happens regardless of the fact whether the design of an interactive system, for instance, was thought, designed and produced for the vast majority of users or a privileged elite [9] [10]. Besides, some claim that there is a creativity myth. Others in contrast, through the arts linked to the technologies, have found an interesting way of making money inside the universities without caring about the working future of their alumni, B.A. in audiovisual, software engineers, specialist in digital music, computer animation technicians, etc.

To talk about the myth or reality of creativity it is necessary to consider it from several points of view and carry out an analysis of the word "creativity". The idea that remains in the economically developed societies about the origins of creative innovation in the sciences and the arts is romantic, because it is based on the belief in the genius. In such a belief underlies the conviction that the original works and the great findings of creative nature are the fruit of great jumps of the imagination, that they take place because the creative individuals have the gift of carrying out extraordinary mental processes [3] [11]. Of course that one thing is to talk about Leonardo Da Vinci and a very different one to talk about an alleged "genius artist" of the audiovisual who may carry out with a computer expert an interactive toboggan on which is projected an interface so that the kids can theoretically interact with it. We say theoretically, because placing the interactive interfaces with the first computer videogames (1980), where there is a battle of Terrestrians, Martians, flying saucers, etc. [12], is something that a child can hardly understand. It is content that requires teenagers and even adults for a correct interaction. However, the latter will not understand why they must jump from a toboggan to destroy flying saucers, for instance. That is, the mental effort of the artist's genius is zero, because it has only been a bid to join several existing techniques with a creativity equal to nil. Joined to the idea of their prodigious mental faculties, the creative artists also posses exceptional personality traits. Both components make up what is known as genius, and one resorts to it to explain the great creations. Evidently, one has always to differentiate in these great creations what is an invention and what is discovery. Keeping up with the genius notion, the creative person suddenly begins to produce something complete and finished, without knowing where it comes from. Such a belief has endured until our days, since the notion of the muses by the Greeks. There is a second implicit presumption in the genius belief, that is, that creative individuals posses a certain indefinable quality which accounts for the manner in which they come to achieve the things they do. Their special kind of creativity enables their possessor to discover the important inside the irrelevant, and to find sense to what is contradictory. Obviously, it is not the case with the interactive toboggan because the quality attributes of a multimedia system, immersive or not, known as empathy, competence and consistence are absent. That is, the premise according to which the creative genius manages to get something out of darkness while we others see nothing has not fulfilled itself.

There is another conception of creativity that has nothing to do with genius, and which can be summed up in the expression that nothing is new. This notion derives from John Watson, one of the main beacons of behaviourism in the USA. For the behaviourists, there is no need to study or explain creativity, since creativity, understood as a specific process which intervenes in the production of something truly new, doesn't exist. Either the product is in fact something ancient, or if new, an accident has happened.

2 Destruction of Creativity in Computer Science, Quality Design and Communicability

In every project related to the software and the hardware, the human capital is the most important to achieve competitive results in the global village of the users of the interactive systems [2]. In the last two decades it has been seen how it is easy to destroy those professionals with knowledge and/or experience in computer science, multimedia, semiotics, education and social communication when workplace mediocrity is not accepted or the lack of respect to the essential rights of the human being such as is dignity [13]. That is, we are in rhombus which seriously damages the future of the tourism industry such as the training of the future professionals in the new technologies which can develop an interest in the safeguard and promotion of the cultural and natural heritage to the community to which it belongs. Graphically it can be depicted in the following way:

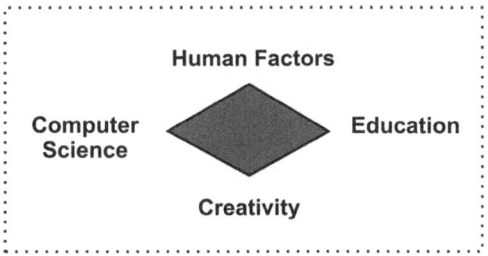

Fig. 1. Future of the tourism industry –main components

Without any doubt, the information and communication technologies have served for the last years to draw the attention of many college students to turn them into professionals who can give support to the industrial sector. One of those industries and which do not have chimneys to pollute the environment is tourism. Now, a series of rhetorical questions will allow us to better know that rhombus:

- Can some members of an audiovisual college institute and/or telecommunications school exert pressure over the team of specialized magazines in software and hardware so that they publish their works?
- Are there university professors who regard as unnecessary or ridiculous the publications in magazines, books, workshops, lectures, international symposiums?
- Is it more important for some colleges the awards got in contests rigged beforehand than the patents of new products or international publications?
- Are there professors related to the computer art, graphic computing, programming, etc. who see themselves as Hollywood stars?
- Is it feasible to destroy the credibility and the professionalism of the scientific journalists who regardless of mercantilist interest try to promote the novelties of the new technologies?

- Are there young graduates or engineers who join in a kind of "holy crusade" to put an end to the motivation of the honest communicability professionals?
- Is it an inconvenience to demonstrate that engineering students in telecommunications can develop creative skills in a HCI lab?
- Is it a nuisance to remark that future B.A in philology or journalism can carry out computer animations within a short time?
- Is it possible that in the linguistics and computing systems the innovating views of a social communicator for the heuristic assessment of multimedia systems are not accepted?
- Are there mathematicians, physics professors, computer science experts who do not accept that a social communicator can set new goals of research inside software engineering?
- Do the science departments us the cloning strategy towards the areas of interest of those professions which are fashionable because of a high work demand?
- Is it feasible that a mathematician or a physics professor, out of educational marketing reasons, turns himself into an expert in computer systems and then in E-learning, E-commerce and E-business strategist?
- Can the panel for the final projects and the PhD theses at the moment of the presentation and arguing be made up by members who are alien to the title to be earned by the future professional?
- Are there associations which do not recognize the true pioneers or leading creators of those areas of science, to which they belong or represent?
- Can an association promote the plagiarism of the works or research of its colleagues by resorting to the trick of using synonymous of the original texts?
- Is it a usual practice in some university environment of the new technologies to constantly plagiarize the works by other researchers without ever mentioning the author directly or indirectly?
- The degree of negation of the creative researchers and the plagiarism of their works can for ever eclipse their existence?
- Are there college presidents and deans who hate the presence of creative professors because they see in danger the status quo of the mediocrity of their institutions?
- Does academic mediocrity –public or private exclude the self-sufficient and creative professors in the face of the fear of having future professionals who are generators of innovative solutions?
- Can multimedia university courses be opened without software or computers for the practice?
- Is it usual to grant doctorates of telecommunications, maths and computer science to people alien to the field of study of these faculties such as can be graduates in psychology or fine arts?
- Can the tutor of a doctor thesis ignore his PhD and even never publish a joint article?
- Can a B.A. or an engineer take the place of a PhD in the territorial committees of such associations as the ACM or the IEEE?

- Is it feasible that just after finishing his studies a student takes a steady post in a public or private college rather than his professors?
- The working instability of the professors with a PhD is greater than that of young graduates and engineers?
- Is there any discrimination of the college professors in relation to their place of birth, physical appearance or economic position?
- Is there a greater training and/or creative quality in the state universities of some developing countries than in certain private or religious universities?
- Do those public or private universities located in territories of a fierce parochialism promote a continuous demotivation of the creative professors?

The answer to all these rhetorical questions is *yes*. This is a first list that will be widened and detailed in future research works with real examples. The reason of this work is to make apparent that many quality works on software engineering [14] [15] are totally obsolete in regard to certain realities of Southern Europe or other realities in the rest of the world. It is striking that some authors assert international dogmas in the context of the software industry and with extensions to the hardware, when these precepts do not have any value for reasons of the human factors that have a negative influence on their setting in motion [16]. Evidently, those negative factors also have a negative influence on cultural heritage and tourism at the moment these new technologies are used.

After analyzing the reality in many universities in the south of Europe for 20 years, the study shows that in 80% of cases creativity is not free to be generated in many departments and/or faculties of computer science, systems, software, audiovisual, literature and languages, education, etc. That is, the law of academic mediocrity reigns in the triad computer science, quality design and communicability. The reason are many and they can be encompassed in the human factors. Some human factors that would be easy to eradicate if there is a will that the EU takes an important place in scientific issues related to the conservation, fostering and safeguard of the huge cultural heritage that it possesses inside its borders. Now it is important to point out that those responsible for the disruption of everything that relates on the one hand the creativity and on the other the above mentioned triad, are not to be found in the university classrooms only, but also outside them, in places such as the mass media that seek revenue sources through publicity or subscriptions: the entrepreneurial sector that tries to cheapen the costs of the services of the professionals in the interactive design; usability engineering, communicability, multimedia programmers, systems analysts, etc. the educational authorities who want to increase quickly the statistic number of people with a college degree without analyzing their quality, etc. In few words, creativity depends on endogenous and exogenous factors inside the computer science, quality design and communicability.

3   What Changes Is It Necessary to Make for a Better Future?

It is necessary to start by revising the human factors inside, whether it is in training, or in the productive sector of the software and the hardware linked to telecommunications. Evidently hardware has always evolved more quickly than the software, as can be seen in the whole history of computer science or artificial intelligence [17] [18]. This evolution has often implied working with professionals stemming from other disciplines and even demanding to obtain better quality in the software, through the incorporation of psychologists, sociologists, anthropologists, etc, something which was very usual in the USA in the 90's, for instance [19]. In a naïve way, many deans of faculties in the Iberian Peninsula or Italy have made a simple copying and pasting of these models in totally opposed realities as we can find in the context of the engineering or software B.A., electronics, telecommunications, systems, usability, industrials, etc.

Oddly enough, those responsible had in many instances a humanistic training, and they know very well that the models of societies vary among themselves and especially so in the educational and professional context. To get back the wasted time with this serious mistake, whose consequences are currently dramatic for a community with millions and millions unemployed, the need prevails to bring about structural and not systematic changes. We understand as systematic changes those that are usually made in the matter of the educational curricula to adapt it to the technological breakthroughs and the new tendencies in the sciences [20] [21]. A structural change is one that modifies the components of formation and their rules and norms.

With regard to the scientific publications where the author or authors do not mention the real sources some kind of post-publication mechanism of scientific verification quality could be established. In this process there should be the option of the elimination of those publications in the databases, such as DBLP –Digital Bibliography & Library Project, since these on-line reference bookshops currently occupy the top spots in the searchers like Google and Yahoo. Besides, the existing trend in some universities that their graduates or engineers to be are presented as scientists, that is, inserting their names at an early time in those databases, damages the credibility of on-line information.

To apply the principles of E-Government at the moment of the presentation of the final year projects and very especially in the defense of the final works of masters or final theses. That is, to impose on the public universities the rules on the transparency of information. There should be direct access to the home page of the Europen universities (not use compressed files of the kind rar, zip, etc.) the schedule with the first and second names of those people who will get university degrees beyond their B.A. and engineering titles for instance. Surprisingly in our days and within the European borders a philologist in Spanish and English in three years can get a PhD in audiovisuals or new technologies. Allegedly in this short time that neo doctor has acquired the sufficient magistral knowledge in specialities of engineering and studies such as: telecommunications, electronics, nanotechnology, computer science, multimedia, cognitive psychology, etc. In many of these colleges where deviations are generated, the research works entail the "butterfly" phenomenon in the originality [13]. Graphically:

The negative consequences are not only negative for the science, but also for the communities where these university centres of study are located from the point of view of ITC.

To avoid asking for personal references of the professors who have passed through educational centres where plagiarism and other unethical behaviour are usually the rule in the context of humanities and/or computing. This is a serious problem inside the EU for those professionals who are victims of plagiarism or the dynamic persuaders, since they can't insert their working references in the university context [22] [23].

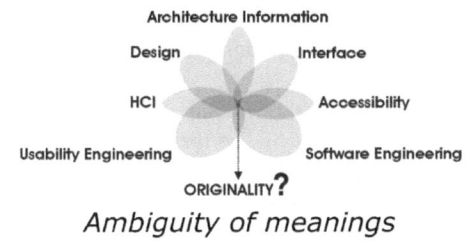

Ambiguity of meanings

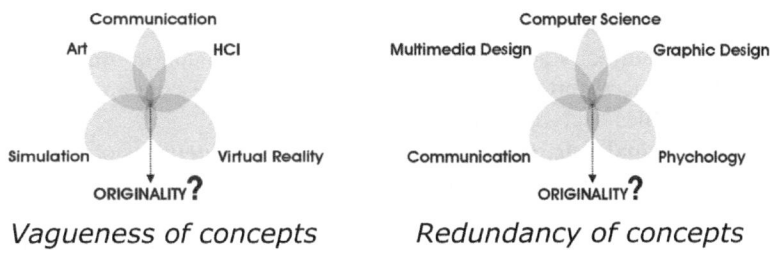

Vagueness of concepts   Redundancy of concepts

Fig. 2. Originality equal to zero in "butterfly" research

Generating a free access database and in the main languages, with the educational institutions and their directors, where the cases of plagiarism of works and the cloning of professional clones can be exposed. This information should be transparent and timeless.

Avoiding that the public universities in the EU play the game of adapting themselves to continuous changes deriving from the lack of knowledge and/or experience of the professor body. That is, without previous knowledge he/she may go from the teaching of office automation to multimedia communication, for instance.

In the presented cases we can see a rhombus of bidirectional relationships among their four components which affect creativity in the future: educative authorities, professors and project tutors, students and scientific researchers. Of course that this list could still be widened. However, we can see in it how sometimes the latest technological breakthroughs in software and hardware can't be applied by their real experts, due to human factors. Consequently, it would be interesting that from software engineering and computer science, before setting dogmas or premises, these factors which we will call "slowdown effect", not only of the bidirectional triad stated at first, but also of the social growth of the local, provincial, regional, national and international community.

4   Measurement of the Slowdown Effect in the Triad Computer Science, Design and Communicability

In the computer science since the 90s the help of the social sciences has been required to increase quality [19]. Currently and luckily the contextual factors in the development of the global interactive systems are considered as very important, regardless of the sector of the new technologies to which the developed products and/or services belong. Inside these contextual factors the slowdown effects can be included which damage a creative future inside the environment of the computer science and the human-computer interaction, for instance.

The other alternative is to include them inside the human factors but as main quality attributes in the productive process of services and products of the on-line and off-line interactive systems. We say essential because they can cheapen or make more expensive the economic or social factors [26] [27]. Next the first analyzed slowdon effects and their matching definitions:

- Opacity in the university portals. The information of the contests for the work places must be directly accessible from the home page and in html pages, that is, without having to resort to third programmes to read the contents such as the text processors or files decompression.
- Linguistic manipulation. It consists in using regional languages or local dialects as a mechanism that bolsters the real computer science professionals, multimedia, HCI, etc. and/or the plagiarism of their works.
- Meteoric regressive metamorphose. It is the change that is detected with the diachronic analysis of the teaching staff in the areas of knowledge related to the triad: computer science, design and communicability. That is, those that allegedly interested them at first and the fast change towards the real areas of interest.
- Dynamic persuader. Those individuals that turn the democratization of the net into "ghettos" inside the Web 2.0 [24]
- Sportive plagiarism: Copying contents using synonymous of the key words of the research works, presenting the same bibliographical references but in a different format, for instance, instead of a book, a magazine or a web portal, and cloning the topics of study including the methodologies and techniques used in the research.

This set of attributes which diminish the quality of the creative future can be broken down into a series of metrics. Metrics which allow to detect these slowdown effects in the Web 1.0 and the Web 2.0 These metrics are based on the design primitives of the interactive systems, whose origins lie in the hypertext, and which have been evolving along the decades, incorporating new notions deriving from interactive design, software, multimedia and semiotics or semiology. Consequently, the degree of analysis is very detailed or granular. Nevertheless, in this case, and in contrast to the metrics used so far such as methodologies or evaluation techniques in the interactive systems aimed at education, e-commerce, tourism, etc., we have approached the issue of quality on the negative sides in order to eradicate them. The goal is that creativity imposes itself again in the immediate future, especially in the triad we are presenting.

4.1   Opacity in the University Portals: Contests and Jobs Accessibility

The quality of hypermedia systems online for the teaching or non-teaching staff requires high accessibility, transparency and equality of opportunity. Consequently, this information must be in the home page, in the shape of an animated news, or with links to direct indexes to the documentation to have access to the summoning for a post. In the colleges of Southern Europe it is necessary to translate the national language into

English and French to reach equality of opportunity for all people in Europe, at least at the moment of the reading of the requisites, for example.

These assessment categories also refer to several quality criteria that must be met in the design of the hypermedia systems with potential users, such as: Accessibility, Behaviour Animation, Coenoscopic, Competence, Consistency, Control of Fruition, Diachronism, Empathy, Inference, Isomorphism, Motivation, Naturalness of Metaphor, Orientation, Originality, Phatic Function, Predictability, Reusability, Richness, Self-evidence, Semiosis, Simplicity, Synchronism, Transparence of Meaning, Triple Dynamic Coherence, Universality, Univocal Phonic, and Unlimited Iconic [13] [24].

In the analysis of the structure of the website it is necessary to take into account a series of primitives related to the design of hypermedia systems, such as: frame, node, link, and index menu. These primitives are related to the common elements in the different existing design models. The models generated through the hypertext, multimedia and hypermedia systems of the eighties, nineties and early years of this century have not allowed the establishment of a single set or an intersection of its main notions among the designers of the multimedia systems.

Currently, through the classical notions, we are making that theoretical framework through the diachronic analysis of the models. In Eye we have used a first group of these primitives. For instance, at the moment of the evaluation we consider whether the website is dynamic or static. Later on we establish topographic and functional groups and subgroups that comprise it. Each of these groups and subgroups are split in areas of unions and intersections with their corresponding elements and relations of inclusion and/or exclusion. Generally, the access to the European university public contest is made up by the following elements: home page, first index links, faculty home page, second index links, collection of links (news and documents), etc. Graphically:

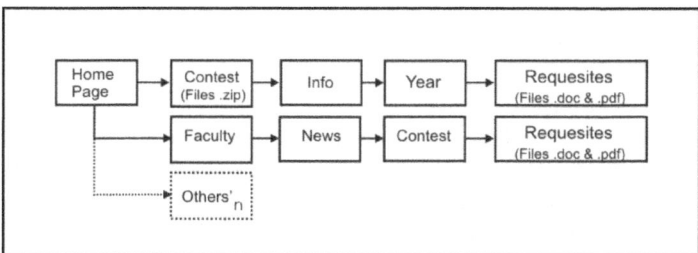

Fig. 3. This is a classical example of opaque website for contests

Directly and indirectly the transparency of access to the information is related to the credibility of the institutional image that in this case are the European and American public and private colleges which make up the universe of study. Besides, the users finds files in different formats: .zip, .pdf, .doc, etc. into contests of the Lombardian university, for instance [28]. We have worked with the websites in France (68 universities), Italy (48 universities), and Spain (64 universities) and the results are into figures 4 and 5 [28].

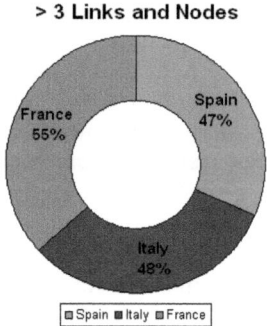

Fig. 4. Contests/jobs accessibility is poor into France universities portals

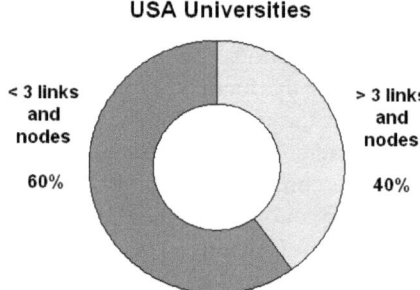

Fig. 5. An excellent media of accessibility into USA universities portals

5 Lessons Learned and Future Works

The human factors described in this work make apparent the deceleration in the R&D sector in the UE, inside the HCI for instance. Besides, both the causes and the consequences are shown why from the highest educational institutions in a civilized community as are its universities there are currently no paneuropean control mechanisms to eradicate the negative human factors, which prevent the growth of creativity. Consequently, in this way the correct development of both the hardware and the software aimed at the new technologies in the EU is slowed down. These human factors directly or indirectly influence the training of the new generations of professionals inside the HCI. Therefore, it is not only an economic factor or of improving the quality of the interactive communicability systems, but it is rather the future of R+D. As a line of work for the future we intend to increase the quality metrics presented in the current work and establish an analysis methodology. This methodology will have a matching computerized interactive system and a free access portal to constantly look up the obtained results.

6 Conclusion

Creativity and originality are the secret for progress in research, through the constant cycle of discoveries and inventions, for instance. It is important that in this dynamic process real professionals intervene, who can distinguish between transdisciplinarity, multidisciplinarity and all the prefixes you can put before the word disciplinarity with purely mercantilist purposes. Disciplines that have to be practiced in the context of the triad presented by those professionals who have a proven training and/or experience demonstrated from the first day they carry out activities related to them. In the same way, those professionals have to detect quickly whether a R+D work is original or not, thus avoiding the "butterfly" effect. The quality metrics have served to determine that little or nothing has changed in the analyzed structures of the south of Europe in the last few years, even with the European plan called Bologna. Evidently, the changes inside a system are much faster than within a structure. However, the results have made it apparent that there are realities that should foster creativity and originality, particularly in those industries with a great power of present and future such as can be the diffusion of cultural and natural heritage in the EU, through the new technologies.

Acknowledgments

A special thanks to Dario Paris (New York University), Jennifer Walsh Freixe (Universidad de Costa Rica), Maria Ficarra (Alaipo & Ainci – Spain and Italy), Simone Manzotti and Carlos for their helps and collaboration.

References

1. Smith, D., Paradice, D., Smith, S.: Prepare Your Mind for Creativity. Communications of ACM 43(7), 111–116 (2000)
2. Edmonds, E., Candy, L.: Creativity, Art Practice, and Knowledge. Communications of ACM 45(10), 91–95 (2002)
3. Csikszentmihalyi, M.: Creativity: Flow and the Psychology of Discovery and Invention. Harper Collins Publishers, New York (1996)
4. Conlon, K.: The Future of Interaction Design as and Academic Program of Study. Interactions 15(2), 38–41 (2008)
5. Wilson, C., Harsha, P.: The Long Road to Computer Science Education Reform. Communications of the ACM 52(9), 33–35 (2009)
6. Denning, P., Flores, F., Luzmore, P.: Orchestrating Coordination in Pluralisctic Networks. Communications of the ACM 53(3), 30–32 (2010)
7. Tedre, M., et al.: Ethnocomputing: ICT in Cultural and Social Context. Communications of the ACM 49(1), 126–130 (2006)
8. Buckley, M.: Computing as Social Science. Communications of the ACM 52(4), 29–30 (2009)
9. White, G.: Designing for the Last Billion. Interactions 15(1), 56–58 (2008)
10. Kantrovich, L.: To Innovate or Not to Innovate... Interactions 11(1), 24–31 (2004)

11. Weisberg, R.: Creativity: Understanding Innovation in Problem Solving, Science, Invention, and the Arts. John Wiley, New Jersey (2006)
12. Berens, K., Howard, G.: The Rough Guide to Videogaming. Rough Guides Limited, London (2008)
13. Cipolla-Ficarra, F.: Quality and Communicability for Interactive Hypermedia Systetms: Concepts and Practices for Design. IGI Global, New York (2010)
14. Kruchten, P.: Casting Software Design in the Function-Behavior-Structure Framework. IEEE Software 22(2), 52–58 (2005)
15. Avgeriou, P., et al.: Architectural Knowledge and Rationale: Issues, Trends, Challenges. ACM SIGSOFT Software Engineering Notes 32(4), 41–46 (2007)
16. Wong, B., Hasan, S.: Cultural influences and differences in software process improvement programs. In: International Conference on Software Engineering, pp. 3–10. ACM Press, New York (2008)
17. Wilson, J.: Toward Things That Think for the Next Millennium. IEEE Computer 33(1), 72–76 (2000)
18. Reddy, R.: The Challenge of Artificial Intelligence. IEEE Computer 29(10), 86–98 (1996)
19. Basili, V., Musa, J.: The Future Engineering of Software: A Management Perspective. IEEE Computer 24(9), 90–96 (1991)
20. Vliet, H.: Reflections on Software Engineering Education. IEEE Software 23(3), 55–61 (2006)
21. Frezza, S., Tang, M., Brinkman, B.: Creating an Accreditable Software Engineering Bachelor's Program. IEEE Software 23(6), 27–35 (2006)
22. Frincke, D.: Plagiarism, Education and Information Security. IEEE Security & Privacy, 5(5), 62–65
23. Rashid, A., Wechert, L.R.: Software Engineering Ethics in a Digital World. IEEE Software 42(9), 34–41 (2009)
24. Cipolla-Ficarra, F.: Persuasion On-Line and Communicability: The Destruction of Credibility in the Virtual Community and Cognitive Models. Nova Science Publishers, New York (2010)
25. Mann, Z.: Three Public Enemies: Cut, Copy, and Paste. IEEE Computer 39(7), 31–35 (2006)
26. Tullis, T., et al.: Measuring the User Experience: Collecting, Analyzing, and Presenting Usability Metrics. Morgan Kaufmann Publishers, Burlington (2008)
27. Bevan, N.: Practical Issues in Usability Measurement. Interactions 13(6), 42–43 (2006)
28. Cipolla-Ficarra, F.: Eyes: A virtual Assistant for Analysis of the Transparency and Accessibility into University Portal. In: DVD-ROM Proceedings Applied Human Factors and Ergonomics. AEI, Las Vegas (2008)

A Trip to Rome: Physical Replicas of Historical Objects Created in a Fully Automated Way from Photos

Luigi Barazzetti

Politecnico di Milano – Rilevamento
Campus Point, Polo Regionale di Lecco
Via Ghislanzoni 24, Lecco (LC) 23900, Italy
luigi.barazzetti@polimi.it

Abstract. It is normal for tourists to take photos during their holidays, which are then printed, loaded into digital frames or shared on the Internet. This paper describes a new methodology to obtain accurate 3D digital models and material replicas of real objects, starting from digital images acquired with consumer and professional cameras. The implemented software is completely automatic and provides detailed reconstructions. It stands out from other existing approaches for the high metric accuracy of the final product, the level of detail obtainable, the speed of the algorithms and its adaptability under different viewing conditions. Several examples relating to an actual trip to Rome are reported and discussed, showing what a tourist can obtain with this package. Obviously, the method can be used for many other applications in which accurate models are needed.

Keywords: 3D model, Automation, Accuracy, Photograph, Physical replica.

1 Introduction

With the rapid diffusion of the use of digital cameras and video-cameras people tend to take numerous photographs during their holidays. Digital images have several advantages with respect to film-based pictures; e.g. the possibility to acquire a great number of images without the need of developing them for simple visualization purposes. These images can be displayed without any extra cost with digital frames. Furthermore, the exchange of information is rapid and the distribution of the data on the Internet is becoming more popular. Several websites offer the possibility to share images (e.g. Facebook, Flickr, …), presenting new opportunities for scientific purposes. As Internet provides billions of photographs, several computer vision researches have tried to reconstruct 3D objects from their projections into 2D images. This is a convenient choice: the data acquisition phase has already been completed by someone else, who has decided to freely distribute his material. In recent years some software for automated reconstruction with digital images have been developed in the field of computer vision (e.g. Microsoft Photosynth, ARC 3D Webservice, Bundler, …). Their aim being to obtain 3D models of very good photographed scenes and objects. The state of the art for such applications is CMVS (Clustering Views for Multi-view

F.V. Cipolla Ficarra et al. (Eds.): HCITOCH 2010, LNCS 6529, pp. 63–72, 2011.

Stereo) [1], which combines a popular software for *Structure from Motion* [2] called Bundler [3] with another one for surface reconstruction coined PMVS2 [4]. The final result obtainable with CMVS is a dense point cloud automatically derived from an impressive number of images downloaded from the Internet. The method was tested on several archaeological sites and then extended towards the reconstruction of whole cities. However, this software was developed for visualization purposes and the accuracy and the completeness of the reconstruction are rarely checked. The use of uncalibrated methods, coupled with orientation strategies based on projective geometry [5], do not always provide a guarantee on metric accuracy.

On the other hand, the possibility to obtain accurate measurements with images is the primary goal of photogrammetry [6]. Here, many procedures for 3D modelling have been developed by taking into consideration the quality of the final product in terms of accuracy, completeness, and level of detail. The automation of the procedure is not a fundamental task, therefore several manual (interactive) measurements must be carried out by an expert operator. The final 3D model is generally a complete and detailed survey, and several examples can be found in technical literature (for a more exhaustive analysis the reader is referred to [7]). However, fully automated elaboration of images is very much in the future. Furthermore, images are often taken by expert operators using high quality cameras. Some fully automated approaches were proposed by [8], but these methods work with targets fixed on the object. Finally, an automated commercial solution for the case of target-less images is still to be developed.

In this paper a procedure for the creation of digital models and physical replicas is presented and discussed. The method was developed combining the traditional accuracy of photogrammetric projects with automation of computer vision techniques. This means that the advantages of both disciplines are mixed, while the disadvantages are strongly reduced. The method is derived from a software for image correspondence extraction and matching [9] and adapted to work with computer vision software for surface reconstruction.

To demonstrate the potential of this methodology some results of a trip to Rome are shown. During this year's Easter holiday the author had the opportunity to visit the city. Several objects were photographed with a low-cost camera (Samsung ST45, costing roughly 120 Euros), starting from the Baths of Caracalla up to the Vatican City, crossing famous squares, bridges, and museums. These images were processed with the implemented software for the automated digital reconstruction of the scene and the creation of material replicas with a 3D printer.

Although the images were taken by an expert operator, this method can be used by people not so expert in the field of computer vision, photogrammetry, and surveying. The main idea is a procedure that can be easily managed by tourists who want to obtain 3D models during their holiday trips, using images taken with non-professional cameras. Obviously, the method can be easily employed by archaeologists, curators, restorers and so on, and not only for touristic purposes but also for technical works. Freeform objects (e.g. bas-reliefs, decorations, and ornaments) are analysed in this paper.

2 The Method for Object Reconstruction and the Path of the Trip

The generation of an accurate model from digital images with the developed methodology is a multi-step approach which includes:

1. image acquisition (at least 2 images)
2. image correspondence detection
3. camera pose estimation & image distortion removal
4. point cloud extraction
5. point cloud interpolation
6. 3D physical replica creation

All these phases can be carried out in a fully automated way in the case of freeform objects, thus allowing a non-expert operator to derive a 3D model for different purposes, not only for visualization and browsing.

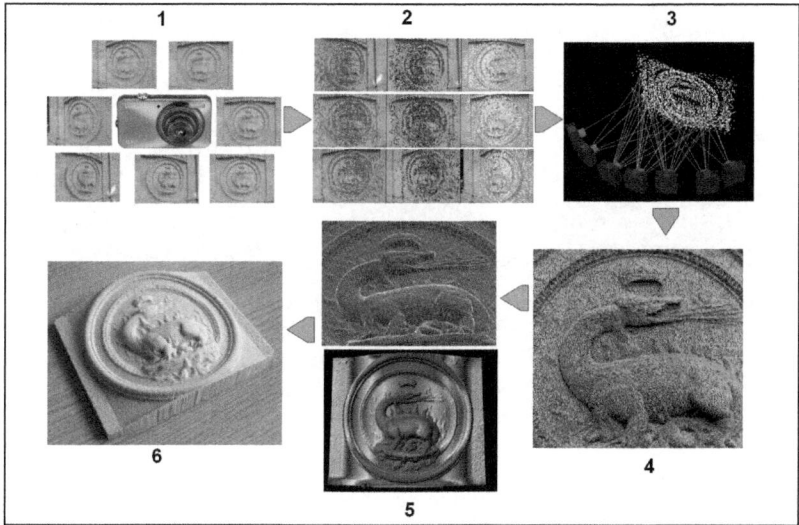

Fig. 1. The pipeline of the proposed procedure for 3D modeling and physical replica creation. It is interesting to notice that the image correspondences in 2 and 4 are automatically detected.

The pipeline for 3D modelling is shown in Fig. 1, with a subdivision into 6 steps according to the phases previously listed. The analysed object is a decoration on the main facade of the Church of St. Louis of the French. Starting from a set of 7 well distributed images around the decoration (and their calibration parameters [10]) the software performs a preliminary automated matching between some particular image pair combinations in order to extract the image points needed for the next step. These pixel coordinates are the input elements for a robust and reliable photogrammetric bundle adjustment [11], which provides an initial 3D reconstruction and the camera poses (position and attitude).

Before running the algorithm for surface reconstruction, the image distortion must be removed in order to make the following phases quicker and more precise. The point cloud is extracted with multi-image matching methods to obtain a reliable solution in an automated way, and a final interpolation of the raw 3D points gives the 3D reconstruction. At this point, the model can be printed. All these steps are described in more detail in the next section.

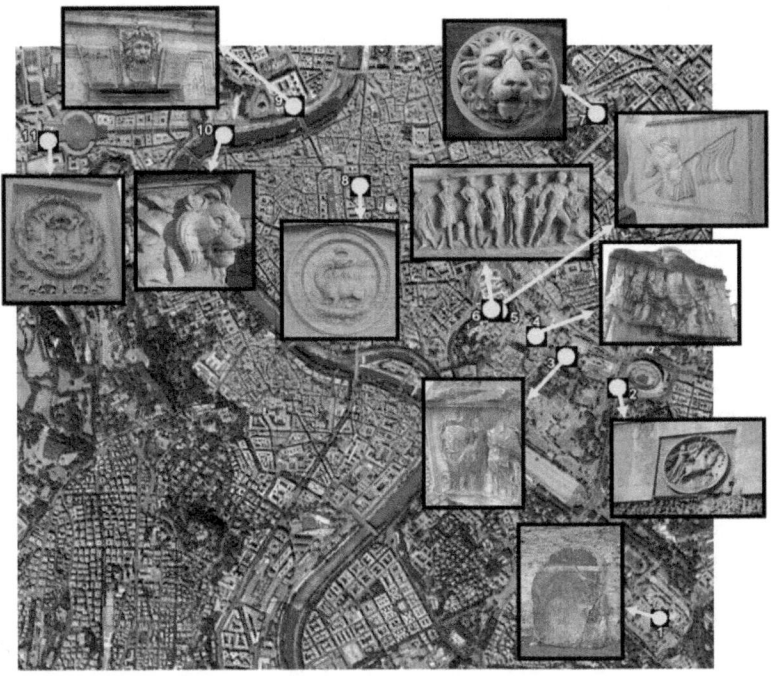

Fig. 2. The objects surveyed during the trip to Rome and their location: (1) Baths of Caracalla, (2) Arch of Constantine, (3-4) Roman Forum, (5-6) Musei Capitolini, (7) Palazzo Barberini, (8) Church of St. Louis of the French, (9) Piazza dei Tribunali, (10) Castel Sant'Angelo, (11) Vatican City.

Figure 2 shows the route taken during the stay in Rome, which crosses some of the most famous tourist attractions; some details of the analysed objects are also shown. These small objects were chosen to offer the possibility of reconstructing what a tourist would see in person, in contrast to the approach based on Internet imagery. With this in mind, in [12] the possibility to reconstruct the most important Roman attractions is discussed. However, a physical replica of big objects like the Colosseum or the Pantheon can be bought from a stand. In this paper an alternative method to derive 3D data for objects that cannot be modelled with Internet photo collections is shown.

The path begins with the Baths of Caracalla, through the Arch of Constantine, the Roman Forum, Musei Capitolini, Palazzo Barberini, Piazza dei Tribunali, Castel Sant'Angelo and the Vatican City. In all, 11 objects were surveyed and presented, but many other datasets were collected. Obviously, these are just a few examples of what a person can find in Rome!

3 The Phases of the Reconstruction

The automated reconstruction of the photographed objects with the proposed strategy is based on advanced techniques for image matching, wrong correspondence detection, orientation and 3D surface measurements. These algorithms are the current state of the art for this kind of applications.

3.1 Image Acquisition and Orientation

All images are taken with a low-cost camera (12 megapixels), similar to those most used by tourists, but the method allows the elaboration of high resolution images used at their original size. In [13] a different version of the software was used to elaborate 24 megapixel images, without any preliminary image compression. It is important to acquire good images, i.e. from different angle shots and with a good distribution around the objects. The camera should be calibrated beforehand. This is not strictly mandatory but is highly recommended. Several low-cost photogrammetric software (e.g. iWitness, PhotoModeler, ...) can solve this task in a fully automated way. An open source implementation is the MATLAB Calibration Toolbox [14].

Images are then automatically elaborated using the green channel only. Matching (between image pairs) based on the SIFT [15] and SURF [16] operators gives the initial pixel coordinates, and the combination of all the pairs of images provides the data for the estimation of the camera poses. The descriptors of both operators are compared with a *kd-tree search* [17] coupled with the *ratio test*, while wrong matches are removed with the robust estimation of the *fundamental matrix* [18] with the MAP-SAC operator [19]. The image points can be refined, decimated and homogenously distributed in the images. The orientation is carried out by exchanging the data with PhotoModeler through a DDE (Dynamic Data Exchange) connection. This link allows the software to send the image coordinates to a commercial package for photogrammetric purposes and its bundle adjustment gives the camera poses used in the next phase.

3.2 Surface Reconstruction

Although the version Scanner of PhotoModeler allows the extraction of point clouds from oriented images, another software (PMVS [20]) is used because of its multi-image matching approach. To run this software some preliminary steps are necessary to modify the typical photogrammetric output (exterior orientation parameters expressed as the coordinates of the perspective centre X_0, Y_0, Z_0 and the attitude angles of the image ω, φ, κ). Distortion-free images are generated to avoid the correction term due to image distortion.

The model used in photogrammetry which gives the alignment between the (i) perspective centre of the image and the (ii) image and the (iii) object points is based on *collinearity equations* and has the form:

$$\begin{bmatrix} x - x_p \\ y - y_p \\ -c \end{bmatrix} = \lambda R \begin{bmatrix} X - X_0 \\ Y - Y_0 \\ Z - Z_0 \end{bmatrix} \tag{1}$$

where x_p, y_p, and c are the *interior orientation parameters*, λ is a scale factor, R is a spatial rotation matrix which depends on 3 rotations and (x, y) and (X, Y, Z) are image and object coordinates for a generic point. PhotoModeler gives all these data, which are automatically exported via DDE.

The input format for PMVS is the traditional computer vision model which describes the transformation from object coordinates $\mathbf{X}$ to image coordinates $\mathbf{u}$ with a 3×4 matrix P (pinhole camera):

$$d\mathbf{u} = d \begin{bmatrix} u \\ v \\ 1 \end{bmatrix} = P\mathbf{X} = P \begin{bmatrix} X \\ Y \\ Z \\ 1 \end{bmatrix} \tag{2}$$

A fundamental difference between both formulations are the units of the image coordinates: in equation (2) image coordinates are expressed in pixels, while for equation (1) metric units are used (generally millimetres), but also the orientation of the axis is different. If p is the pixel size (in metric units), the transformation to pixel units can be performed with the following relation:

$$\mathbf{u} = \begin{bmatrix} u \\ v \\ 1 \end{bmatrix} = \begin{bmatrix} 1/p & 0 & w/2p \\ 0 & -1/p & h/2p \\ 0 & 0 & 1 \end{bmatrix} \begin{bmatrix} x \\ y \\ 1 \end{bmatrix} = D\mathbf{x} \tag{3}$$

where w and h are the width and the height of the sensor (in metric units). With these assumptions, equation (1) can be cast in the form:

$$C\mathbf{x} = \begin{bmatrix} 1 & 0 & 0 \\ 0 & 1 & 0 \\ 0 & 0 & -c \end{bmatrix} \begin{bmatrix} x \\ y \\ 1 \end{bmatrix} = \lambda R \begin{bmatrix} 1 & 0 & 0 & -X_0 \\ 0 & 1 & 0 & -Y_0 \\ 0 & 0 & 1 & -Z_0 \end{bmatrix} \begin{bmatrix} X \\ Y \\ Z \\ 1 \end{bmatrix} \tag{4}$$

and, with a compact notation (without the scale factor):

$$\mathbf{u} = DC^{-1}R[I, -\mathbf{X_0}]\mathbf{X} \tag{5}$$

Thus, ignoring the scale term, the projection matrix which contains the exterior orientation parameters can be written in the more familiar computer vision form:

$$P = \begin{bmatrix} 1/p & 0 & w/2p \\ 0 & -1/p & h/2p \\ 0 & 0 & 1 \end{bmatrix} \begin{bmatrix} 1 & 0 & 0 \\ 0 & 1 & 0 \\ 0 & 0 & -1/c \end{bmatrix} R \begin{bmatrix} 1 & 0 & 0 & -X_0 \\ 0 & 1 & 0 & -Y_0 \\ 0 & 0 & 1 & -Z_0 \end{bmatrix} \tag{6}$$

For each image a P-matrix must be estimated, then PMVS can automatically detect homologous points to create a dense point cloud.

3.3 Completion of the Model

The point cloud derived from the images can be interpolated in order to obtain a continuous representation. For objects like bas-reliefs (e.g. 1-2-4-5-6-8-11 in Fig. 2 and 3) the interpolation of the 3D points onto a regular grid can be a convenient choice. The final result is a 2.5D model normally known as *Digital Surface Model* (DSM) in which the object is divided into regular squared cells with an associated depth value. For other objects (e.g. 3-7-9-10) the best solution is the generation of a *mesh*, i.e. a network of triangles which connects the points. The method used to generate the mesh is the *Poisson interpolation* [21].

Finally, the 3D digital model can be printed to obtain a prototype. The user has to select the portion of the object and the scale of the model. For flat-like 3D models a base should be added to strengthen the replica. The machine used to print the digital models is the Spectrum Z510 Full Colour system, with a print-head resolution of 600×540 dpi and maximum object size of 254×356×203 mm.

4 Results

Fig. 3 shows the objects reconstructed with the proposed methodology. Each digital model can be completed in roughly 2-3 hours, while the creation of the replica took several hours, according to the size of the model and the level of detail. All models are made up of more than 100,000 points with an estimated accuracy superior to 1:1000 (i.e. 1 mm for an object 1 m wide). The comparison with other matching techniques provided satisfactory results and confirms the previous statement.

All objects were reconstructed with more than 2 images to obtain a reliable solution. From a theoretical point of view, 2 images are sufficient for a complete 3D survey. However, fully automated methods must be able to work with incorrect data. The use of multiple images provides additional equations for the same unknown value, with the consequent possibility to check the quality of the solution. The robust estimation techniques implemented in the procedure showed a good resistance against outliers, without increasing significantly the computational cost. For these reasons, a minimum number of 4-5 images per objects seems a good choice. In addition, more images than those strictly necessary allow the analysis of the partially occluded parts, that are not visible in the case with a few images. The digital model can be saved using different file formats for an efficient distribution and a quick visualization with free viewers. As the accuracy of the model is similar to that achievable with photogrammetric techniques, these models can be used for metric purposes, after setting an opportune scale factor.

70   L. Barazzetti

Fig. 3. The reconstruction of the objects photographed during the trip (their location is shown in Fig. 2). For some of them (8, 10), a physical replica was created (Fig. 4).

If the user wants to obtain a physical replica, the accuracy of the 3D digital model is normally superior to the printer resolution. This is useful for touristic applications, but also for accurate and detailed real surveys in the field of Cultural Heritage preservation, with an extension towards many other possible applications.

Figure 4 shows some of the printed models. In both cases the printing took more than 6 hours, then the models were refined with a resin to strengthen the chalk.

Fig. 4. Two replicas printed with resinated chalk. The undulate edges are due to an automated elaboration (exception made for the scale of the model, the selection of the printable area, and the thickening of the reconstructed surface). To obtain sharp edges a manual editing is needed.

5 Conclusion

The proposed method for 3D object reconstruction is capable of creating accurate 3D models from photos in an automated way. It is based on software for image correspondence detection, which controls other packages for image orientation and surface reconstruction. Software as described is not yet available on the market.

In this paper a possible application to images taken with a low-cost camera during a trip was presented. However, this method can be used for many other purposes, where 3D models are desired other than the normal visualization requirements. Further developments concern the implementation of a robust photogrammetric bundle adjustment in order to create a stand-alone package. There are also some additional considerations, involving several disciplines, which can improve the proposed procedure. For instance, as some modern digital cameras have an integrated GPS receiver, the location of the images can be measured with a precision of a few meters. The knowledge of the geographic coordinates can be useful to visualize the data with digital maps (e.g. Google Earth). Furthermore, the transformation into particular file formats and the direct link between the model itself and an opportune metadata file could improve the exchange of information. The main idea is an extension of the EXIF format associated with digital images towards digital models, offering new opportunities for a future employment and distribution of the model itself. An exhaustive description encapsulated into the file could give more information to understand the content of the model, including simple data (e.g., name, location, time of creation, …) but also advanced information (e.g., method of image matching, point cloud interpolation algorithm, …) that would be useful for professional activities.

References

1. Furukawa, Y., Curless, B., Seitz, S.M., Szeliski, R.: Towards Internet-scale Multi-view Stereo. In: IEEE Conference on Computer Vision and Pattern Recognition CVPR, San Francisco (2010)

2. Pollefeys, M., Nister, D., Frahm, J.-M., Akbarzadeh, A., Mordohai, P., Clipp, B., Engels, C., Gallup, D., Kim, S.-J., Merrell, P., Salmi, C., Sinha, S., Talton, B., Wang, L., Yang, Q., Stewenius, H., Yang, R., Welch, G., Towles, H.: Detailed Real-Time Urban 3D Reconstruction From Video. Int. J. Comp. Vis. 78(2), 143–167 (2008)
3. Snavely, N., Seitz, S.M., Szeliski, R.: Modeling the World from Internet Photo Collection. Int. J. Comp. Vis. 80(2), 189–210 (2007)
4. Furukawa, Y., Ponce, J.: Accurate, Dense, and Robust Multiview Stereopsis. IEEE Transactions on Pattern Analysis and Machine Intelligence 32(8), 1362–1376 (2010)
5. Faugeras, O., Luong, Q.T., Papadopulo, T.: The Geometry of Multiple Images, p. 646. MIT Press, Cambridge (2001)
6. Kraus, K.: Photogrammetry: Geometry from Images and Laser Scans. Walter de Gruyter, Berlin (2008)
7. Remondino, F., El-Hakim, S.: Image-based 3D Modelling, a Review. The Photogrammetric Record 21(115), 269–291 (2006)
8. Jazayeri, I., Fraser, C.S.: Interest Operators for Feature-based Matching in Close-range Photogrammetry. The Photogrammetric Record 25(129), 24–41 (2010)
9. Barazzetti, L., Remondino, F., Scaioni, M.: Orientation and 3D modelling from Markerless Terrestrial Images: Combining Accuracy with Automation. The Photogrammetric Record (in press)
10. Remondino, F., Fraser, C.S.: Digital Camera Calibration Methods: Considerations and Comparisons. IAPRSSIS 36(5), 266–272 (2006)
11. Granshaw, S.I.: Bundle Adjustment Methods in Engineering Photogrammetry. The Photogrammetric record 10(56), 181–207 (1980)
12. Agarwal, S., Snavely, N., Simon, I., Seitz, S.M., Szeliski, R.: Building Rome in a Day. In: International Conference on Computer Vision, Kyoto (2009)
13. Barazzetti, L., Remondino, F., Scaioni, M.: Automation in 3D Reconstruction: Results on Different Kinds of close-range blocks. IAPRSSIS WG V/4, Newcastle upon Tyne (2010)
14. MATLAB Calibration Toolbox: http://www.vision.caltech.edu/bouguetj/calib_doc/
15. Lowe, D.: Distinctive image features from scale-invariant keypoints. Int. J. Comp. Vis. 10(56), 181–207 (2004)
16. Bay, H., Ess, A., Tuytelaars, T., Van Gool, L.: SURF: Speeded Up Robust Features. Computer Vision and Image Understanding 110(3), 346–359 (2008)
17. Arya, S., Mount, D.M., Netenyahu, N.S., Silverman, R., Wu, A.Y.: An optimal algorithm for approximate nearest neighbour searching fixed dimensions. Journal of the ACM 45(6), 891–923 (1998)
18. Hartley, R.I., Zisserman, A.: Multiple View Geometry in Computer Vision, p. 672. Cambridge University Press, Cambridge (2004)
19. Torr, P.: Bayesian Model Estimation and Selection for Epipolar Geometry and Generic Manifold Fitting. Int. J. Comp. Vis. 50(1), 35–61 (2002)
20. Furukawa, Y., Ponce, J.: Accurate, Dense, and Robust Multiview Stereopsis. In: IEEE Computer Society Conference on Computer Vision and Pattern Recognition (2007)
21. Kazhdan, M., Bolitho, M., Hoppe, H.: Poisson Surface Reconstruction. In: Symposium on Geometry Processing, Sardinia, pp. 61–70 (2006)

Advances in Human-Computer Interaction: Graphics and Animation Components for Interface Design

Francisco V. Cipolla Ficarra[1,2], Emma Nicol[3], Miguel Cipolla-Ficarra[2], and Lucy Richardson[2,4]

HCI Lab. – F&F Multimedia Communic@tions Corp.
[1] ALAIPO: Asociación Latina de Interacción Persona-Ordenador
[2] AINCI: Asociación Internacional de la Comunicación Interactiva
[3] University of Strathclyde
[4] Electronic Arts
Via Pascoli, S. 15 – CP 7, 24121 Bergamo, Italy
ficarra@alaipo.com, emma.nicol@cis.strath.ac.uk,
ficarra@ainci.com, lucy.richardson.ea@gmail.com

Abstract. We present an analysis of communicability methodology in graphics and animation components for interface design, called CAN (Communicability, Acceptability and Novelty). This methodology has been under development between 2005 and 2010, obtaining excellent results in cultural heritage, education and microcomputing contexts. In studies where there is a bi-directional interrelation between ergonomics, usability, user-centered design, software quality and the human-computer interaction. We also present the heuristic results about iconography and layout design in blogs and websites of the following countries: Spain, Italy, Portugal and France.

Keywords: Interface, Icon, Computer Graphics, Computer Animation, Human-Computer Interaction.

1 Introduction

In the 90s the momentum of the multimedia systems in the international commercial sector prompted the population of the economically developed societies to the acceptance of the virtual reality systems [1–4]. However, in that very same decade it was seen that it would not follow the expansion road of the off-line and on-line multimedia systems. In the mid nineties the university educational sector in Barcelona, for instance, received significant financial aid from the EU for R+D projects which would only become more audiovisual prototypes or in the paper support of industrial or computer engineering. Automatically, this failure of the democratization of virtual reality, as it happened with the multimedia systems, would generate the same distortion of concepts with commercial purposes, for instance, immersive multimedia is equal to virtual reality [4]. With the passing of time and making a diachronic analysis it can be seen that several factors have prevented the advance of virtual reality, outside the scientific environment; the cost of the equipment (gloves, helmets, computers capable of processing a high volume of images in a short time, etc.), the lack of professionals in

F.V. Cipolla Ficarra et al. (Eds.): HCITOCH 2010, LNCS 6529, pp. 73–86, 2011.
© Springer-Verlag Berlin Heidelberg 2011

and outside the educational sector in the context of virtual reality and the feeling of balance that the user has in these tridimensional environments. At that time one could speak of immersive multimedia in attractions of Discoveryland in Eurodisney, for instance. In some of those attractions the audiovisual effects were joined to the movement of the armchairs, with which the degree of realism was greater. In these attractions the user does not suffer from the problem of the feeling of loss of balance because he/she is sitting on a chair, although immersed in a context that simulates outer space. Once again, the multimedia entertainment sector went ahead of virtual reality. Now many inside and outside the educational environment saw in immersive multimedia a solution by using it as synonymous to virtual reality, when in fact they couldn't tell the difference between the real and the virtual [4]. Here is one of the reasons why the multimedia notion flooded all the sector of R+D in the Mediterranean since the 90s until the beginning of the new millennium.

Obviously those who ran after a commercial and non-scientific purpose didn't know the differences among hypertext, immersive multimedia and virtual reality [5]. Those were interactive systems that required different interfaces, because of the limitations in the hardware and/or software, for instance in the timings of access to the information stored in the databases in a CD or DVD or in the Internet. To such an extent that in the first systems of virtual reality, the quality of the images is inferior to the computer-made 3D animations. The navigation through virtual environments required a great speed to generate those images [6]. Consequently, in that navigation there was a tendency to the emulation of reality rather than simulation. Besides, those were environments where the navigation icons were similar to those used in the multimedia systems for the videogames or encyclopaedia consultations.

In the current work is made a study of static and animated iconography in the navigation of the interactive systems. With this purpose are described each one of the main categories that make up the layout or presentation of the information on the screen of the interactive systems, making a special stress on bidimensional and three-dimensional animation, such as the combination of both. The impact of the iconography on the interface is also measured from the perspective of the metaphor and the different existing models in the current hypermedia systems. Simultaneously communicability, acceptability and novelty of the metaphors are analyzed, through a set of quality metrics that make up a heuristic model named CAN (Communicability, Acceptability and Novelty).

The method represents a confluence of practical and theoretical knowledge about ergonomics, usability, user-centered design, software quality and the human-computer interaction [7–11]. The CAN method is being applied in a set of on-line websites randomly chosen among blogs or websites of the following countries: Spain, France, Italy and Portugal, with the purpose of determining those websites where the human-computer interaction from the prospect of the quality of the layout is superior, average or inferior (including icons and metaphors) and the animations. Its qualitative metrics are the result of a long period of evaluations and realizations of hypermedia systems. Addtionally, the obtained results make it possible to establish a first guideline of qualitative design for the next years, from the point of view of human-computer interaction and communicability.

2 New Interfaces Design and Human-Computer Interaction

One of the main problems to be solved in the design of interfaces for the new mobile multimedia interactive systems and virtual reality are the icons [12–17]. Many of these icons have been carried out by ready-made experts coming from the computer sector, copying the operative systems of the personal computers of the eighties and then the apogee of Windows and Macintosh [18] [19] (figures 1 and 2).

Fig. 1. Windows icons with Spanish text

Fig. 2. Macintosh icons

In the nineties with the appearance of the design guide for the Macintosh environment many multimedia systems in on-line support started to use that book as a vademecum or ready reckoner [20]. However, in the context of Windows and the operators who did not use commercial applications for their hypermedia productions aimed at art encyclopedias, museums, teaching, etc. [21–24]. In this context started to interact in Southern Europe two groups of professionals: artists and technicians. Among the first were the professionals and amateurs of the fine arts, and in the second group the programmers, systems analysts, computer engineers, etc. [25].

The human-computer interaction labs had not started to train professionals yet. In some exceptional cases and within the context of telecommunications and multimedia engineering the first theoretical and practical bases of these professionals could be seen through subjects such as: Introduction to the Human-Computer Interaction; Dynamic and Static Means in the Multimedia Systems; Multimedia Production; Hypermedia Programming; Computer Animation; Usability Engineering and Design Models in the Multimedia Systems. The purpose was to obtain professionals who represented the intersection of the formal, factual sciences and experience in real projects through a technology transfer between the academic sector and the entrepreneurial or industrial context. Obviously the qualitative design factor required some time in the context of the human-computer interaction due to the to the human factors, that is to say, the relationship among the different factors. The quality in the first interfaces of those interactive systems shows whether the human-computer interaction is high or low [25]. For the analysis of the interfaces one resorts mainly to semiotics since this discipline allows to split each one of the components from both the systematic and the structural point of view [26]. In the present context of study and in some cases, the linguistics notions allow one to establish the structural components of the minimal units of the information mainly in the signs and the symbols [26] [27]. Obviously inside the framework of human-computer interaction we have the cultural factors among the potential users of the interactive systems. Once more the instruments stemming from semiotics, some methods of heuristic evaluation, software engineering and the communicability professionals may make easier the task of detecting the failings and determine the possible solutions to increase the quality of communication between the user and the on-line off-line interactive system.

The communicability analyst has a series of knowledge and previous experiences that allow him to quickly detect the main problems of the interface in relation to the potential users. This ability of analysis is very important in the whole evolution of the products and/or services of the interactive services and where the predominance of the dynamic means has been chosen. Dynamic means which may have different costs in regard to the contents and the speed in generating them. For instance, a video about cultural heritage of a tourist zone may have a lower cost than the tridimensional reconstruction in a virtual reality environment in which reality is simulated. Evidently if we don't consider the copyright variable or permits of the local authorities to film those places as it may happen in some places in the South of the Mediterranean [28]. The advantage of working with images instead of the audio or the text, is that an image is worth a thousand words, although we have to remember that the veracity of the images has lost its value with their self-editing. Not for nothing some scholars sustain the need of going back to the text to get back the veracity of the digital information [29]. Once again semiotics plays a very important role at the moment of inserting the contents in the interface and most especially in the design of the icons which activate or deactivate functions inside the interactive traditional system or the new ones where micro computing prevails and besides, the micro interfaces, such as wristwatch phones (figure 1) or multimedia phones. These interfaces will spread not exponentially, but rather geometrically in the next few years, due to the OLED (Organic Light Emitting Diode) sheets.

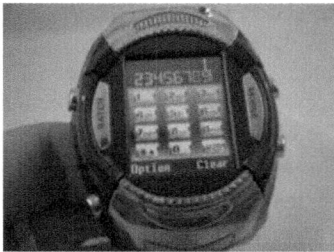

Fig. 3. Wristwatch phone interface –classical keyboard

The new dimension of the screen which is considerably smaller than those existing in the PC desktops, mobile PC, Tablet PC and PDA have led to structuring the presentation of the information on those screens through single-function or multifunction icons. A single-function icon is that in the operating systems such as Windows,

Linux, Mac OS X, etc., and which has assigned a single operation. In contrast the multifunction icons are those which can be assigned more than one function and which are used in the mobile phones, for instance. Inside the operative systems for mobile phones we have the Subian S60 v5, generally installed in Nokia [30]. In the new version, there is an attempt to leave the pencil behind as much as possible, to adapt to the interaction using the fingers. This is the reason why on the main screen we come across with big-sized icons even if it is for the main menus, but unfortunately the vertical scrollbars are still used like in Windows, which prompts the use of a pointer. In contrast, in the Blackberry phone the menus are clear and simple with a minimalist interface and a really practical conception of design. With the incorporation of animations and 3D emulations of the keyboards in the interface, the communicability of the new version is optimal. Besides, it incorporates the possibility of having the whole QWERTY keyboard available. Many young and adult potential users are grateful for having single-function icons and even the option of the traditional keyboard, whether it is to write or calculate, as we can see in the image of the wristwatch. However, the problem of ambiguity of the visual information in the mobile phone icons of the iPod 4 persists, especially for those users of Windows operative systems who interact with it for the first time. An heuristic experiment with a group of 25 adult Italian users, whose ages ranged between 40-50 years, randomly selected from an universe of 150 and experts in computer science, in front of an iPod 4 have had problems to identify the 83% of the functions of the icons which are in the following screen (title of the icons were omitted):

Fig. 4. iPods 4 –ambiguity of the icons when the texts or titles are omitted

Therefore, title and/or subtitle for an icon is not the ideal solution. Besides, it shows that the novelty of a product and the acceptability on the side of the computerwise public is not a total guarantee of the success of the communicability between the user and the interactive system.

3 Communicability, Acceptability and Novelty

Currently designing for the Web 2.0 and the Web 3.0 isn't easy, because the profile of the potential users has quickly changed in the last few years. In the off-line and on-line multimedia systems of the late 90s and early 2000 it was feasible to have a defined profile of the potential users such as are the eventual ones (less than an hour of navigation, for instance, consulting a topic of tourist information, intentional users (between one and two hours, generally, are users interested in the content of a subject and want to go deeper into it) experts (unlimited time, such as can be a scientific researcher), inexpert and intentional (unlimited time, for instance, students who have no experience in the use of computers but who are keen on learning). Now and in many occasions not even they know how to differentiate between seeking information to broaden their knowledge or navigating with the purpose of spending their time. Here is one of the reasons why many Web designs have adopted the strategy of designing as if they were advertising products and/or services. From the point of view of the distribution of the elements inside the interface, the concepts deriving from Leonardo Da Vinci about the divine proportion, are currently usually left out because of the scarce room available on the screen, as in the case of a multimedia mobile on a wristwatch or in the standard formats. These concepts must be kept as much as possible, especially in the PC tablets or e-Books, for instance.

It is striking to see the size of the icons and the distance among them in the home-page of the iPad, since their use requires having sufficiently long fingers. This ergonomic factor in the case of the Asian market and its potential users requires that the screen resolution must be adjusted at the start to make them smaller and closer among them. In the opposite side we have the multimedia mobile phones or the PDA (Personal Digital Assistant) phone, anwhich need a pencil to activate the functions through the pressure to the matching icons. Those who prefer the solution of adapting the resolution of the interface are the adult and old users, usually called single-media. Whereas the teenagers, young and adults expert in the interaction of the multimedia systems, that is, multimedia users, prefer the small screens of microcomputing.

Some single-media adult and old people are used to using a maximum of 8 buttons on the screens of the ATMs. These keys are aligned in two rows of 4. This is the ideal organization for the iPad screens. In the case of a horizontal reading, you can shift the icons downwards to make two groups of four. The ideal disposition can be seen in figure 5. Number 1 indicates the area of the most important visual centre of interest and number 4 that of the least important one [31]. Besides, it is necessary to remember that the reading direction of some Asian countries (from left to right) is contrary to the Western one (from right to left). Therefore, the icons should change their position inside the screen bearing in mind Leonardo Da Vinci's divine proportion notion.

The momentum of the social networks has boosted the presence of ambiguous icons in the net. Consequently, these icons need to be accompanied by text so that the anchoring principle is maintained in the image-communication relationship. This is a clear example of the involution of the icons starting with the new millennium, if compared with the off-line systems of the 90s, systems that were designed by professionals hailing from the graphic arts in paper support and with decades-long experience in analogical communication, especially in Southern Europe. The principles of analogical communication must be kept in the digital media, especially in microcomputing because of the small size of the screens. It is also easy to realize how communicability is impossible with the user who lacks an experimental background or of knowledge with mechanical objects which in many cases are already museum pieces. In the modern devices we can find a wind-up alarm clock with Roman numbers, a landline phone with a frontal disk and an English candlestick model, etc. The communicability is equal to zero because a diachronic cultural factor of the users, even though the images of these icons are tridimensional with an excellent rendering and accompanied by shadows of the contours, light details or other lighting effects.

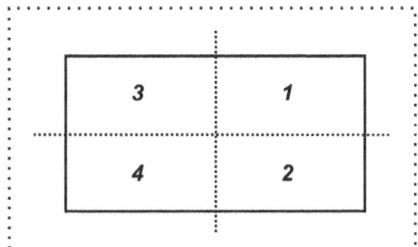

Fig. 5. Ideal disposition of the information on the screen

The context also has an influence in the choice of the different kinds of interfaces to access interactive content. Currently there is a tendency to the use of interfaces which are integrated with the space where the potential users are, such as for example a part of an interactive wall. Besides, in the case of organic interfaces they are being used in a progressive way to have access to the contents of cultural heritage in some science museums in the USA, Europe and Asia. The possibility of making interfaces in any way or shape is something that could change the traditional way of interacting in the immediate future. We should also not forget the possibility of having interfaces which can be doubled. In all these type modalities of interfaces, the problem of the distribution of the icons or active zones for the interaction lies in the height of the potential users. For instance, a standing person is not the same as a person sitting on a wheelchair. In these cases to guarantee a greater accessibility to the potential users it would be possible to work with the navigation icons or active zones between 1.10–1.30 metres. In regard to the shapes and the colours it is important to make previous assessments of the real and/or virtual environments where these interfaces will be inserted.

Now in the analyzed interactive systems in the social networks it can be seen how the standardization in the design templates has made easier the interaction among millions of users spread all along the world. The simplicity of the shapes, the universality of the distribution of the information on the screens of the main applications of the Web 2.0, the minimalist design in several free access applications evidently has also changed the diffusion of the new Internet era. However, from the point of view of communicability and design some problems belonging to the usability era persist. Our field of work has focused on three quality attributes which keep among them a bidirectional relationship which can be depicted graphically in the following way:

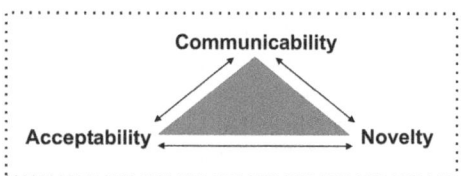

Fig. 6. Bidirectional relationship between communicability, acceptability and novelty

In the upper part of the pyramid is communicability. Communicability is a qualitative communication between the user and the interactive system, such as hypermedia, mobile phones, virtual reality, multimedia immersion among others. Communicability is the extent to which an interactive system successfully conveys its functionality to the user.

The novelty is that set of elements which attracts the user's attention through the senses, especially audio and visual (80% of messages are perceived by the combination of the audiovisual in the off-line interactive systems, for instance [31]).

Finally, the accessibility to the interactive information is stored in the hyperbase. The ergonomics of the design as well as its size (due to the momentum of microcomputing in some cases) may leave out or bolster the factual function, that is, the direct communication in the interaction process between the user and the computer, without generating mistakes.

As a rule, direct communication is that which takes place through the different entrance peripherals of the interactive information (keyboard, microphones, arms movement, etc.) and which belong to the highest interdependence level in the dynamic process of user-computer communication.

4   Objectivity in the Choice of the Universe of Study and Results Obtained

One of the problems that is always latent in the heuristic evaluation works is objectivity and the margin of error of the results obtained. In our case, we have overcome both problems through the notions of descriptive statistics and the techniques used in the heuristic evaluation with some strategies deriving from the methods used in the social sciences [32] [33].

Methods and techniques which have been perfected along the years and which allow one to carry out evaluations of the interactive systems in an economic way and with 100% reliability. For the choice of the universe of study it has been generated in a random way a database with keywords.

Later on these keywords were inserted in the Google and Yahoo search engines, choosing the ten first entries of the first page. A new listing was generated with all of them, and a new random selection was made, until making up a universe of study of 100 Spanish, French, Italian and Portuguese blogs and/or portals –results heuristic evaluation in figure 7.

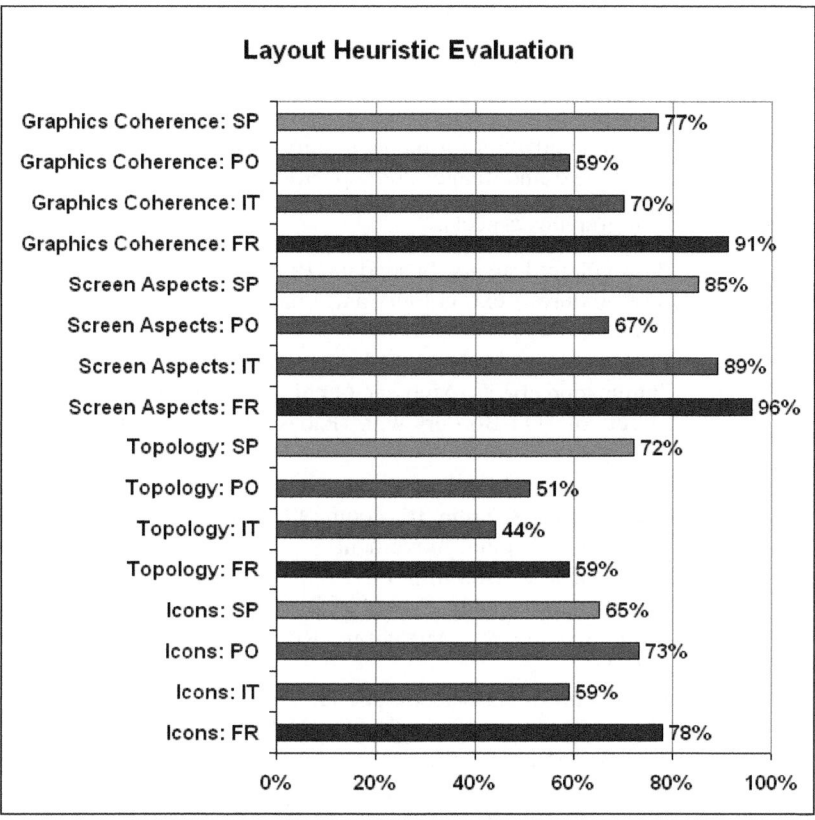

Fig. 7. Results layout heurist evaluation (metric binary of presence): FR = France, IT = Italy, PO = Portugal and SP = Spain

A table of heuristic evaluation aimed at the design category named "layout" has been applied to this universe of study. In it the main components have been analyzed of the static and dynamic images which are next listed:

1. Icons:
    - a. Dynamics (animation). Static. Wire.
    - a. Disposition of the icons upon changing the visualization/orientation of the screen. The icons remain in the same disposition reducing its size. The icons keep their size and shift downwards in the shape of a column.
    - b. On-line connectivity icons. The icons for connectivity to internet depict the operative systems. The connectivity icon is associated to the phone company/ies.
    - c. Explanation of the functions of the navigation icons: Title or name. When the cursor is placed over them. In the help. None.
    - d. Gesture icons for multi-touch interactions: Classical hand. Emulation hand.

  e. Style: Universal for PC and microcomputing. Special for trademark, i.e. Apple. Mixed: PC, microcomputing, multimedia phone, etc.

2. Topology:

  a. The same position for the navigation keys.
  b. Shared text and image screen position.

3. Coherence of graphics aspects:

  a. Base colour: Primary. Secondary. Primary and secondary combination.
  b. Base texture: Text, colours and images. Only text and image. Only images.
  c. Transparencies: All screen. Frame. Windows. Icons.
  d. Illumination effects: Ambient. Omni-directional. Indirect illumination.
  e. Effects of 3D : Borders with shades. Reflection of light. Diffuse of the image.
  f. Video: Colour. Black & white.
  g. Camera effects: Zoom in. Zoom out. Horizontal movement. Vertical movement. Angular movement.
  h. Plane: General. Medium. First.
  i. Emission movement: Constant. Stop or break.
  j. Animation classes: Morphing. Rotation. Only 2D. Only 3D. 2D and 3D.
  k. Typographies: Classical. Special.
  l. Object or image presentation: With rendering (a perfect finish). Without rendering. Wire.
  m. Photographies: White & Black. Colours. Wire.
  n. Pictures format: Panoramic. Spherical. Plane.
  o. Drawings: White & Black. Colours. Wire.
  p. Key of navigation: 2D. 3D. Static. Animation. Arrows or cursors. Special icons. Draws.

4. Screen aspects:

  a. Transition types (2D): Cut. Dissolve. Random bars horizontal. Split vertical out. Split Vertical in. Wipe up. Vanish. Binds vertical. Blinds horizontal. Blinds central. Checkerboard. Diagonal. Spiral. Uncover. Strips. Cover. Box in. Box out. Fade throught black.
  b. Transition types (3D): Balloons. Bifolding backdrop. Box in box. Breaking up. Camera shutter. Closing box. Counter rotating disks. Counterrotating panels. Crushing slide. Cubic formation. Double cross. Dual screens. Fall out. Flip. Four square. Getting file from folder. Hyper slides. Infinite horizon. Mass production. Open up. Opening cylinder. Paddle wheel. Paint ball. Pods. Racing rectangles. Reassemble tiles. Revolving cube. Revolving frames. Rubic's cube. Shattering glass. Space cubes. Spring away. Starburst. Swap. Tunnel travel. Turning billboard. Turning page of book. Twirling circles or panels or rectangles or squares. Undulating bars.
  c. 3D simulation of the frames.

    d.   Screen content attention elements: Special symbols (circle or ellipse; squared or rectangle; arrows; and icons). Sounds. Words.

    e.   Space occupied by animations and videos on the screen: Full screen. A frame on the screen.

This table has allowed us to establish a metrics of binary presence of the element which had to be traced inside the analyzed portals, whose results are in the graphics divided up by countries (figure 7).

Later on, with the binary presence metrics being applied to the three quality attributes and to the design primitives, for instance; link, structural links, node, guided tours, index, frame, collection, etc. the metrics have been carried out to evaluate the systems again.

The procedure to generate these metrics can be checked in the following bibliography [9] [25] [32]. In this case a random sample of 50 portals for every country has been chosen and our final results of the three quality attributes are in the following graphic:

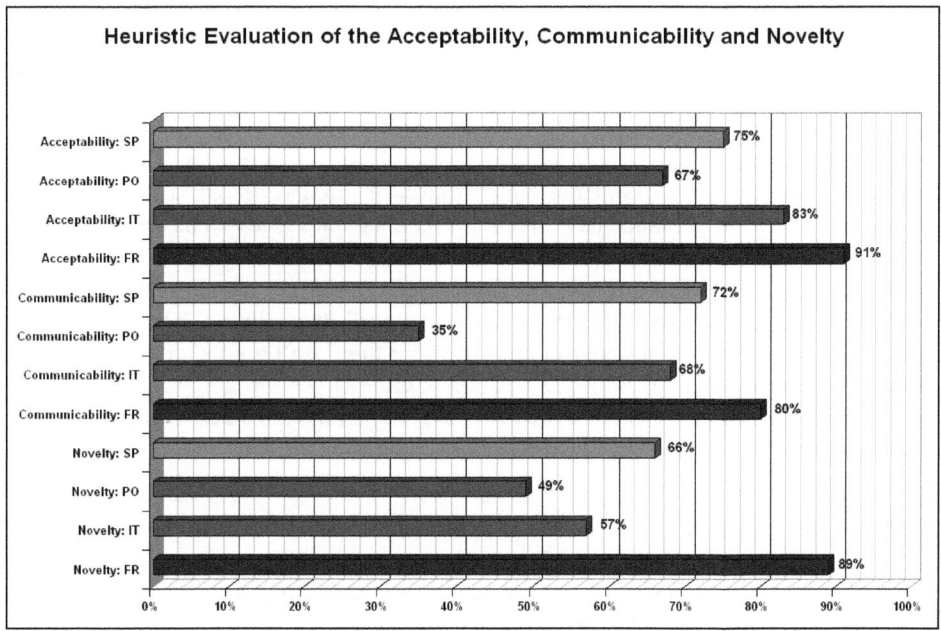

Fig. 8. Results layout heurist evaluation (metrics acceptability, communicability and novelty): FR = France, IT = Italy, PO = Portugal and SP = Spain

These results allow us to be optimistic to broaden our universe of study towards microcomputing interfaces such as mobile phones, for example, or the organic interfaces aimed at the promotion of cultural heritage and tourism.

5 Lessons Learned

In the study methodology it has been seen the constant evolution of the social networks from a quantitative point of view. However, in the last five years there is no great news from the design point of view in the Web 2.0. The minimalist style to occupy the first positions inside the search engines because the text prevails over the dynamic image, has boosted digital photography, where one tends to make not a spontaneous photograph but rather a marketing type, even with people. Where one tends to make not a spontaneous photograph but rather a marketing type, even with people. That is, there is a marketing of the human being in the Web 2.0 from the point of view of design. Consequently, the notions deriving from semiotics applied to marketing are very positive to carry out evaluations of the layout, applying the CAN methodology.

6 Conclusion

The obtained results make it apparent that the Web 2.0 has grown in quality in France because there is a greater tradition in the layout of the interactive systems and also in the use of the computer animations in the portals. Perhaps its websites do not occupy the main places in the Google or Yahoo engines, for instance, but its quality is superior to the rest of the analyzed countries. The reason also has to be found in a historic issue where more PCs for design were sold, such as the Macintosh in the 90s. The 90s were a key decade because they meant the digitalization of graphic design. The 2D and 3D digital images sector in France have lived this as a natural process. The other countries we have analyzed have plumped for other solutions aimed at managing computing, such as the storing and access of information, for instance, leaving in the background the layout. The minimalist design of the Web 2.0 has allowed that solution. Nevertheless, the layout has to be bolstered in those countries where there isn't a good communicability in the computer-made images in 2D and 3D. Currently we are going towards a new momentum of the new interfaces which emulate and simulate the 2D in great spaces or in small screens of micro computing that can even be doubled.

Acknowledgments

The authors would like to thanks Electronics Arts, Maria Ficarra (Alaipo & Ainci – Spain and Italy) and Carlos for their support and helps.

References

1. Jacobson, J., Hwang, Z.: Unreal Torunament for Immersive Interactive Theater. Communications of the ACM 45(1), 39–42 (2002)
2. Kumar, S., et al.: Second Life and the New Generations of Virtual World. IEEE Computer 41(9), 46–53 (2008)

3. Lee, Y., Kozar, K., Larsen, K.: Does Avatar Email Improve Communications? Communications of the ACM 48(12), 91–95 (2005)
4. Maldonado, T.: Lo real y lo virtual, Gedisa, Barcelona (1994)
5. Cipolla-Ficarra, F., Cipolla-Ficarra, M.: Interactive Systems, Design and Heuristic Evaluation: The Importance of the Diachronic Vision. In: Cipolla-Ficarra, F., Cipolla-Ficarra, M. (eds.) New Directions in Intelligent Interactive Multimedia, pp. 625–634. Springer, Berlin (2008)
6. Luebke, D., Humpherys, G.: How GPUs Work. IEEE Computer 40(2), 96–100 (2007)
7. Nielsen, J., Mack, R.: Usability Inspections Methods. John Wiley, New York (1994)
8. Pfleeger, S.: Software Metrics: Progress after 25 Years? IEEE Computer Software 25(6), 32–34 (2008)
9. Cipolla-Ficarra, F.: Communication evaluation in multimedia: metrics and methodology. In: Proc. Human-Computer International, vol. 3, pp. 567–571. LEA, Mahwah (2001)
10. Salvendy, G.: Handbook of Human Factors and Ergonomics. John Wiley, New York (2006)
11. Sears, A., Jacko, J.: The Human-Computer Interaction Handbook: Fundamentals, Evolving Technologies and Emerging Applications. LEA, New York (2008)
12. Frohlich, D.: The Design Space of Interface. In: Proc. Eurographics Workshop Multimedia: Systems, Interaction and Application, pp. 53–69. Springer, Berlin (1991)
13. Billinghurst, M., Grasset, R., Looser, J.: Designing Augmented Reality Interfaces. Computer Graphics 39, 17–21 (2005)
14. Blundell, B., Swartz, A.: 3-D Display and Interaction Interfaces: A Trans-Disciplinary Approach. John Wiley, New York (2006)
15. Galitz, W.: The Essential Guide to User Interface Design: An Introduction to GUI Design Principles and Techniques. John Wiley, New York (2007)
16. Colman, D., Vertegaal, R.: Organic User Interfaces: Designing Computers in Any Way, Shape, or Form. Communications of the ACM 51(6), 48–53 (2008)
17. Saffer, D.: Designing Gestural Interfaces: Touchscreens and Interactive Devices. O'Reilly, Sebastopol (2009)
18. Caplin, S.: Icon Design: Graphic Icons in Computer Interface Design. Watson-Guptill, New York (2001)
19. Cipolla-Ficarra, F.: A User Evaluation of Hypermedia Iconography. In: Compugraphics, pp. 182–191. GRASP, Paris (1996)
20. Apple: Macintosh Human Interface Guidelines. Addison-Wesley, Massachusetts (1992)
21. Shirley, P., et al.: Fundamentals of Computer Graphics. Peters Ltd., Wellesley (2005)
22. O'Rourke, M.: Principles of Three Dimensional Computer Animation. Norton, New York (2003)
23. Kerlow, I.: The Art of 3D Computer Animation and Effects. John Wiley, New York (2009)
24. Birn, J.: Digital Lighting & Rendering. Indianapolis, New Riders (2000)
25. Cipolla-Ficarra, F., Cipolla-Ficarra, M.: Computer Animation and Communicability in Multimedia System: A Trichotomy Evaluation. In: Studies in Computational Intelligence, pp. 103–115. Springer, Berlin (2009)
26. Sebeok, T.: Global Semiotics. Indiana University Press, Bloomington (2001)
27. Saussure, F.: Course in General Linguistics. McGraw-Hill, New York (1983)
28. Cipolla-Ficarra, F.: Copyright for Interactive Systems: Stratagems for Tourism and Cultural Heritage Promotion. In: Proc. HCITOCH 2010. Springer, Berlin (2010)
29. Debray, R.: Vie et mort de l'image. Gallimard, Paris (1995)
30. Cipolla-Ficarra, F.: Mobile Phones, Multimedia and Communicability: Design, Technology Evolution, Networks and User Issues. Nova Publishers, New York (2010) (in printer)

31. Cipolla-Ficarra, F.: Evaluation and Communication Techniques in Multimedia Product Design for On the Net University Education. In: Multimedia, pp. 151–165. Springer, Berlin (1996)
32. Cipolla-Ficarra, F.: Quality and Communicability for Interactive Hypermedia Systems. IGI Global, New York (2010)
33. Cipolla-Ficarra, F.: The resolution of the problem of objectivity in a method of evaluation for interactive applications. SIGWEB Newsletter 5(2), 6 (1996)
34. Cipolla-Ficarra, F.: Dyadic for Quality in Hypermedia Systems. In: DVD-ROM Proceedings Applied Human Factors and Ergonomics. AEI, Las Vegas (2008)

Information Design in Natural Surroundings

Oriol Camacho-Díaz

Department of Drawing, Design and Aesthetic, FineArts College
University of La Laguna, Spain
oriolcamacho@yahoo.es

Abstract. In the current work is presented the importance of information design in natural surroundings on two key concepts: accessibility (offering usefulness, without any modifications, for as many people as possible) and usability (easiness of use, in order to reach a specific aim). A set of measures and guidelines are presented to facilitate processing information in a complex environment.

Keywords: Sign, Communication, Environment, Nature, Orientation.

1 Introduction

Signs help the visitor to know the new place through a visual system of communication, combining the recurrent factors, the variable aspects and the relationship between them, through a specific "repertoire"[1]: typography, signs –arrow, pictogram, logo– and colour. Nature manifests two important variables. On the one hand, the subjective impressions based on the very movement in the perceptive field; on the other hand, the different experiences perceived along the path, facing adverse lighting conditions and a topography which transforms the vision's scale and angle of some elements of reference such as swift temperature changes due to height differences, varying vegetation, etc. According to P. Wildbur and M. Burke"[2] [2], the study of orientation in a complex environment requires "the selection, organization and presentation of the information for a specific audience".

Questions such as, "Which direction to follow?" or "Which is the best way?" are constant doubts when we have to make a decision going through unknown places with plenty of stimuli. Thus, the designer has the responsibility for helping the citizens in this task.

2 Information Design

The designer undertakes a task with an obvious public purpose, linked to the duty of informing and being of use to the whole of the society. Another aspect to take into consideration is time: we want to get everywhere quickly, to make the most of our

---

[1] Costa, J: Señalética, p. 126. Ceac, Barcelona (1987). Term referring to the "simple elements that organize themselves, making up meanings within the graphic space".

[2] Wildbur, P., Burke, M.: Infográfica, p. 6. Gustavo Gili, Barcelona (1998).

F.V. Cipolla Ficarra et al. (Eds.): HCITOCH 2010, LNCS 6529, pp. 87–99, 2011.

everyday activity, which involves looking for instant, increasingly detailed information, especially in an urban context, even though humankind also creates order in the natural landscape: it is an intuition-guided attitude, a self-protection mechanism that transmits us self-confidence and independence so we can consequently understand our environment to a better degree.

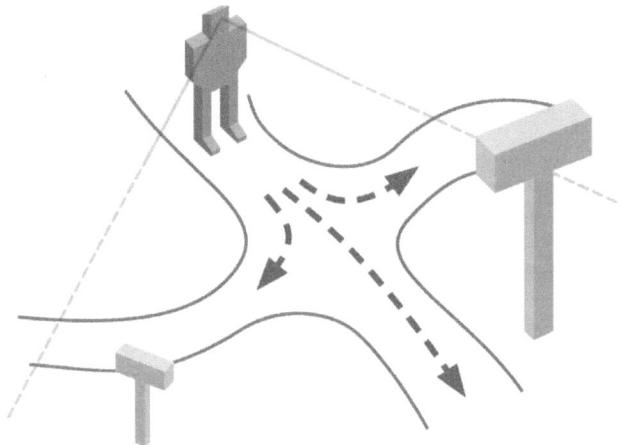

Fig. 1. To move forward is to take decisions

The difficulty of designing information is to make easy what seems complex at first sight. According to Yves Zimmermann[3] [3], "it is impossible to personally meet the needs of orientation of a large mass of people", referring to signposting. It requires an initial global inception that must take into account specific peculiarities, from a plain graphic language that acts as a reminding rule in the directional design of paths –more dynamic due to a greater rate of action–, as well as in interpretation centres, that involve a pause before resuming the course, with a more static use. We must not forget that we are addressing a fairly heterogeneous group, within wide age span and education levels; therefore, we must remain aware of those conditions that could have an effect on visual perception.

Designing information relies mainly on two key concepts: accessibility (offering usefulness, without any modifications, for as many people as possible) and usability (easiness of use, in order to reach a specific aim). Designing is a complex procedure, and requires a constant and meticulous studying, even though many of the stops –especially as a consequence of experience– are based on intuition; quite the contrary, the attained maturity should not be an impediment for a renewed creation, since it then becomes a deficiency and not a virtue. As a consequence, there is a tendency to systematize the process within the useful bounds of action to know how to analyse the reasons that lead us to choose our outlines for creating.

---

[3] Chaves, N.: Zimmermann Asociados, p. 91. Gustavo Gili, Barcelona (1993).

2.1 Determining Factors

Graphic schematization is a group of data, values, etc., that the designer must visually organize through a previous selection. It is necessary to know the receiver's profile beforehand, in order to determine the visual and assimilating effort that he is about to do (*what* has to be communicated, *to whom* and *how*). Arranging disperse data starts with a mental stage which becomes formal afterwards, on which closeness, size and connecting lines between elements have all an effect. In any case, information in the two-dimensional organisation will appear layer after layer in a linear way, namely defining the principle (proposition), a middle part (development) and an ending one (resolution) that must all be either perspicuous –such a narrative– or non-linear, but always with a hyerarchy which sets up the necessity's priorities[4] –those that must work– more than higher ones such as creativity [4].

We can use the term "visual semiotics"[5] to allude to the depuration of marks and elements, expression analysis and assessment of the ensemble [5]. The validation will determine the level of acceptance and comprehension by means of a test, increasingly requested in the infographic resources and widespread information, based on the thematic and formal variation, degrees of iconicity, legibility, decoding and universality. There is a descriptive interpretation that asserts that beauty –something so subjective that gives to us the impression of being a spiritual delectability or a rule of the process of creation–, is simply a result of the purity of its function, based on nature (however, natural selection does not intendedly transfer genetic patterns from one generation to the next). Nevertheless, a design's functional aspects are considered more objective than those aesthetic, and as a result of that, designs endure longer in time even if they are perceived as being simple and of relative interest.

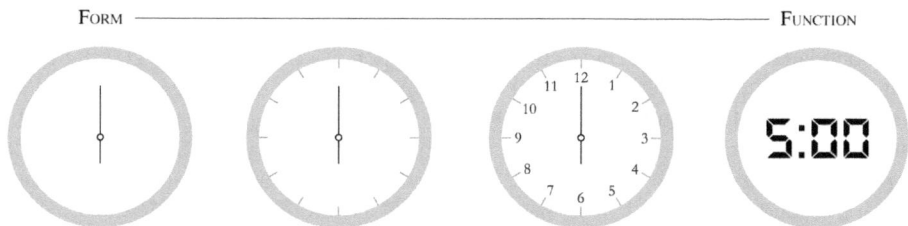

Fig. 2. Form and function depending on the criteria of success as primary aim

Prescriptive interpretation stems from the latter and additionally considers the aesthetic aspects on a secondary level, even if it suggests that, in order to get a successful design, it is not enough to follow the function, but it is necessary to implement a method that manages to be as unobjectionable as possible to achieve success: in some cases, the main factor will be aesthetical and in others it will be functional. At any rate, it is worth to avoid using both interpretations –descriptive and prescriptive– in a rigid way, in view of the fact that decisions may vary because of the relative ensemble of aspects

---

[4] An essential work on the concept of hierarchy of needs is: Maslow, A.: Motivación y Personalidad. Díaz de Santos, Madrid (1991).

[5] Phrase quoted in: Costa, J.: La Esquemática, p. 131. Paidós Estética, Barcelona (1998).

there are to design (form and function) depending on the criteria of success as primary aim (figure 2).

In the same way that, in design for publishing, information can be distributed by means of different types of mesh –manuscript, columns, modular, hierarchic, and so on–, which configure multiple templates each customized for a given section, the way of displaying data must comply with a specific order within the bounds of the architecture of two-dimensional space. Even in order to achieve the deconstruction of a visual structure –e.g., to induce a specific emotional reaction– it is required to foreknow the rational signification associations that set up between the diverse graphic components. We usually expect a certain type of information to appear at a specific place and not another; that being so, modifying its logical order can result in an unexpectedly favourable result; that is to say, an involvement on behalf of the observer, that perceives this emphasis as a relevant sign, directly related to the hierarchization of contents. However, if the breaking of basic composing rules does not follow an intentional asset, order becomes unintelligible.

When it comes to signalling, it is frequent to use a hierarchic guide of modules which organises a multiple message into diverse simpler messages [6], especially if it is a directional directory in which "the basic square unit can be used on its own, or else combined with others to create independent informative panels, of every type or complexity"[6]. Modularity is then assumed as a useful structural principle, in which the designer needs to know the setting thoroughly, in order to be able to dissociate it into modules and, in turn, to make them work as a whole altogether. As a result of that, this kind of systems becomes wider when we increase our knowledge, without the necessity of thus limiting the creativity; quite the opposite, it acts as a control me-chanism to release oneself from dispensable tasks, allowing at the same time to focus our effort where it really matters.

Information always needs to be designed with a "progressive revelation"[7] as a basis, independently of the surface on which it happens to be, shall it be graphic representation, editorial mesh, modular line for signalling, etc. [7]. Those examples are even more useful the more efficient the whole of signalling, signs or symbols that naturally linked to a communication is and, in order to achieve that, it is compulsory to plan a strategy which controls the complexity of the information, showing only what is needed or required in a specific moment. Thereby, the complexity of given data will be exposed in a gradual and progressive way, addressing not only the experts in the subject but also those who are still in the learning stage, that is to say, making progressive attempts to come closer as a reinforcement to a due behaviour.

It is difficult to teach a complex specific conduct on processing information. Because of this, an adjustable process is needed, which fragments knowledge into simpler subcategories to be comprehended independently before understanding the whole. It is frequent for the learning process to happen in an unconscious way; for instance, a videogame reveals each different difficulty level as the player gets through a series of increasingly difficult tasks, with a natural progression in acquiring new information, thanks

[6] Samara, T.: Diseñar con y sin Retícula, p. 103. Gustavo Gili, Barcelona (2004).

[7] Assigned term to explain the dissociation of information in various layers and represent just the ones that are necessary or relevant, quoted from: Lidwell, W., Holden, K., Butler, J.: Principios Universales de Diseño, p. 154. Blume, Barcelona (2005).

largely to cumulative reinforcements, which have been analyzed to emerge in specific moments. Practice is, in itself, an intrinsic reinforcement to the very game, based on the experience the player gets through a reiteration effect, which enhances procedures and complex motional skills, allowing eventually intuitive responses to emerge.

Fig. 3. Active visual message

With the aim of ensure the efficiency of the visual message it is then necessary to avoid the feeling of redundancy in the search for clarity, it being defined at different levels:

- Diverse: the variety of elements avoids a single flaw, but it is complicated to put into practice. For instance: using different types of signals in a common area reinforces the message's continuity (directional, interpretative, continuousness, etc.).
- Homogeneous: with a high risk of single flaws –due to the domino effect–, it is composed of various elements of the same type. For instance: the disappearance of a signal within a chain of even typology interrupts the sequential reading.
- Active: flaws are evenly distributed between all the elements, with a minimal risk of an interruption of the system. For instance: the use of informative dashboards and panels with a same or quite similar message in the same place (sightseeing spot, leisure area, etc.) If any sign gets disproved, there always are alternative ones that will accomplish its function (figure 3).
- Passive: suitable for secondary elements that may take over only when an active element fails. It is the simplest and most common redundancy. For instance: the immediate renovation of a faulty signal.

3 Spatial Orientation

The user's psychological disposition remarkably varies from a close space to an open one. As long as the individual is endowed to a panorama, he will have the need for a recognisable frame, but once he walks into a greenery-surrounded path, and the light intensity dims, he will be forced to follow the proper instructions to resume the itinerary. It is not the same thing to move within a controlled enclosed zone than to experience the thrill of nature: weather conditions in a given area vary along the seasons, and even along the day –showers, humidity, solar radiation, etc.–, the topography of the land compromises the scale of reference elements –and the visibility angles–, the differences between heights can cause sharp changes to the temperature, the orientation of slopes determines the side of predominant winds, the greenery varies, not to mention that it is necessary to anticipate the existence of mid-climates, and so on. All those factors, among many others, must be taken into account (figures 4, 5 and 6).

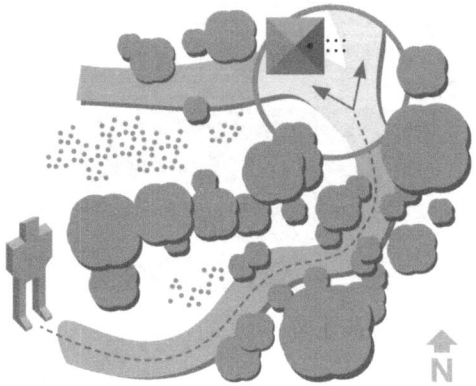

Fig. 4. Setting

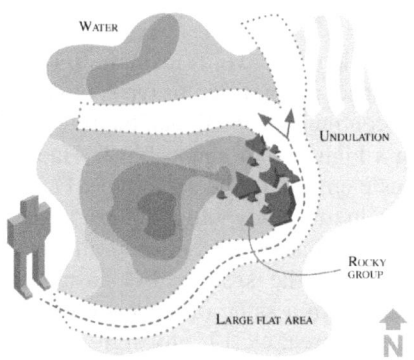

Fig. 5. Topography

The spatial orientation that Lynch & Myers [8] propose incorporates two funda-mental aspects:

1. Subjective and changing impressions based on own movement (apparent movement inside the perception field, spatial impressions, proportions and scale, lighting)
2. Orientation experience (appearance and disappearance of the image of the surroundings: paths, fringes, etc.)

Any perception of space is always subjective, therefore it becomes essential to link the place's nodal points; that is to say, in a map equipped with a reference system, the

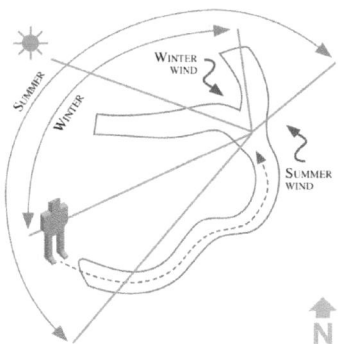

Fig. 6. Climate

coordinates' whole numbers. The characteristic elements will assemble themselves into a sign system for some experiences of movement, such as "up" and "down", spinning, stifling or loosening spatial impressions; and to achieve this, it is crucial to comprehend *in situ* the rambler's experience taking in the surroundings' image through the user's vision. When all the variables are assessed as a whole, it will be easier to define the effective range of view, placing the sign so it can offer an optimal reading from every angle [9], and also to reduce the time required to take a decision as the number of options increases (Law of Hick-Hyman[8]).

Knowledge of space is therefore a strategic skill to plan movement or identify the best zone to place oneself. When we visit a town for the first time we get a very different image of it that the one we do when we get a street map which changes our perception of the place (fig 7). We seek connection links: wide avenues as main arteries, the watercourse of the river that sets down a particular laying, the historic centre that acts as a strategic nucleus inside the whole, etc. Due to our inability to fly, we lean on the street map's view from above from a global perspective –a bird's eyeview– to understand the dynamic behaviour of our environment.

Fig. 7. Symbolic map of a city

---

[8] Additional information: Hick, W. E.: On the Rate of Gain of Information, vol. 4, n° 1, March, pp. 11-26. Quarterly Journal of Experimental Psychology, London (1952).

Interpreting a map, when understood as a "process of using spatial and environmental information as a mean to get to a destination"[9], will follow the same procedure disregarding the medium in which it is set: a webpage, a college campus or in our case, in the middle of a thick forest. Four stages can be defined thus [10]:

- Orientation: As main factor, it is in charge of placing the position and the direction connected to the surrounding elements. The best way not to get lost is to locate strategic spots that can be a reference in unique subspaces that minimise the options, so it will give us a memorable image of the place and a global identification of space: signals are essential for fixing destinations and setting out zones.
- Determining the route: to move forward is to decide, and in order to get to our destination we need to choose between the different available options. On account of that, with the aim of trying to avoid to increasingly confuse the user by setting up too many choices, it is advisory to supply specific signs, strategically placed in the decision spots: it is preferable to point towards a short route, even if it is more complex, than towards a longer one, because it eventually proves to be more efficient when it comes to comprehend narrative directions [11]. On the other hand, a well-designed map[10] provides a long-lasting mental representation of the place, especially if it is an extensive space.
- Controlling the route: confirming that the path leads to the chosen destination, using tracking markers at regular intervals, connected to the two spots that distinctly identify the distance's boundaries: beginning and end. As the person moves forward, he or she needs to be allowed visual clues, to calibrate his or her progress, and in case of long or slow routes we can insert striking visual elements that encourage to keep moving forward (think of the breadcrumbs that guide us at every moment, but also allow us to go back in our tracks in case of mistake).
- Identifying the destination: we examine the space until we are able to set it apart from others. To achieve this, the general delimitation of it has to state the reaching of the end by way of a clear and steady halt.

Generally speaking, there is a tendency to favour panoramic environments that allow us to visually track the zone and, in another sense, the areas of privacy and retreat, as shelters in which we can feel safe so our survival instinct does not acknowledge intermediate stages. The panorama-shelter theory[11] is connected to this idea: in unobstructed views we attempt to see the whole surroundings at a glance; whereas in reduced spaces, we attempt to hide for our safety's sake (in both cases, the concept of swiftness underlies in an intense way). If a background has any of these elements, it is considered better suited to explore and dwell, as has been the case since prehistoric times. By this means, when we reach a new place we favour edges over central spots, besides looking for strategic views from multiple locations, preferably over a roof and with clearly identifiable points of access (entrance, way out) which we can easily reach in case of danger.

---

[9] Definition found in: Lidwell, W., Holden, K., Butler, J.: Principios Universales de Diseño, p. 208. Blume, Barcelona (2005).

[10] An essential work on the interpretation of maps is: Lynch, K.: La Imagen de la Ciudad. Gustavo Gili, Barcelona (1998).

[11] More information on said theory in: Appleton, J.: The Experience of Landscape. John Wiley and Sons, Chichester, New York (1975).

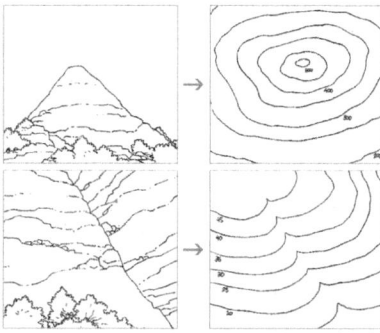

Fig. 8. Contour lines (top: summit; bottom: valley) –Villarrasa, A., Colombo, F.: Mediodía. Ejercicios de Exploración y Representación del Espacio. Graó, Barcelona (1988)

In a natural environment we immediately locate the hills, mountains and trees in an effort to delimit the void, as well as caves or thick masses of trees to climb and get a panoramic view before resuming the route. Therefore, the goal is to be able to see without being seen by means of balancing both elements: panorama (wide open space) and shelter (reduced, protected space). There are certain keys to get orientated in open land. For instance, to carry out a calculation of gradient on a hiking day trip, after studying the contour lines in a topographic map to determine the best trail:

- Figure 8: top, peak or summit, represented by concentric curves, the smallest one being the highest; bottom, valley or stream, whose line –by which the waters flow– is represented by the widest curved spots in concave curves.
- Figure 9: top, crest, dividing waters between two streams, represented by the closest curved of convex curves; bottom, mountain pass or hillock, the lowest point between two crest's peaks, represented by the spot where equally high curves diverge.
- Figure 10: top, cliff, ridged spot represented by overlapping curves; bottom: flatland or plain, represented by lines far apart.

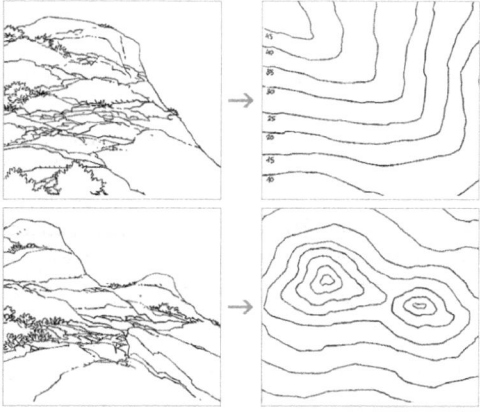

Fig. 9. Contour lines (top: crest; bottom: hillock) –Villarrasa, A., Colombo, F. [13]

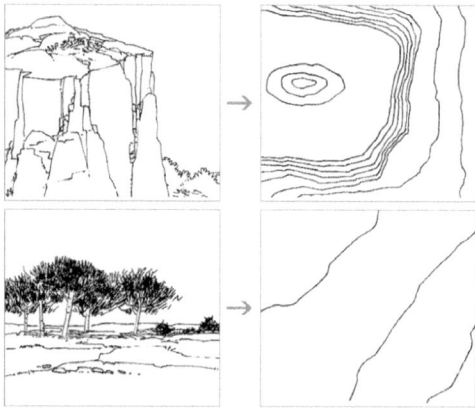

Fig. 10. Contour lines (top: cliff; bottom: plain) –Villarrasa, A., Colombo, F. [13]

The shortest way is not always the right one: the slope may be too steep, or pass over a river, dividing it into sectors according to relief shapes (a sharp elevation of the ground, a higher density of vegetation, etc.). Sometimes we can assist ourselves by watching man-made landscapes (ploughed fields, roads, pipelines, etc.).

4 Technology and Innovation

Designing information in natural surroundings can also be implemented on several innovative cases for a larger scale use[12]. For instance, we come across a logbook for those travellers who want to write down every one of their experiences. It is a prototype created by Eric Zhang that works as a digital version of the old travel journals, providing weather forecasts, time and destination of the route (figure 11). For long outdoor journeys it includes an extendable, unfoldable solar panel that can be attached to the backpack, as well as another with light that can be dimmed and can be entwined to make it stand as a table lamp in the chosen camping place. Finally, a zoom helps understanding the orography of natural spaces through a wireless Internet connection to Google Earth[13].

In the same lines we can also find *Touch & Go*, by Natalia Ponomareva, a navigation system for blind people which allows them to be self-reliant outdoors that combines a hand-attached device and a headphone, although it is also possible to attach it to one's shoulders or hang it from the belt. It features a tactile screen and displays directions in a map made of strings of raised-points on a 1:1.000 scale, similar to the Braille system. The position of the user remains at a central spot, while an arrow points the way while connected with a hearing aid equipped with an ultrasonic transmitter that creates an electromagnetic pulse field: it detects any obstruction ahead the user and informs him or her with an alarm, using Bluetooth (figure 12).

---

[12] More information on the quoted examples on: http://www.yankodesign.com

[13] Computer programme similar to a Global Positioning System (GPS) that allows the visualization of 3D images of the planet, combining satellite images, maps and Google searching engine.

Fig. 11. Digital Book Mark (prototype) –http://www.yankodesign.com

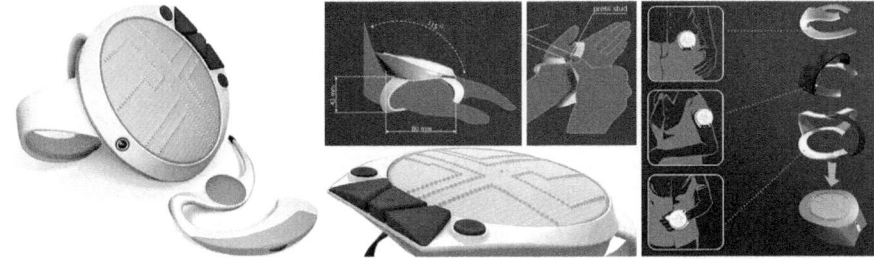

Fig. 12. Touch & Go (prototype) –http://www.yankodesign.com

Fig. 13. Compass, Show Me The Light –http://www.yankodesign.com

Compass, Show Me The Light (fig 13), by Francisco Lindoro, is a digital compass that works with a dynamo that turns mechanical energy into electric, by electromagnetic induction (it also features an electronic device with an infrared sensor). It can be configured through the computer, programming locations by USB connection or by pushing a button to record any position –it rings right afterwards– and so be able to return in the future to the same place. The red disc is an indicator of battery charging and the light inside the ring displays the chosen way on screen, and turns from blue to red according to the distance to destination: blue when further and red when closer.

Those are some samples that have recently come out for a better positioning in the environment, preferably natural, by means of new ideas or projects that help create infographic languages concerned with the promotion of a planned teaching of knowledge in the field of observation and orientation in space.

5   Lessons Learned

This is a consideration aimed to the development of a plausible line of investigation on information design in natural surroundings, especially in signposting and its various elements, both from the strategic and the operative point of view. Therefore it stresses on defining, planning and modelling the component parts of a message and its background, with the aim of achieving specific goals linked to the users' needs. The analyzed topic involves touching on numerous areas of knowledge, to different extent:

- Graphic design: visual communication, and by extension, designing information connected to orientation and accessibility. It is necessary to bear in mind the knowledge related to two-dimensional shape psychology, which directly affects the user's visual perception on his journey.
- Industrial design: researching new breakthroughs connected to techniques and materials for external communication, especially emphasizing the whole set of signs within public space (support + board surface)
- 3D Design: virtual space simulation that allows evaluating and interacting with the researching field before the definite setting, thus ensuring a greater chance of succeeding. Also ideal, for instance, as a programmed teaching of knowledge in visitor centres.
- Architecture and landscaping: global concept of space. In that case, it refers to the whole physical world that surrounds human life in a natural background (actual sight distance, setting, route design, etc.)

6   Conclusions

Starting from this studio we can establish, in a brief and concise way, some considerations:

- The unpredictability of being out in the open in a natural environment implies environmental and related variables (peculiar). The vandalising factor is regarded as a random variable conditional on the subjective action of the factor person (individuals).
- Classifying and distributing signs determine the orientation system, since the afore-mentioned variables affect the user's visual perception. In order to give a solution to this problem, the following measures should be taken: 1. General signalling (sign posting) plan which detects the centres of interest through space prospecting, with a suitable cartography for the features of the area based on a graded priority analysis that would manage the public's needs (classification); 2. Technical dossier with specific instructions for sign posting (distribution).
- There must be a designer with an action of devising, programming, outline and implement visual communications, bringing together collective means and efforts, which must be mainly aimed at investigating graphic language from a semantic dimension. It is necessary to assert what may possibly be the most analytic side of the creative process: 1. To know where and how to seek information, so the

invested time pays off; 2. To know how to transmit it to others in an efficient way, improving the production expenses through information design (the designer is above all a transmitter of useful knowledge by means of the educational image).

The general conclusion is that it is necessary to combine multiple human factors and materials to establish control strategies for designing information in natural environments. This involves taking into account at least three groups of interest: enjoyment of surroundings, acknowledge of the importance of physical and ecological processes, and sustainable resources that allow human wellbeing.

The occurrence of random variables additionally implies a profound knowledge of the physical and biological surroundings, thus the need to configure a multitask team whose professional feature is diversified and heterogeneous, following the production chain and its degree of financial benefit.

References

1. Costa, J.: Señalética: de la Señalización al Diseño de Pictogramas. Ceac, Barcelona (1987)
2. Wildbur, P., Burke, M.: Infográfica. Gustavo Gili, Barcelona (1998)
3. Chaves, N.: Zimmermann Asociados. Gustavo Gili, Barcelona (1993)
4. Maslow, A.: Motivación y Personalidad. Díaz de Santos, Madrid (1991)
5. Costa, J.: La Esquemática. Paidós Estética, Barcelona (1998)
6. Samara, T.: Diseñar con y sin Retícula. Gustavo Gili, Barcelona (2004)
7. Lidwell, W., Holden, K., Butler, J.: Principios Universales de Diseño. Blume, Barcelona (2005)
8. Aicher, O., Krampen, M.: Sistemas de Signos en la Comunicación Visual. Gustavo Gili, Barcelona (1979)
9. Hick, W.E.: On the Rate of Gain of Information. Quarterly Journal of Experimental Psychology, London (1952)
10. Lidwell, W., Holden, K., Butler, J.: Principios Universales de Diseño. Blume, Barcelona (2005)
11. Lynch, K.: La Imagen de la Ciudad. Gustavo Gili, Barcelona (1998)
12. Appleton, J.: The Experience of Landscape. John Wiley and Sons., Chichester (1975)
13. Vilarrasa, A., Colombo, F.: Mediodía. Ejercicios de Exploración y Representación del Espacio. Graó, Barcelona (1988)

Usability, Communicability and Cultural Tourism in Interactive Systems: Trends, Economic Effects and Social Impact

Francisco V. Cipolla Ficarra[1,2], Emma Nicol[3], and Miguel Cipolla-Ficarra[2]

HCI Lab. – F&F Multimedia Communic@tions Corp.
[1] ALAIPO: Asociación Latina de Interacción Persona-Ordenador
[2] AINCI: Asociación Internacional de la Comunicación Interactiva
[3] University of Strathclyde, UK
Via Pascoli, S. 15 – CP 7, 24121 Bergamo, Italy
ficarra@alaipo.com, emma.nicol@cis.strath.ac.uk,
ficarra@ainci.com

Abstract. We have developed a set of techniques and an analysis methodology aimed at boosting the quality of interactive tourism systems. The details of it will be presented in full and with real examples which have yielded interesting results in the last few years, both from the social and economical point of view, but with a huge wealth of cultural and natural heritage. We will also present a first guidelines to foster tourism in those villages that are willing to promote themselves in the national and international market at a low cost.

Keywords: Communicability, Usability, Software, Outsourcing, Cultural Tourism, Hypermedia, Web 2.0, Evaluation.

1 Introduction

Tourism is a very important source of financial revenue. There are countries that promote cultural tourism, as well as natural and cultural tourism [1] [2]. The first one via the cultural patrimony of ancient civilizations that have left a very important imprint in the history of humankind. The second, that is to say, natural tourism, especially in those countries where nature still prevails over human beings. Lastly there are those scientific breakthroughs and discoveries that have changed the quality of life of the inhabitants. Currently, there is a tendency to combine these three models.

Through the new interactive multimedia/hipermedia technologies on-line and off-line this goal has been boosted in the last decade, to such a degree that in the official websites of every country we have witnessed constant evolutions. Obviously each one of the stages of this evolution has been accompanied by a continuous growth of software and hardware, whether it is on the side of the official bodies which promote their cultural, natural and scientific heritage or on the side of the users [3] [4] [5].

In this process of constant change it is important to analyze the speed of adaptation in the time of these new trends in the interactive design and communicability, for instance, which carry out the regions that because of their economica wealth, based on

F.V. Cipolla Ficarra et al. (Eds.): HCITOCH 2010, LNCS 6529, pp. 100–114, 2011.
© Springer-Verlag Berlin Heidelberg 2011

other productive industries, usually leave the touristic industry in the background. Besides, it is interesting to examine how those regions called poor or underdeveloped in regard to the productive average inside a given state, use the latest technological breakthroughs to foster tourism, since usually it is an important source of financial resources. At the same time it is essential to study the adaptation of the touristic localities to the new technologies, especially in the areas far away from the traditional circuits. These are towns and villages that do not have big budgets for tourism promotion as compared to the regional bodies to which they belong. We present the results of a first comparative work of the official on-line websites analyzing the presence of the Web 2.0 resoruces in the design.

The Web 2.0 and the Web 3.0 are boosting new mechanisms of interactive communication among the users and the microcomputing devices (i.e., iPhone, iPod, Palm, PC tables, etc.) where the contents of the interactive systems must be adapted not only to the new dimensions of the screens, but also to the new requirements of the potential real and virtual visitors of the cultural heritage of a state, region, province, city or town. These mind-boggling changes force those responsible in the tourism offices to hire services that are alien to their institutional structures through what is known as outsourcing services [6] [7]. Theoretically these are businesses that know very well the territory and the cultural heritage where they have to contribute original, simple and universal solutions. However, in many instances these businesses are based on simple comparative studies of other tourism environments and they try to apply the same communicative strategies in diverse realities, even inside the European Union. That lack of attention to the real problems of the customers of the businesses which offer outsourcing services has led to this kind of solution being advised against when it comes to solving problems related to the new technologies [8]. The reason that has generally justified resorting to these services was the lack of great financial resources to set up the structure and train the staff to carry out the tasks that are performed by the employees of these outsourcing businesses in a short time. The equation "shorter time in solving a problem related to tourism" may mean higher costs along time. That is, it can generate a kind of boomerang effect with said businesses. The problem is that the solutions offered by these businesses is based on techniques used by the usability engineering such as the comparative tables. That is, the sampling of a universe of study which is also made in sociology with the help of descriptive statistics. There are many studies that talk about the quality of the web aimed at cultural tourism [9] [10]. However, almost all of them refer to the usability engineering as stated by Nielsen in the early nineties [11] [12]. Currently the new mobile technologies are putting at the disposal of millions of users throughout the world the possibility of having quick access to tourism information. This speed and accessibility of these new devices requires communicability. Communicability is essential to gather the highest possible amount of tourists in the least possible time, for instance. The tourism industry requires the latest technological breakthroughs in its museums, hotels, airports, information stands, etc. in order not to lose national and international competitiveness. Many of these new technologies are integrated in interactive systems. These are systems that must be within the reach of the greatest possible amount of potential users with a design that respects the communicability principles. Therefore, every component of the different design categories is important to reach communicability, both in the traditional interactive communication systems (computers,

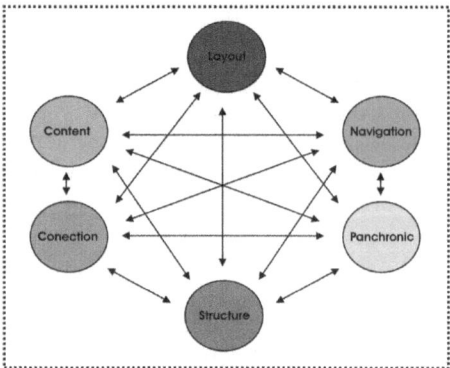

Fig. 1. These categories are constantly being updated in relation to the new requirements deriving from the new devices where multimedia interactive systems work

digital terrestrial television, off-line multimedia supports, etc.) and in the new supports: mobile phones. In the following graphic the bidirectional relationship between the design categories can be seen:

A specialist in communicability, analyzing the on-line and off-line interactive systems with these design categories, establishing quality attributes and its corresponding quality metrics is able to determine in a short time the degree of usability and communicability existing in the interactive system. All of that without resorting to usability labs or special equipment. The results obtained with our analysis reveal the presence or the lack of communicability in all those contents tending to foster cultural heritage, tourism, ecology, etc. The interested sectors may go deeper into these notions in the following bibliography [13].

To reach the stated goals, the work is structured as a state of the art of tourism and the new technologies in Italy, Spain and in other Southern Europe countries; a diachronic analysis of the design of the on-line and off-line multimedia systems aimed at the promotion of cultural, ecological heritage, etc. since the 90s until our days, the presentation of heuristic assessments results.

2   Pictures: Diachronic Evaluation

One of the main aspects of that diachronic examination is the picture, since it allows one to see how via two images of the same place along time, places that are qualitative to the tourist are built or destroyed, whether from the cultural heritage or ecological point of view. In the following example we can see how a simple coastal town of the European Mediterranean has become in a short time a sort of "little Manhattan" because of the high buildings that have been built on its coastline.

Oddly enough, some concrete businesses in the Lombardy region have introduced as marketing campaigns everything related to ecology, such as electronic bicycles or mini cars for the city. However, nobody has made a study of the impact on the natural landscape of those concrete tons thrown on the Italian peninsula for decades or an interactive systems about this topic, for instance. That is, there is no diachronic vision

Fig. 2. The comparative pictures of the digital newspaper *El País* (www.elpais.com) make apparent the negative impact on the ecology of the coast area in Alicante, Spain

of pictures or films of those places. There is a trend to present in the Web 2.0 great photographs where apparently nature prevails over concrete.

The value of photography, as in the maps, illustrations, etc. lies in the design principles in analogical support that have been shifted to the digital supports and which allow interactive communication. That is, it is a component of the static means which added to the dynamic ones (video, computer animations, etc.) and to communicability may boost local, provincial, regional national and international tourism.

Our work context is in the framework of the quality of the computer systems with a special stress on the human factors (social and economic), the human-computer interaction and the interactive communication means. Among these last the traditional aspects of analogical communication will not be left behind. In this regard, we consider that many aspects of the traditional design must be considered or boosted in the new technologies [14].

Therefore, we focus on the user's point of view of those technologies whose contents are related to the cultural heritage, ecology, nature, rural tourism, the uses and customs of the villages, etc. [15] [16]. That is to say, we intend to give a U-turn to the issue as it was approached, focusing on the economical and social aspects.

In this overall view of the issues surrounding tourism we make a special emphasis on its synchronical vision, after a diachronic assessment of the on-line and off-line phenomena in the interactive multimedia systems in the last two decades [13]. The goal is to try to eliminate those falsehoods concerning the alleged humanism that many content creators are trying to sell us at the moment of presenting them to the virtual community and the potential user of those systems.

In the south of Europe tourism in the official bodies –that is, city halls, provinces, autonomous regions, ministries, etc- aimed at its promotion are almost always under the internal management of people who are not related to touristic training, but are humanists with a scarce technical knowledge of the aspects related to tourism. However, in a myriad cases, we can find professionals with a degree in history, or in psychology for example. Next they register to make a PhD in audiovisual sciences, but after a short time they may leave it after having obtained a master in journalism, but without ever having made an interview or published an article, book, etc. Later on they may get in another university a PhD in telecommunications without knowing how a parabolical aerial or digital television work [13].

All of this happens in semi private or semi public universities. For instance, universities managed under the bias of a local neo-nationalism but with state funds, or also state universities under the rule of the highest church authorities wherever they are located. That is, that the secularism of teaching practically does not exist, but even these training realities (or rather, training-distortion generating) link to each other through collaboration projects, agreement signings, students interchange, etc. in order to enhance the disorientation and the rock-bottom quality of the multimedia interactive systems, All of this under the billing of interdisciplinarity or multidisciplinarity. These last two terms are a source of endless contradictions and loss of financial resources in the tourism sector, for instance. Consequently, we have a checkered professional who can define himself as a humanist and technologically trained for the new challenges in the context of international tourism, but in fact he lacks the experience or the necessary knowledge for the new challenges in design and communicability with the users at the moment of broadcasting touristic contents. This lack of experience may slow down the introduction of the latest breakthroughs in the interactive design in the official tourism websites in wealthy regions or generate communicaiblity problems with potential losses for that region from the touristic point of view.

3   Tourism Local and Software "Canned"

Europe is without any doubt a space of great cultural interchanges throughout the centuries with a remarkable wealth in cultural heritage as compared to other continents of our planet. In those other continents, they do not have such a variegated cultural heritage, but they have natural and ecological wealth that have lasted until our days, and which are a major source of income in the tourism sector.

Now this wealth is such in some states in the European basin of the Mediterranean that there is no complete or official catalogue in digital support, that is, a database, of the Italian cultural heritage, for instance. Evidently, lacking that digitalized information does not boost the promotion of that wealth in the on-line and/or off-line multimedia/hypermedia systems. A quick solution to the problem could be an active census of the pictorial works, monuments, buildings, etc. as if they were people.

The lack of that information damages in a remarkable way the small towns in their provincial, regional, state-wide and international promotion. As a rule, the small towns, wealthy because of their cultural and natural heritage, do not usually have available the economic or technical means to carry out of their own accord promotion campaigns of their landscapes, holidays, gastronomy, etc. Consequently, they usually buy off the shelf or canned software to solve the tourism problem.

Fig. 3. Home page has not components of the Web 2.0 –July 2010

Nevertheless, these are solutions that are not adapted to their realities, and therefore can be activated in a long process of modifications to that "canned" software which in time may turn out to be more costly. The human factors that are entailed in the "canned" solution are resistance to change and not reflecting the reality of the tourism environment. That is, a sort of emulated virtual reality is churned out that does not simulate the reality of that town, for instance. The momentum of commercial software in the tourism, cultural heritage and ecological portals (and others) entails a spate of considerations related to the momentum of the Internet and the interactive language.

If we analyze the portals in Northern Italy, where some are derived from commercial software, especially in the Italian-Swiss-Austrian alpine triangle, that is, the autonomous region of Trentino-Alto Adige in Italy (www.visittrentino.it –figures 3, 4 and 5). In those portals we can see how little or nothing has changed when it comes to interactive design and communicability since the off-line interactive systems of the 90s. In the summer vacations of 2010 the first changes related to the Web 2.0 have been introduced.

In the following table are summed up the main components from the point of view of design of the tourism official portals, which have been made with programmers, system analysts, etc. from the public institutions and/or commercial software:

Fig. 4. Home page has components of the Web 2.0 –August 2010

- Orienting the tourist, that is, how to reach the spot, the places to be visited, etc.
- Drawing up a tourism roadmap in relation to the days available and the tourists' preferences.
- Visualizing the route on a map or in a mobile device, for instance, telephone, Tablet PC, etc.
- Informing and indicate the range of the different hotels, boarding houses, restaurants, etc. with their respective timetables, prices in high and low season, etc.
- Having updated information concerning the weather and public safety conditions.
- Having available the timetables, routes and fees of the transportation means.
- Creating and managing a community of potential visitors and former tourists taking notes of the vacations of the tourists on-line, through on-line forms for the sending of catalogues, brochures, etc. to the home of the potential visitor, for instance.
- Informing about the offers, cultural and sport events and other news related to the surrounding area and territory.
- Storing and updating the dynamic and static means related to the tourism in the area, that is, pictures, videos, animations, webcam, etc.

This listing of components can be found in commercial support versions and it has been marketed up to the first decade of the new century just like the CD-ROMs Amsterdam [17] and New York [18] interactive systems. Now the main reason for this lack of evolution in time can be tracked back diachronically to two earlier stages. The first in the 90s, when the off-line interactive systems appeared with the boom of the CD-ROM support multimedia, which prompted a high cultural production in the whole of Europe, since the contents of the museums, artists', musicians' etc. were presented in this support with excellent works such as the Thyssen-Bornemisza Museum of Art [19], Renoir [20], Le Louvre [21], etc. many of them internationally awarded because of their original approach or the adaptability of the paper support to the analogical one.

That was the breakthrough of the multimedia/hypermedia systems aimed at the cultural heritage and indirectly at tourism. The production of the first interactive systems aimed at tourism presented maps and many of the options there are currently in the Internet. Some excellent examples of that time are Amsterdam [17] and New York [18]. In the second, which has its origin in 2000 with the on-line multimedia systems and which volatilize all the existing wealth up to then in finding creative solutions in less than 1 Gb, since the interactive language was quickly aimed towards the Web 1.0, thus leaving behind the off-line supports. Now the great problem inside the educational sector, tourism context, cultural heritage, ecology, etc., is that it is not feasible to make profitable these creations that waste endless human, technological and therefore financial resources [22]. Conceptually, the contents in the Internet and the access should be free, although we are going through an era where these assumptions are beginning to be rather a myth than a reality, as in the Web 2.0 and the Web 3.0. At the same time, this philosophy about the contents related to cultural heritage in CD-ROM support and specially the interactive language are now stranded in time, that is, there are no breakthroughs from the standpoint of design or the conception of interactive contents, and the interactive language in the new devices. All of this is easily detectable if the interfaces of some last generation mobile phones are analyzed that still keep the Windows system scroll bars, for instance.

In the Internet, the world wide distribution of broadband may prompt a new momentum from the point of view of the interactive language, because the dynamic means will be enjoyed with an excellent end quality of image and interaction. A proof of this are the videogames. These have given rise to a new culture of interactive systems where millions of users can get wired from any place in the planet and can interact with other users who are thousands of miles away, in real time [23]. It will be perhaps from the interactive games that the interactive language now stranded in the 90s is to be boosted [3] [24].

3.1   Outsourcing for Tourism Local

Local tourism usually adopts two options in the face of the new technologies: hiring the minimal services to private firms through outsourcing or keep on using the resources granted by the public administration and boost promotion through the traditional mass media, such as the press, the radio, television, the Internet, etc. In both cases they will claim to be the focus of attention for the whole year to the potential tourists. The ideal thing would be that these small towns could unite with each other, through a global offer, aimed at the Internet and the new devices stemming from micro computing. Evidently in both options the linguistic factor must be considered with extreme caution, since it is just another resource of communicability. Less than five years ago the regions with a strong presence of the textile, chemical, steel, agribusiness, etc. regarded the tourism industry as something of secondary or tertiary interest, and even in some provincial capital towns in Northern Italy there weren't enough notices to indicate the places of tourist interest or only two languages were used in the on-line portals tending to promote tourism, for instance [25]. It was enough to circulate through the highways in Southern Europe and see how the traffic signs were written in a single language, even in border areas with other states.

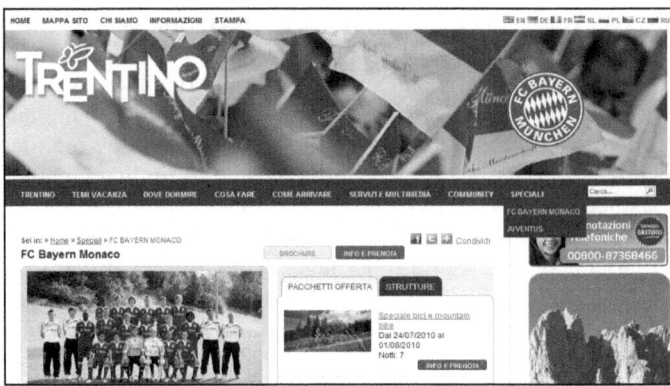

Fig. 5. Trentino Tourism Official Website and the soccer clubs –July 2010

In the last few years with the removal of those industries to other emerging markets of the Asiatic continent, human and technological globalization has taken shape in some of those areas with the gathering momentum of the local dialects [26]. Consequently, instead of using state-wide languages to boost the wealth of the cultural and ecological heritage the few economical resources are invested in boosting said dialects. As a result, there are cities in the Lombardy which are within 15 minutes car distance of an international airport, and with over seven million passengers per year but which have hardly any tourists, because they have decided to go back to their linguistic roots, that is, local dialects. A dialect that even within the borders of the national estate nobody understands, since they lack a written tradition and have been maintained along time through an oral tradition [27]. Evidently, a passenger who receives information in the tourist office of that airport can only be interested in its medieval holidays. Oddly enough it is a reality that is frequently repeated in those regions regarded before the financial crisis as the four great economic engines of Europe: Baden-Württemberg, Rhône-Alps, Lombardy and Catalonia. For instance, in the figure 3 made with canned software, we can see how the language selection does not consider two languages which are grow ingexponentially in the world such as Chinese and Spanish. In contrast if we compare that portal with the Andalusian one, we see the presence of Chinese and Japanese (www.andalucia.org). Additionally, the on-line tourist, because of the universality degree of the linguistic contents, can detect the presence of certain factors that tend to prompt a greater or lesser acceptance in those places.

Undoubtedly, another serious mistake from the point of view of communicability is to insert the preferences in the tourism portals from the sports point of view, such as can be the soccer clubs (see figure 5). In short, from the category of the content one can gather how the universal communicability of the portal of figure 5 is aimed at seizing determined potential tourists in detriment to the rest of the tourists of the world. Now this portal is about a region which usually has available more resources than a town of fewer than 5,000 dwellers, for instance, but which in the course of time has known how to profit from its experience in the tourism business becoming a kind of model to be followed because of the successes it has achieved with its modest financial resources.

4 Unions and Intersections of the Territories with Multimedia

The splitting of a territory may sometimes be an obstacle to boost the tourism of those natural resources that exceed those geopolitical borders, such as rivers, seas, mountains, etc. In a diachronic vision we see how cartography has played a very important role in the development of the first interactive systems aimed at tourism, including cultural and ecological heritage, for instance. In our days, Google Maps is a tool of great usefulness which upon the basis of satellite photography may help to find and visualize squares, monuments, facades of historical buildings, etc. In those places where a river, for instance along the centuries, has been an important engine for economical and social development of the inhabitants of its banks, it can be a link at the moment of designing and developing an interactive multimedia product, based on literary works which tell stories, create funny characters, describe a whole political and social crossroads, etc. This can be a starting point so that a community understands which is its tourism potential and starts to catalogue and value the cultural heritage where it is immersed, with special attention to the audiovisual and multimedia sector [28]. Starting by the archaeological aspect, following by sculpture, painting, etc. until reaching movie productions with prestigious national and international artists, such as Fernandel, Gino Cervi in the role of Don Camillo and Peppone (www.mondoguareschi.com) but maintaining through the decades the cinematographic body that a town has been. Starting from this basis, several museums are opened where the deeds of these main characters are enacted and the whole context of movie production, archaeology is boosted and also the international projection of a town, through on-line and off-line first generation interactive systems, coupled by other cultural products such as DVDs, books, etc.

In the design of the interactive systems aimed at tourism, cultural heritage, ecology, etc., one can start by answering several rhetorical questions, such as: What is the main goal and the secondary goals of our interactive system? How long is the time we have available to reach those goals? What type of contents do we want to present? What are the strategies we will use to reach those goals? What kind of contents do we want to present? Who are the potential users of our system? Where are these users to be found? What are the services or products we want to sell or promote? Inside the on-line tourism context we may find some topologies or classifications: the hospitality of the destinations, that is, lodging linked to other activities such as food, health, etc; the distributors who are responsible for organizing and distributing tourism packages, that is, the tour operators, travel agencies, etc.; the recreation or pastimes which are focused on a given geographical area such as museums, theatres, exhibition halls, natural parks, pathways, cycling pathways, etc.; the tourist operators who physically move the tourists, such as the means of transportation.

Obviously, these activities must be focused or distributed in different ways, making up diverse subsets. Nonetheless, the priority goal in the Internet, regardless of the Web 1.0, Web 2.0 or Web 3.0 is the client or potential tourist, who must get the highest amount of possible information in the least possible time. Evidently this action entails the communicability of the interactive system, whether in the design stage or in the maintenance and adaptation to the new demands of the tourism market, for instance.

4.1 Local Tourism: Numbers versus Quality

Locally there is a tendency to regard cultural heritage as something that has to be cloistered within the walls of a museum and in which everything that is kept and exhibited is a work of art: exhibits which may use the latest breakthroughs deriving from the immersive multimedia/augmented reality in real-time 3D environments or not [29] [30]. However, this remains a primitive view of what is currently understood as cultural heritage. In this sense a good definition is the one coming from UNESCO [31]. Now this is the theoretic aspect and there are endless studies made in this regard. However, if we analyze the local aspect of tourism, including the notions of agritourism in Europe or rural tourism in America, we may come up with situations where figures rule and not quality. Although from the scientific point of view figures have an important value, in the case of tourism and promotion of the cultural heritage an exception should be made, with the purpose of turning the area into a touristic interest zone, during the four seasons of the year. For instance, in many towns and villages inside countries of the southern cone of America, that is, Argentina, Chile and Uruguay, with regions with a centenary touristic tradition, now they are trying to imitate exogenous models, such as concentrating the greatest amount of visitors in the least possible time, for instance, to practice extreme sports, or by concentrating period cars without promoting the local museums where allegedly, according to them, the cultural heritage is stored. The same thing usually happens in some areas in Central and Northern America, as in the EU. In the diffusion of the cultural and natural heritage the local tourism bodies play an essential role and supported by the new technologies they can reach economic results which are far superior to the current ones both in amount and quality. The secret lies in the originality of the touristic projects in the mid and long term, leaving aside the near-sighted short term vision. In the Italian case, the new technologies and the "Pro Loco" play a very important role in the next decades. Since the origin of these associations there has been a goal of managing the festivities of the community. Consequently, they entailed the development of tourism activities, specially the diffusion of gastronomy, craftsmanship, popular traditions, etc., that is, activities or components which we can find also as options of tourism information in many websites in the Internet when we talk about a region, city, locality or village. Moreover, they were responsible for the tutoring of the cultural and natural heritage of the area where they were located.

The assessment of the quality in the interactive systems for cultural and natural heritage requires a methodology and techniques which have proven in the course of time a 100% reliability in the obtained results and contained costs which can help the promotion of local tourism, for instance. In our cases the used techniques that have had their oorigin in the usability era have been oriented towards the era of communicability and very especially in the era of the expansion of communicability as the one we are living now.

5 Results and Lessons Learned

In the figure 6 are the results of the analysis made in the tourism portals among the main traditionally touristic regions (T) compared to those where tourism activity takes a secondary role (S), since their main revenues derive from other industries. The universe of study has been made up with the official portals of the Spanish and Italian regions, and some local ones, which have been randomly picked, using the techniques of descriptive statistics. The methodology of study that has been used is partial, since the work has been done in the home pages of the websites [32].

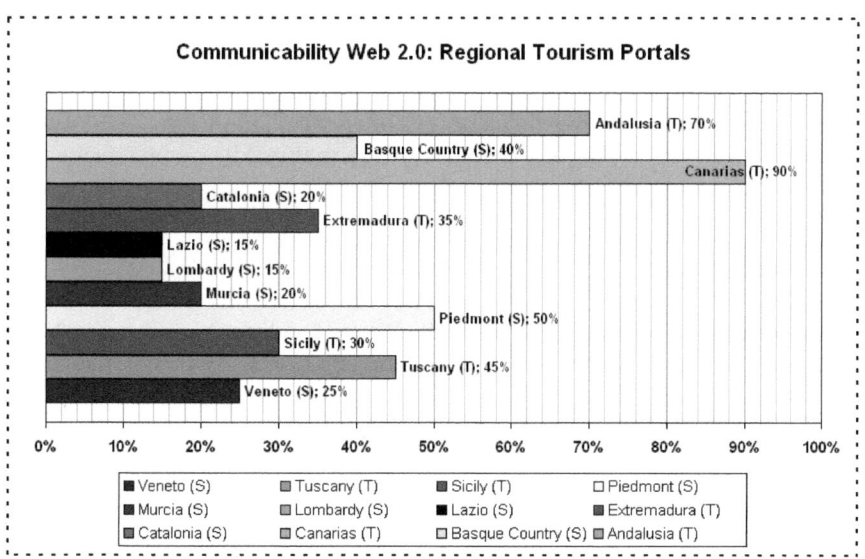

Fig. 6. Heuristic evaluation of the communicability Web 2.0 in the home page

These websites have been under direct observation for the last 12 months by communicability experts and they have seen the presence or not of the main components of the Web 2.0 split into the main categories of design (figure 1). We analized the following components of the social media networks: blog and microblog communities, collaborative tools, forum, knowledge sharing, message boards, networking sites, news aggregators, photo sharing, podcasting, social bookmarking and videocasting. A first guide is presented in annex #1 for the evaluation of communicability in the official tourism websites of the local bodies.

Usability and communicability applied to the interactive systems have been essential in leading the tourists to many places that eluded the traditional circuits in the last two decades. However, in many portals a slowness to introduce the novelties in the Internet is visible. The reasons are not always financial, but rather of the training of those responsible to introduce those changes, especially in the regions of a high wealth rate per capita. The trend in the next years is that the new users will be acquainted with the use of microcomputing and consequently they will feel the need to have access to a greater volume of digital information from any place in the planet. In the case of tourism, that information is varied and multimedia by itself. It is necessary that the experts in communicability participate more actively in the diffusion of tourism and of the cultural heritage on-line.

6 Conclusion

The results obtained show that the analyzed Spanish regions take a longer time in improving on-line tourism and in a special way with the open source software. The guide elaborated from the analyzed websites makes apparent the importance of regarding the design of the interactive systems as a unit made up of several categories that interrelate among themselves, in a bidirectional way. A failing in one of these categories can bring about many losses among the potential tourists, especially in those areas where rural, alternative or ecological tourism is promoted. Regrettably it has been seen how the scarce financial resources available to the local authorities have been wasted with false professionals of the multimedia communication sector and/or outsourcing enterprises.

Acknowledgments

A special thanks to Gabriele Carpi, Raffaella Rozzi, Giuditta Carpi, Simone Manzotti, Maria Ficarra (Alaipo & Ainci – Italy and Spain) and Carlos for their collaboration.

References

1. Park, J., Gretzel, U.: Success factors for destination marketing Web sites: A qualitative meta-analysis. Journal of Travel Research 46(1), 46–63 (2009)
2. Toyama, K., Dias, B.: Information and Communication Technologies for Development. IEEE Computer 41(6), 22–25 (2008)
3. Cipolla-Ficarra, F., Cipolla-Ficarra, M., Harder, T.: Realism and cultural layout in tourism and video games multimedia systems. In: Proc. of the 1st ACM international workshop on Communicability design and evaluation in cultural and ecological multimedia system, pp. 15–22. ACM Press, New York (2008)
4. Jung, T., Butler, R.: Perceptions of Marketing Managers of the Effectiveness of the Internet in Tourism and Hospitality. In: Information Technology & Tourism, vol. 3, pp. 167–176 (2000)
5. Ishida, T.: Communicating Culture. IEEE Intelligent Systems 21(3), 62–63 (2006)
6. Schuff, D., Louis, R.: Centralization vs. Decentralization of Application Software. Communications of the ACM 44(6), 88–94
7. Govindarajulu, C.: The Status of Helpdesk Support. Communications of the ACM, 45 (1), 97–100
8. Oh, W., Gallivan, M., Kim, J.: The Market's Perception of the Transactional Risks of Information Technology Outsourcing Announcements. Journal of Management Information Systems 22(4), 271–303 (2006)
9. Carstens, D., Patterson, P.: Usability testing of travel websites. Journal of Usability Studies 1(1), 47–61 (2005)
10. Powell, T.: Web Site Engineering. Prentice-Hall, Upper Saddle River (1998)
11. Nielsen, J., Mack, R.: Usability Inspection Methods. John Wiley & Sons, New York (1994)
12. Zhu, W., Vu, K.P.L., Proctor, R.W.: Evaluating Web usability. In: Handbook of human factors in Web design, pp. 321–337. Lawrence Erlbaum Associates, London (2005)

13. Cipolla-Ficarra, F.: Quality and Communicability for Interactive Hypermedia Systems: Concepts and Practices for Design. IGI Global, Hershey (2010)
14. Baskinger, M.: Pencils Before Pixels: A Primer in Hand-GeneratedSketching. Interactions 15(2), 28–36 (2008)
15. Cipolla-Ficarra, F.: Tourism Promotion in Rural Areas: Tools for Quality Design. In: Proceedings of the CollECTeR, pp. 83–91. UNC, Córdoba (2007)
16. Cipolla-Ficarra, F., Cipolla-Ficarra, M.: Multimedia, User-Centered Design and Tourism: Simplicity, Originality and Universality. In: New Directions in Intelligent Interactive Multimedia, pp. 461–470. Springer, Heidelberg (2008)
17. CD-ROM I viaggi su misura: Amsterdam. Simulation Intelligence – RCS Editori, Milano (2001)
18. CD-ROM Città del mondo: New York. DeAgostini, Novara (2000)
19. CD-ROM El Museo Thyseen-Bonemisza. Quadrivio, Madrid (1997)
20. CD-ROM Galleria d'arte: Renoir. DeAgostini, Novara (2001)
21. CD-ROM Le Louvre. Montparnasse Multimedia, Paris (1995)
22. Wilson, C., Guzdial, M.: How to Make Progress in Computing Education. Communications of the ACM 53(5), 35–37 (2010)
23. Zyda, M.: Computer Science in the Conceptual Age. Communications of the ACM 52(12), 66–72 (2009)
24. Edvardsen, F., Kulle, H.: Educational Games: Design, Learning and Applications. Nova Science Publishers, New York (2010)
25. Cipolla-Ficarra, F.: Guided Tour for International User Interfaces: Multimedia Design in Ecological and Rural Regions. In: DVD-ROM Proc. Applied Human Factors and Ergonomics, AEI, Las Vegas (2008)
26. Saussure, F.: Course in General Linguistics. McGraw-Hill, New York (1983)
27. Sebeok, T.: Global Semiotics. Indiana University Press, Bloomington (2001)
28. Veltman, K.: Understanding New Media: Augmented Knowledge and Culture. University of Calgary Press, Alberta (2006)
29. Rosenbloom, A.: Toward an Image Indistiguishable from Reality. Communications of the ACM 42(8), 28–30 (1999)
30. Lok, B.: Toward the Merging of Real and Virtual Spaces. Communications of the ACM 47(8), 49–53 (2004)
31. UNESCO. Mexico City Declaration on Cultural Policies, P. 4 (1982), http://unesdoc.unesco.org/images/0005/000546/054668MB.pdf
32. Styliaras, G., Koukopoulos, D., Lazarinis, F.: Handbook of Research on Technologies and Cultural Heritage: Applications and Environments. IGI Global, Hershey (2010) (in printer)

A   Annex #1: Guidelines for Tourism Local –Communicability, Design and Users

- Modification of the contents in an autonomous way by the heads of the computer and/or information services of the city hall or the local tourism secretariat.
- Presence of the main European and/or international languages, excluding the local dialects.
- Approximate inventory of the contents of the museums in a visual way (tables, graphics, etc.) that is, natural and cultural heritage catalogue of the place.

- Map of the area with the main elements (emulating 3D) of the cultural and ecological heritage.
- Approximate dimension of the museums rooms.
- Tourism information focused on a single entity of institutional and official communication.
- Differentiation among the public, private, mixed bodies, profit and non-profit organizations, etc. which manage the cultural and ecological heritage of the area.
- Timetables for the museums visits, closing schedules because of bank holidays or other events, prices of the tickets, etc. Communication channel on-line to know the last news in the museums openings.
- The information in the digital and/or analogical supports of the tourism office matches the reality of the place being visited.
- Prices table of the hotels, restaurants, excursions, etc. and dates of last updating as contact information for them.
- Updated information of the transportation to reach and move inside the town being visited.
- Virtual guides to know on-line and off-line through interactive systems the main places to be visited.
- Interactive information points and the possibility of making a map of potential visits to be made (museums, touristic itineraries, recreational aspects, etc.) in relation to the time available to visit the town.
- Schedule of the main events through the year.
- Splitting of the main tourism activities offer in relation to the time of the year, economic resources, profile of the potential tourists, etc.
- Links network associated of the official tourist sites on-line between the local, provincial, regional, nationwide and continental heritage.
- Inclusion of the set quality attributes of the communicability into on-line and off-line interactive/hypermedia system.
- Management of the design and contents of the local tourism information systems by a communicability expert.
- A small difference between reality and visual information (digital and/or analogical support), for instance, photographies, draws, pictures, postcards, etc.
- Transparency between textual and visual information about services and costs.

Sharing e-Learning Experiences: A Personalised Approach

Andrea Clematis, Paola Forcheri, Maria Grazia Ierardi, and Alfonso Quarati

Istituto di Matematica Applicata e Tecnologie Informatiche del CNR - Genova, Italy
clematis@ge.imati.cnr.it, forcheri@ge.imati.cnr.it,
quarati@ge.imati.cnr.it

Abstract. A two-tier architecture is presented, based on hybrid peer-to-peer technology, aimed at providing personalized access to heterogeneous learning sources. The architecture deploys a conceptual model that is superimposed over logically and physically separated repositories. The model is based on the interactions between users and learning resources, described by means of coments. To support users to find out material satisfying their needs, mechanisms for ranking resources and for extracting personalized views of the learning space are provided.

Keywords: Distance Learning, Distributed Architecture, Sharing Learning Experience.

1 Introduction

The availability of a high number of reusable resources, due to the diffusion of learning repositories (LR) accessible via the web, combined with that of sharing them by means of web 2.0 applications, considerably increases the potential of ICT technology as a means to realise innovation in learning [1]. The exploitation of this potential, however, is still a difficult issue. Firstly, the overabundance of resources at disposal is often disorienting for the user. In fact, especially in the case of multiple search in interrelated repositories, queries can produce a high number of results, thus requiring considerable labor and effort to find relevant material of interest. A possible solution to facilitate users in discriminating amongst results is by ranking resources with some viable function, for example taking into account others' experience [2].

Ranking, however, is not enough to discover sets of objects that are relevant with respect to the task to be performed by a user who deals with a LR. Repositories, in fact, can be a fruitful source of resources for a number of learning-related activities: for example, users can look for ideas to design a lesson in a traditional or blended context; or, they would like to find suggestions for structuring and deepening the learning of a topic; in other situations, they intend to collect ideas for realising interdisciplinary approaches, and so on. In their current practice, users often avail themselves of recommendations expressed by others as hints and orientations to address these kinds of tasks [3,4].

Moreover, the efficacy of a material depends on its adequacy to heterogeneous audiences of students, each one with strict and specific learning requirements. Adaptive

F.V. Cipolla Ficarra et al. (Eds.): HCITOCH 2010, LNCS 6529, pp. 115–124, 2011.
© Springer-Verlag Berlin Heidelberg 2011

systems customize their behaviour to the goals, interests and tasks of individual users or groups of them [5]. Particularly relevant are systems that aid users to realize tailored learning paths by applying sort of personal filters on the suggestions or experiences of others [6,7].

As an integrated approach to address the previous issues, our paper introduces, in Section 2, a "thin" overlay network, that superimposes on existing learning repositories. This network aims to supply users with facilities: 1) to access to distributed heterogeneous knowledge sources as a whole, using comments about learning resources; 2) to exchange personal viewpoints, upon their experience in dealing with a certain learning resource (hereafter also referred to as *leaning object* – LO) . This constellation of personal acquired lessons allows one to build up a shared and comon view about learning activities carried out on a set of repositories; and 3) to create personalisable learning paths – according to actual user needs – based on other users' experience. On this basis, Sections 3 and 4 present the design of a functional framework that enables personalised access to distributed repositories by deploying a hybrid peer to peer architecture. Section 5 concludes the paper.

2   Adding Value to Learning Activities

Learning repositories are a strategic asset for e-learning, for their offering of high quality re-usable materials, characterized in terms of educational features, context of use, technical aspects etc. As a matter of fact, in a quite short period the scenario of use has quickly changed from an initial scarcity of learning resources to an overwhelming abundance. To cope with this complexity some mechanism should be devised to address users toward their own learning target.

Our proposal stems from noting that users' activities carried out with a set of learning material (possibly belonging to different LRs) establish a conceptual network that links those resources to each other. We believe such a network may be used, as a map, to guide (other) learners to find their (right) direction. To this end, learning resources are enriched with the expressive power deriving from the interactions with the users and other LOs and described with comments.

Relationships between a user u and a given learning object lo can be classified into two levels: 1) a *reflection level,* represented by the variety of users' perceptions about lo; 2) an *interconnection level,* represented by the conceptual network of learning resources, including lo, dynamically created by users during the search and the interaction processes further refines these levels.

According to Table 1, for any relationship expressed by a user upon relevant learning objects we determine a *relationship tuple r*:

$$r = <User, Relationship, Comment>, \text{where:}$$

- *User* is any suitable reference to identify the user annotating the object;

- *Relationship* $\in$ {u,p,e,s,c,a};

- *Comment* is the annotation associated with the relation.

Before we proceed, we briefly introduce some notions that will be helpful in what follows. Given two sets V and E, $V \neq \varnothing$, a multigraph[1] is a triple $G=(V,E,\phi)$ where ϕ is an application defined as:

$$\phi : E \rightarrow B_{1,2}(V)$$

The notation $B_{1,2}(V)$, denotes the collection of the subsets of V having one or two elements.

Given a multigraph $G=(V,E,\phi)$ for a vertex $v \in V$, the *degree* of v, denoted as $d_E(v)$, is the number of edges in E having v as a vertex.

A multigraph $G'=(V',E',\phi')$ is said a *subgraph* of G if $V' \subseteq V$, $V' \neq \varnothing$, $E' \subseteq E$ and $\phi' = \phi|_{E'}$ denote the restriction of ϕ to its subdomain E'. Moreover G' is said *induced subgraph* of G, if $\forall$ u,v $\in V'$, {u,v} $\in$ image(ϕ) $\Rightarrow$ {u,v} $\in$ image(ϕ').

Table 1. Levels of user-resource interactions, related to the user u and to the LOs lo and λo

	Relationship	Case of use
Reflection	Peer review (p)	the opinion of an expert officially entrusted with the task
	Results of the experience (e)	the description of a realm where lo has been used and the students' reaction
	User opinion (u)	a non-qualified comment of a generic user
Interconnection	Specialisation (s)	λo is seen by u as a specialisation of lo if u thinks λo could be used to go in deep or to show an example of a concept which is tackled by lo
	Complementary (c)	λo is seen by u as a complement of lo if u thinks the two LOs can be coupled in the same context or she/he experienced this use
	Affinity (a)	λo is indicated by u as similar to lo if u thinks that λo and lo could be used indifferently

Let us consider now L as the union of learning objects sets belonging to n distinct LRs: $L \equiv \bigcup_{i=1}^{n} LR_i$ and R the set of relationship tuples related to comments upon L.

We define *graph-of-comments* (about L) the multigraph $GoC \equiv (L,R,\lambda)$, where λ is the (labelling) application that assigns to each relationship tuple the object(s) involved.

The graph-of-comments GoC expresses a conceptual model, that we superimpose over logically and physically separated LRs. These repositories are generally owned by third organisations and managed by tools (e.g. Learning Management Systems - LMS) that support the creation and updating of learning resources, under precise utilization criteria and strict access policies. Even the LOs discovery process is bounded by the searching modalities allowed by LR managers (e.g. metadata based

---

[1] Note that different definitions of multigraph are admitted, depending if graph loops are allowed or not (http://mathworld.wolfram.com/Multigraph.html). In this latter case ϕ has to be defined as $\phi : E \rightarrow V \times V$.

query). Thus, it is not feasible nor practical to assume any architectural hypothesis or any other constraint over the typology of LRs. For these reasons, the design and implementation of *GoC* is orthogonal to LRs. Through *GoC*, LRs are queried independently from the discovery mechanisms deployed by the underlying LMSs.

Relying on *GoC*, LRs may be queried via the bare content of the comments, via some reference about the author of an annotation or the kind of relationship. For example the result of the query "find all LOs commented by Prof. E.Smith") may be transcript as the set $S \subseteq L$, $S = \{ l \in L \mid \exists\ r \in R, r = <$"Prof. E.Smith",_,_> and $\lambda(r)=\{l,\_\}$ or $\lambda(r)=(l)\}$, where the underscore symbol "_" stands for "any admissible value of the parameter". Similarly, based on the interconnection relationships among LOs envisaged by prior users, the query "find all material similar to LO *l*", can be translated as the result set $S \subseteq L$, $S = \{ l \in L \mid \exists\ r \in R, r = <\_,s,\_>$ and $\lambda(r)=\{l,l\}\}$.

The neat separation and the reciprocal independence between LRs and the graph-of-comments allow one to define and realize a portable and autonomous distributed infrastructure. Indeed, operations on this infrastructure (e.g. graph traversal) will benefit from the adjacent lists data structure representation for graphs. This structure allows one to smoothly and efficiently deal with the complex and (possibly) huge amount of interconnections established by users.

To make the potentiality supplied by *GoC* effectively exploitable by users, we designed two mechanisms aimed to profitably access an enriched learning space: 1) the ranking of LOs, based on comments; and 2) the creation of personalized walkthroughs.

2.1 Comment Supported Ranking

The use of ranking to help the user to select suitable learning objects is suggested in [2], with the creation of a ranking function expressing the relevance of learning objects according to a specific user and context. Merlot (www.merlot.org) and DLNET (www.dlnet.vt.edu) provide tools to rate LOs on a five-point scale. Some of these rating mechanisms require LOs users to explicit express their vote on LOs. By contrast, our solution bases its ranking facility in an automated way, by examining the overall comments about LOs.

The process is quite simple: as a result of the comment activities, to each LO a *rank* is associated, in accordance with the total number of comments it received. Ranks along with comments establish a new, and more exhaustive user-centric view of LOs and of their dynamic interrelations. Ranks are used to order the LOs resulting from users' queries. Given the graph-of-comments $GoC = (L,R,\lambda)$, for a learning object $l \in L$ we have its rank equal to the degree $d_R(l)$.

Differently from other systems, the rank for a given LO is not given by averaging the votes of distinct users to obtain a relative value, but by assigning an absolute "popularity" weight. It may be objected that this ranking technique does not adequately capture the "real" willingness of the user to suggest or discourage the use of a LO. Actually, we observe that the relative interest of a LO with respect to another may be significantly synthesised by its rank. Besides, we note that a heavily hit LO is probably more pedagogically interesting. Moreover, it is reasonable to think that people are generally willing to express their comments on valuable items. By contrast, as an experience with a LO may regard multiple perceived aspects, it is arguable whether an explicit expression of a vote could be more objective and less prone to mistakes or misinterpretations.

2.2 Personalised Walkthroughs

Based on the interconnection relationships established by users of a given set L of LOs as expressed by the graph-of-comments $GoC=(L,R,\lambda)$, we can define the following subsets of L and R:

- $EA = \{r \in R \mid r = <\_,a,\_>\}$, $VA = \{l \in L \mid \exists r \in EA, \lambda(r)=\{l,\_\}\}$;

- $EC = \{r \in R \mid r = <\_,c,\_>\}$, $VC = \{l \in L \mid \exists r \in EC, \lambda(r)=\{l,\_\}\}$;

- $ES = \{r \in R \mid r = <\_,s,\_>\}$, $VS = \{l \in L \mid \exists r \in ES, \lambda(r)=\{l,\_\}\}$;

It is easy to affirm that $IA=(VA,EA,\lambda|_{EA})$, $IC=(VC,EC,\lambda|_{EC})$ and $IS=(VS,ES,\lambda|_{ES})$ are the induced subgraphs of GoC representing the different per-object views of the interconnections among LOs (namely *interconnection graphs*) summarizing at the community level the network of relationships among objects.

By means of the *complementary* graph IC it is possible to get help for identifying a set of LOs that represent a corpus of (alternative) available resources on a given domain. One of the possible uses of the *affinity* graph IA is to set up a catalogue of learning objects that have a similar content and approach in addressing a selected topic. The *specialization* graph IS allows one to identify objects that constitute a specialization process from some general content to a set of specific information and vice versa. Indeed, if we consider that the *specialization* relationship is not symmetric we should treat IS as a direct graph, and λ should be changed in $\lambda : R \rightarrow L \times L$, so that $VS=\{l \in L \mid \exists l' \in L, \exists r \in ES, \lambda(r)= (l,l')$ or $\lambda(r)= (l',l)\}$.

By visiting (an implementation of) an interconnection graph the user may avail herself of the experience of previous 'navigators'. The idea is to supply learners with a sort of *personalised* roadmap, to help them to find the right direction, starting by the node at hand, namely the *root*, to reach new and possibly unexpected destination, without having to do blind-moving in the LOs space. The meaning of *personalised* is twofold: it refers to the individual and actual perspective of the exploring user who chooses her own direction, as well as to the personal observations of prior users who traced the path.

3   A Distributed Architecture for Sharing Learning Experience

The conceptual model supplied by the graph-of-comments guides the design of a learning platform aimed to assist users in accessing distribute repositories, sharing their experiences and following personal itineraries. Moreover, the quantity of comments about LOs, generated by independent stakeholders, asks for strong requirements on management and organization of the content. These facts lead us to consider peer-to-peer architectures as natural candidates to provide the supporting environment for distributed comments on learning objects. The intrinsic collaborative nature of GoC, in fact, straightforwardly finds in P2P a suitable implementing counterpart.

Moreover, in our opinion, P2P are preferable to centralized solutions as these latter suffer of several drawbacks (e.g. bottleneck, lack of scalability, single point of failure).

3.1 Hybrid P2P Systems

Peer-to-peer (P2P) emerged as a lightweight interaction paradigm finalized to share resources among individuals in a rapidly changing environment. Thanks to its collaborative paradigm, peer-to-peer attracted the attention of researchers involved in e-learning and different proposals and research projects were developed [8,9]. According to their structural design P2P networks may be classified as: structured, unstructured and hybrid. Hybrid solutions aim to combine the achievement of structured (e.g. efficient responses to keyword searches) and unstructured (e.g. allowing to perform exact-match lookup operations) P2P networks, by mixing their technical and topological solutions (random structure vs. highly structured key space), were proposed. Brocade [10] is a hybrid overlay network, where a secondary overlay is layered on top of a primary Distributed Hash Table (DHT); SHARK [11] employs a hybrid DHT solution for rich keyword searching.

Other forms of *hybrid* architectures adopt some form of centralization at least to keep an index or directory of relevant information. SuperPeerNetworks (SPN) [12] introduce the concept of super-peers, i.e., peers with additional capabilities. Super-peers (SP) nodes form the backbone of the overlay network having normal peers placed around them. SP nodes act as a query server with respect to a set of clients (normal peers) and as peers with respect to the other super peer nodes. Each client node is connected exactly to one super peer node. To post a query, each client has to contact only its super-peer node, which in turn passes the client request to its neighbours SP.

3.2 A Two-Tiers Architecture to Deploy the Graph-of-Comments

Being informed by collaborative-pedagogical requirements (e.g. sharing, mining, and updating heavy weighted comments widespread on the network) and by technological constraints (e.g. distributed nature of the learners, heterogeneity of clients' machines) emerging from the community of users, our choice to implement the graph-of-comments in an efficient and effective way led us to design a *two-tier* P2P architecture, which follows an hybrid approach. The first overlay (namely Tier1) provides the ground to develop the basic mechanisms for sharing and discovery comments about LOs and, as a consequence, to access LRs in a platform independent way. The second overlay (Tier2) supplies the infrastructure for managing and distributing storage of the graph-of-comments that is necessary to build up personalisation paths.

Tier1 relies on a super-peer node infrastructure. User-created comments about LOs are managed by simple peer nodes which store them. Besides, the information labelling the interaction arcs relating to the LOs commented are transmitted to the SP node responsible for the publication on the network and interacting with other SP nodes in the discovery process. The connection between SP nodes of Tier1 is unstructured, so allowing the execution of multi-attribute and range queries in a straightforward way respect to that offered by DHTs topologies.

The structured network realized on the second overlay offers two support functionalities aimed respectively: 1) to order the set of results based on ranks; and 2) to extract personalised paths from the graph-of-comments. Tier2 establishes a DHT overlay upon the super-peer nodes of Tier 1. To build-up the graph-of-comments, the adjacent list data structure is mapped on the DHT. To this end, the URI of each commented LOs is hashed and indexed in the appropriate node of the distribute table along with its rank and all its neighbours. The rank of a LO is immediately updated as soon as a new comment on the LO is created by a user. Moreover, to take into account the presence of the three subgraphs *IA*, *IC* and *IS*, three adjacent lists are assigned to each LO. The choice of adopting DHT for implementing Tier2 is due to its efficiency in executing keyword searches: the look-up of a key, into a N nodes network, requires $O(\log N)$ hops.

4 Accessing LRs by Means of the Graph-of-Comments

To access learning resources through the graph-of-comments, we consider two types of *canonical* queries. The former mines the content of comments to obtain LOs. For example the query "find all LOs related to comments speaking about WWII", will return the ranked list of LOs associated to such comments. The latter queries are of the form: "find comments about *topic*"; in this case comments are queried per-se, and users probably are more interested in the opinion of other learners about a learning experience than in the related LO itself.

Depending on the type of querying capability that has to be granted to the users, the kind and the granularity of the information spread out in the two-tiers framework vary. If a full text search is desired, inverted index technology [13] should be adopted. For each term contained in a comment, a list of the identifiers of comments that contain that term has to be pre-computed and stored. If a query involves more terms the related lists are intersected. In all other cases where full text format is not feasible (e.g. comments in audio or audiovisual format) or required, the discovery of comments may be driven by metadata about the content of comments [9].

A further typology of queries includes those aimed to obtain, starting from a given *root* LO, a personalised roadmap, through one of the three interaction graphs (see 2.2). This case is more specific and concerns queries reflecting the pattern: "return all the LOs *relationship root*", where *relationship* is one of 'specialising', 'complementing' or 'similar to'. From an architectural point of view, these 'relationship' queries only involve Tier2 as they uniquely depend on the interconnection relationships between LOs.

In the following an overview of the tasks required to building up and querying *the graph-of-comments* is given, by highlighting the main operations carried out by the services involved.

4.1 Deploying Comments

The building of the graph-of-comments originates from the creation of a new comment by a user that invokes the `CreateComment` service of the peer. After the editing, the comment is saved on the user node and the *comment-record*

$c=$ <*user,relationship,commentid,source,destination,Data*> is built. There is a clear correspondence between comment record and relationship tuple. Indeed, the former implements and extends the latter by adding the *Data* field and explicits, by their insertion, the LO(s) subjects of the relationship. In other words, c may be considered as the mapping of a relationship tuple $r=$<*user,relationship,commentid*>, $r \in R$ and $\lambda(r)=\{source,destination\}$. Note that *commentid* identifies the file storing the comment inside the local peer file system. *Data* is the extra info required to execute searches on the content. *Data* may range from a set of metadata, to the complete inverted list of the words belonging to the comment, needed to exploit a full text search.

In either cases, once created, c is advertised to the network by calling the `T1Indexer` service that resides on the SP node responsible for the peer. `T1Indexer` is in charge to accomplish the indexing operations necessary to respond to canonical queries (e.g. to create and maintain the overall inverted lists of comments indexed by the peers managed by the node), and to build-up Tier1 overlay, by organizing and storing list of adjacent SP neighbours.

Moreover, Tier2 is updated by invoking `T2UpdateRank&BuildRelation` on the same SP node. Given the LO *source*, the key $k=hash(source)$ is computed (where *hash* is the hashing function adopted by the DHT environment). Let spn_k be the SP node in the DHT responsible for the key k (we remind that in a DHT the nodes are mapped to the keys space). If *source* is in spn_k (i.e. the *source* vertex already belonged to the graph-of-comments), 1 is added to the rank of *source*. Otherwise, a new vertex with label *source* is created and its rank is set to 1. If *source* ≠ *destination* a new arc from *source* to *destination* is inserted into the appropriate interaction graphs. If *relationship* ∈ {c,a} one arc from *destination* to *source* is also inserted in the node responsible for *hash(destination)*. The total cost of this operation, in number of exchanged messages, is $O(\log(SPN))$ (where SPN is the number of SP nodes), and is related to the lookup into the DHT of nodes *destination* and *source*.

4.2 Searching for Comments and LOs

A canonical query is submitted by invoking the `DiscoveryAgent` service running on users' peers. To reduce latency, occurring when visiting the whole network, we allow users to set a threshold (*thres*) to the total amount of objects returned. The `DiscoveryAgent` is a two-phases service that, at first, looks for satisfying objects by exploring Tier1; then, it orders the results relying on their ranks managed by Tier2.

The first phase is initiated by calling the `T1Discovery` service residing on S, the SP node responsible for the query-emitting peer. This service (generally) executes a local and a global search. The first look-up is executed by `T1LocalSearch`, that checks whether the required objects (being comments or LOs references) are identified in the comment-records stored and indexed in S. If rs objects are found and $rs > thres$, the search on Tier1 is finished and `T1Discovery` returns. Otherwise, a call to `T1QueryDispatcher`, aimed to retrieve the remaining *thres-rs* objects, is activated. `T1QueryDispatcher` is based on a random-walk algorithm [14] that, starting from some of the neighbours of S, visits the network. For each of the neighbours visited, a call to the residing `T1Discovery` service is made. The discovery process terminates when *thres* objects are found or the network is entirely examined.

Once the `DiscoveryAgent` gets the result set, it invokes `T2DHTRankLookUp` which is in charge of the rank-based ordering of the resulting LOs. To this end, for each comment-record, in the result set, the referred LOs are extracted and their ranks retrieved from the DHT ring of Tier2. The resulting order list is finally returned to the user.

The performance of the query mechanism is related to the execution times of the two look-ups. Search into Tier1 is affected by the overall number of comments, the quantity and the granularity of the data managed by each super-peer node and the total amount of super-peer nodes composing the first overlay. The execution time also depends on the threshold value, limiting the number of objects returned and hence the number of possible network hops. As to the Tier2 look-up, as already pointed out, a DHT requires $O(\log N)$ hops (N number of nodes in the network) to search for a key; thus it is possible to extract the rank or the neighbours of a given LO in $O(\log SPN)$.

4.3 Following Personalised Roadmaps

The user constructs a personalised roadmap rooted in a given LO *lo* by invoking the `BuildGraphs(lo,r)` service, with *r* identifying the desired interaction graph. `BuildGraphs`, running on the user's peer, calls the `T2BuildPaths` service residing on the corresponding SP node. It starts the construction algorithm by visiting, via a Breadth First (BF) search the graph-of-comments stored in Tier2 and returning a (partial) spanning tree, rooted in *lo*, to the requiring peer. BF is preferred to Depth First visit. This latter in fact, returns objects starting from the ones that are more far in the graph from the root – while BF proceeds by retrieving as broadly as possible all objects adjacent to the root. Considering the meaning of the relationships originating the edges of the graph, it is evident that, from a knowledge point of view, a distant object is somewhat in a weaker relationship with the root than a closer one. Even amongst *similar* objects someone are more "similar" than others. BF is better appropriate also when heuristics would be applied to limit the size of the returned subgraphs. In fact, as known, the running time for BF to visit a whole graph with *n* vertex and *e* edge is $O(e)$ if $e{\geq}n$, when using an adjacent list to store edges. To further reduce the computation time, it is possible to use a parameter *height* that determines the level at which to stop the computation (construction). This way, once execution interrupts the more significant (closer) object are retrieved. A second technique filters out learning resources that rank below a certain threshold.

5 Conclusion

The paper focuses on a framework aimed at providing personalized access to heterogeneous learning repositories. To help users to overcome the feeling of disorientation in dealing with a considerable quantity of learning resources, we propose to leverage on a network of users-created comments, that enrich learning resources with mutual relationships envisaged by users. Mechanisms for ranking LOs and for building up personalised roadmaps based on prior users' experiences, are discussed. As both LRs and users are expected to belong to different communities, to allow the navigation on LRs, we designed a two-tier architecture based on hybrid peer-to-peer technology.

Acknowledgments

This work is partly supported by the MIUR-FIRB Project Learning for All (L4A) of the Italian Ministry of Education, University and Instruction.

References

1. LI, F.W.B., Qing, L., Lau, R.H., Shih, T.K., Li, F.W.B.: Technology supports for distributed and collaborative learning over the internet. ACM Trans. on Internet Technology 8(2), 1–24 (2008)
2. Ochoa, X., Duval, E.: Relevance Ranking Metrics for Learning Objects. IEEE Trans. Learning Tech. 1(1), 34–48 (2008)
3. Margaryan, A., Littlejohn, A.: Repositories and communities at cross-purposes: issues in sharing and reuse of digital learning resources. Journal of Computer Assisted Learning 24, 333–347 (2008)
4. Busetti, E., Dettori, G., Forcheri, P., Ierardi, M.G.: From LOs to educational itineraries: helping teachers to exploit repositories. In: Leung, H., Li, F., Lau, R., Li, Q. (eds.) ICWL 2007. LNCS, vol. 4823, pp. 496–507. Springer, Heidelberg (2008)
5. Broy, M., Leuxner, C., Sitou, W., Spanfelner, B., Winter, S.: Formalizing the notion of adaptive system behaviour. In: SAC 2009: Proc. of the 2009 ACM symposium on Applied Computing, pp. 1029–1033. ACM, NY (2009)
6. Carchiolo, V., Longheu, A., Malgeri, M.: Reliable peers and useful resources: Searching for the best personalised learning path in a trust- and recommendation-aware environment. Inf. Sci. 180(10), 1893–1907 (2010)
7. Dolog, P., Simon, B., Nejdl, W., Klobučar, T.: Personalizing access to learning networks. ACM Transactions on Internet Technology (TOIT) 8(2), 1–21 (2008)
8. de Santiago, R., Raabe, A.: Architecture for Learning Objects Sharing among Learning Institutions - LOP2P. In: IEEE Trans. on Learning Technologies, IEEE computer Society Digital Library. IEEE Computer Society, Los Alamitos (2010)
9. Nejdl, W., Wolf, B., Qu, C., Decker, S., Sintek, M., Naeve, A., Nilsson, M., Palmer, M., Risch, T.: Edutella: A P2P Networking Infrastructure Based on RDF. In: Proc. 11th Int. Conf. on World Wide Web, pp. 604–615 (2002)
10. Zhao, B.Y., Duan, Y., Huang, L., Joseph, A.D., Kubiatowicz, J.: Brocade: Landmark routing on overlay networks. In: Druschel, P., Kaashoek, M.F., Rowstron, A. (eds.) IPTPS 2002. LNCS, vol. 2429, pp. 34–44. Springer, Heidelberg (2002)
11. Mischke, J., Stiller, B.: Rich and Scalable Peer-to-Peer Search with SHARK. Active Middleware Services, 112–121 (2003)
12. Yang, B., Garcia-Molina, H.: Designing a super-peer network. In: Proc. 19 Int. Conf. on Data Eng., pp. 49–60 (2003)
13. Zobel, J., Moffat, A.: Inverted files for text search engines. ACM Comput. Surv. 38(2), article no 6, 56 (2006)
14. Lv, Q., Cao, P., Cohen, E., Li, K., Shenker, S.: Search and replication in unstructured peer-to-peer networks. In: Proc. 16 Int. Conf. on Supercomputing, pp. 84–95 (2002)

Building Didactic Applications for the Teaching of Practical Content in a Virtual Campus

Daniel A. Giulianelli, Graciela S. Cruzado, Rocío A. Rodríguez,
Pablo M. Vera, and Edgardo J. Moreno

National University of La Matanza
Department of Engineer and Technological Research
School of Continuing Education - Department of Education
Buenos Aires, Argentina
{dgiulian,rrodri,pablovera,graciela,ejmoreno}@unlam.edu.ar

Abstract. Distance teaching becomes a tough task when its goal is to explain topics with high practical contents because it is necessary for the student to have the teacher's guidance in order to understand the steps and method to solve a particular problem. On the other hand, theoretical contents adapt themselves more easily to this methodology by the use of tools such as text with hyperlinks, synoptic charts, etc. This paper demonstrates a solution that facilitates the virtual teaching of practical contents by the use of multimedia material specially designed to fulfill this task. This material not only allows the student to learn the practical contents, but also provides him with an overview method and several ways of automatically checking his knowledge and comprehension of content.

Keywords: Distance Learning, ICT, Tutor, Pedagogic Material, Multimedia.

1 Introduction

Distance learning can be defined as: "… a no face training which, through technologic platforms, allows and makes access and time more flexible in the teaching-learning process, adjusting it to the skills, necessities and availabilities of each student, also it grants collaborative learning environments by the use of synchronic and asynchronic communicational tools, powering, finally, the skills based management process" [2].

Distance education allows students to learn while managing their available times at their own pace and rhythm, but, to achieve this goal, it is necessary to have discipline and perseverance and arguably, both of these can be encouraged by a good tutor.

The National University of La Matanza, has adopted face-face learning with a requirement of 75% of assistance as one of the conditions for passing a course. Although, being conscious of the benefits that distance learning can bring to students, the university offers, in some courses, the possibility of passing the whole course or some units of a course by attending distance learning. A research group of the university, projected, developed and implemented the MIEL System, an acronym that stands for Interactive Courses On Line, which incorporates learning material in pdf format. This material is

F.V. Cipolla Ficarra et al. (Eds.): HCITOCH 2010, LNCS 6529, pp. 125–135, 2011.
© Springer-Verlag Berlin Heidelberg 2011

published in a "virtual campus", that allows students to attend distance learning and pass the courses.

In those courses in which almost all the contents are theory oriented, it is very easy to see the advantages that distance learning offers. A virtual campus allows the downloading of material, asking the counsellor questions about the unit that the student is not able to understand and also asking questions to all the other students through a forum, creating debates. However, the idea has now gone beyond the theory oriented content of the course and questions have been generated as follows: Will it be possible to teach practical content, such as: integrals, derivations, function simplification, etc., to the students within a virtual environment? This paper proposes a methodology in which, by the use of the ICT it is possible to teach practical content in a virtual way.

2 Distance Learning Bases

The teacher in a school room has the mission of teaching course content. This mission is based around the transmission of content, allowing the students, based in the development of the teaching – learning processes, to take notes in order to reach new knowledge. However, in distance learning the teacher, called a tutor, only monitors the student. The tutor doesn't have to teach, because the student reaches the knowledge by himself through the learning material. The monitoring requires that the tutor will be able to answer all kinds of questions made in a virtual way by the student. The tutor also has the possibility of contacting his students by email in order to remind them for example, that assignments' due dates are close, because he is the one that controls these assignments. There is no doubt that the tutor's task is a very tough one, and, in a way, the key facts of distance learning success are: how didactic and clear is the provided material added to the tutor-student relationship. The tutor, in a virtual way, goes along with the student through the whole learning process, building an important link between both of them. If a student doesn't deliver a practice task by its expiration date, the tutor is the one who will communicate with the student to ask the reasons why the student has not performed the task. The same tutor can decide to give the student a new submission date according to the kind of problem. The environment where the contents are hosted must allow the students to download these contents and also to communicate with the tutor.

One important fact that was added to MIEL, was the display of the student's last access date in order to monitor each student's activity. Figure 1 shows a part of the list where can be seen a particular student with his last login date and his state.

In addition, the learning environment must give the possibility of:

- Sending emails to the designate tutor
- Taking part in opinion forums.
- Downloading class material.
- Including chat to allow the campus members to communicate.

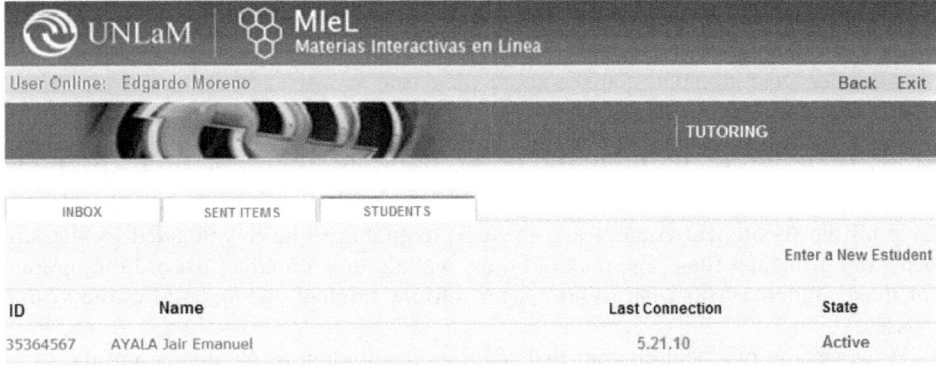

Fig. 1. A student view with date and state of his last connection[1]

Figure 2 shows a logged in student and the courses that are offered in the virtual campus. Each of these courses includes different content. It can be seen that some of them have implemented more resources than others.

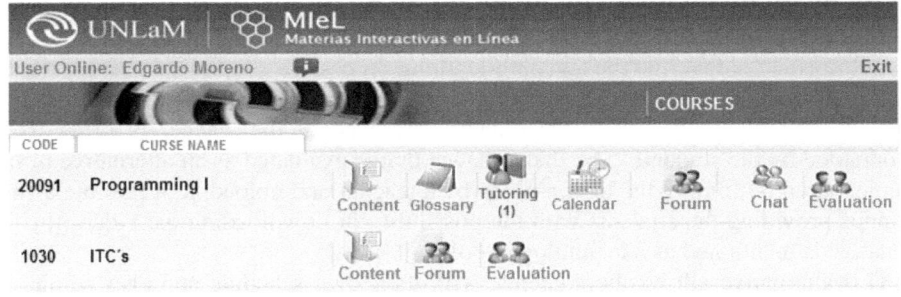

Fig. 2. Distance learning offered courses

Although several authors point that "this kind of learning is based strongly in the independent learning, where the student takes an active and independent behavior to face the learning" [3], the goal pursued by our research is to decrease the student's independent behavior making him feeling more supported by his tutor and his university. Experience has shown that forums can really allow the idea interchange among distance learning students, however it has proved to be an important initiative to include a chat feature, in which each student logs in with a registered username, preventing anonymity and involving the students with the serious use of the academic chat. This chat can be used as a communication channel among tutors and students who can fix a date and build a dialog space.

---

[1] Screenshots have been translated from their original language (Spanish) to English.

3 From Face Class to Virtual Class

The teachers had attended courses about their role as tutor and training with MIEL. The courses led them to understand the main difference between face and distance learning. As was explained before, the tutor's task is very tough and it is necessary to use a trained teacher to perform the task. The second key that leads to distance learning success is the kind of material provided by the virtual campus. This material must have all the theoretical content and must be available to be downloaded by the students in pdf format files. The material must include too, a reading list or bibliography for those students who wish to go deeper into the content encountered in the virtual classes.

However the practical content that requires the student to be able to see the steps that the teacher would traditionally write on the blackboard to solve an exercise, can't be given expression in a comprehensive way by means of written plain text, as the student would not be able to understand the contents in the same way as with face-face learning. This leads to the necessity of including other methods to achieve the goal of reaching the student with material with added value, that is, the material would not only transmit the content's concept, but it must be equally dynamic as the methodology that the teacher would use in a face-face situation way. It means that the perception that plain text is enough for the student to understand only by the reading of text guides or text lessons is changing, especially when the content is practical and of a certain level of difficulty. There is a move towards considering the incorporation of multimedia content into the teaching-learning processes.

The proposal begins by choosing those practical contents that have any comprehension difficulty and require the didactic presence of the teacher in order to be understood by the students. The first instance that is evaluated as an alternative of implementation is: filming the lesson given by a teacher and uploading it into the virtual campus providing the students with the possibility of downloading the video (this alternative is mentioned as a technologic tool in [1]).

This alternative allows the students, with their own schedule and also within the comfort of their own home, to listen to and watch the lesson. It is important to highlight that this methodology is not capable of being applied due to the following reason: a good quality video, with quality enough to read what is written on a blackboard, although it is compressed with advance compression techniques such as "divx codecs", will take approximately 700 MBytes for a 120 minute long class. In addition, the time that is taken in downloading the video classes, although the students have broadband connections, is very high indeed. Streaming seems to be the solution; nowadays we can post a video with good quality to youtube or another streaming service, but the problem with streaming is that the student loses the possibility of carrying the material with him, for example in a laptop, because a permanent high speed connection is required, and if the connection is lost the student will not be able to see the material.

Based on that first proposal, the research team begins to consider the possibility of generating multimedia contents in which, by the use of animations it would be possible to underline, highlight and gradually add parts of information. That means, removing the filmed blackboard and turning it into animated information that is gradually shown, while the teacher's voice explains the content. This way, the written text will not be very long and it will be possible to hear the teacher's explanations multiple times as per the student's own requirements.

4 Multimedia Environment

All these alternatives become reality by the development of multimedia applications that can be accessed by the students within the virtual campus. The inclusion of these applications transforms distance learning into a pleasant way of studying. The goal is to allow the student to choose the content that he wants to see and download it alone instead of downloading a complete lesson. This option allows file sizes to be decreased making their download faster.

The virtual campus offers a file list, where, as in a face-face class, the student is supposed to have understood the previous contents. The student is the one who is able to choose the contents he wants to download. This way of working allows the student to choose his own learning level according to his requirements. In addition, the virtual campus offers exercises and more detailed materials about the learning content, which is recommended to be read after he has studied the introductory material and the virtual class. If a student considers that his or her own knowledge allows him to access the material without seeing the virtual class, he or she is free to do it. Each virtual class shows the time that would spend the student while participating in it, so he/she can plan his or her time. This was added to allow each student to download several classes and to build his or her particular schedule for learning them because he or she can then know how much time he or she has to spend with each class.

Figure 3 shows the list of contents that can be downloaded. A team of experienced tutors guides new teachers in the development of multimedia content.

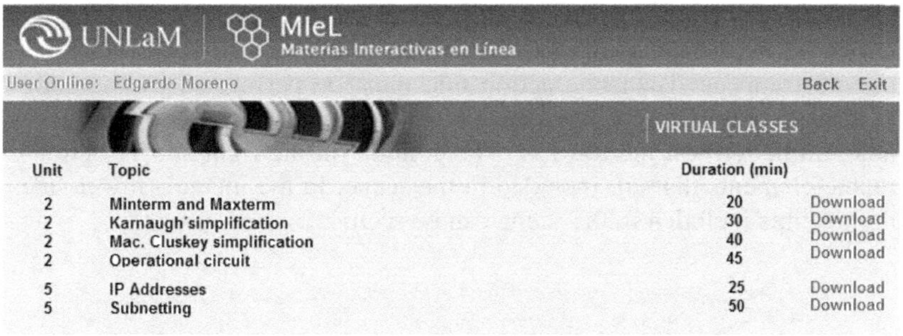

Fig. 3. Virtual classes list

Some practical content of the course "Introduction to Information Technologies" has been uploaded to the website. During the year 2006 text material was incorporated in the virtual campus with the contents of Unit 3: Logic Circuits and Unit 8: Networking. 50 students for Unit 3 and 48 for Unit 8 enrolled in distance learning during that year. This proposal was offered only to repeating students. During 2007 new students (that haven't attended the course yet), were invited to join the proposal with the possibility of attending one or both of the units uploaded. These students didn´t have previous knowledge of the content, and distance learning would an additional support for face-face learning. 62 and 63 students respectively joined the proposal. During 2007, 2008 and 2009 multimedia content was added to the virtual material, in particular, practical content. It is important to highlight that the new students that attended virtual classes that included multimedia materials didn´t need to attend face-face classes because they said that they had understood all of the content by watching and working with the multimedia resources.

5 Virtual Class Development

The product Flash by Adobe, was chosen for the creation of the virtual classes. Its main advantage, over PowerPoint, is the possibility of generating an executable file that includes sound, allowing a better use of the different elements to be displayed during the presentation. The audio is recorded using a microphone plugged into the computer. Later, it is necessary to reduce, using specific software, the audio file's quality in order to obtain a "lighter" file.

The different scenes are made using Flash. Each one of them represents a "slide" of Power Point. Each scene must have, at least, three layers:

1. Animation: It will include the elements that will appear in the presentation (text, graphics, equations, etc.).
2. Buttons: basically includes all the elements that are going to remain in sight during all the content explanation (buttons, content title, content length, etc.).
3. Sound: includes the audio with the teacher's explanation that will last during the whole scene presentation.

Afterwards, each element that must be animated is recorded specifying the time at which it must appear. Then, the action that must be performed by the code (action script) must be added to each button. Figure 4 shows the three layers (Sound, Buttons, and Animation) on the top left. The column on the right shows buttons sounds and graphic elements that are included in the scene. In the image's lower side, one of the button scripts included in the scene can be seen.

Fig. 4. Part of a screen built with Flash

6 Didactic Question Papers

With the unique goal of providing the students with a tool to check their own comprehension of the content, Flash executable files with question papers were created. They don't represent an evaluation tool as such. Simply, once the student, guided by his tutor, has studied the whole unit and has fulfilled the written practice, he/she is then able to use the question papers as a review tool.

Each question is presented with different answers. The student chooses the answers, in a didactic way (clicking over an answer, dragging a graphic, or linking concepts by arrows or lines). Then, the student clicks the validation button to check if his answer was correct. If the student answered in an incorrect way, he would be able to review the content or even contact his tutor. The question paper is only one more tool provided to the student, that's why it is not given a grade. The question papers are executable files, so the student has to download them only once, and can use them as many times as he wants to, without being connected to Internet.

The questions included in the question papers, were developed according to the following methods:

- By several options using multiple choice (the student can select all the options he wants). Figure 5 shows an example.

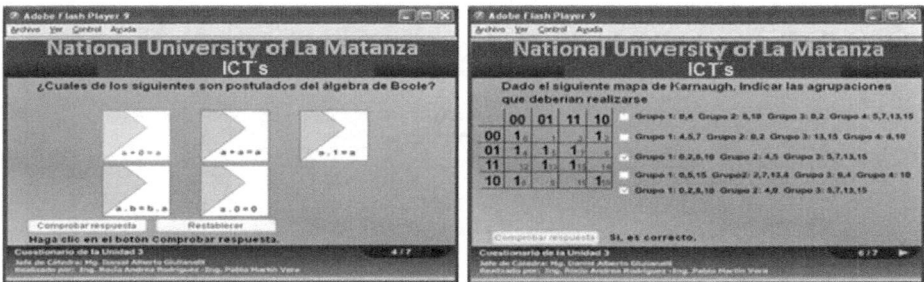

Fig. 5. Screen captures where the student answers are selected by multiple choice

- By simple choice. The goal is that the student selects only one possible answer, among several options. For example: which is the best method for…? The options include all the methods but the student has to select only one.
- Typing by keyboard the requested word (the student can write the correct word using uppercase, lowercase, or using a synonym; all of them are taken as a correct answer). Figure 6 shows a circuit and the student must provide its name. The correct answer "half adder" can be written in Spanish or English, using uppercase or lowercase, capital letters, spaces between words, etc. All of them will be taken as correct answers.

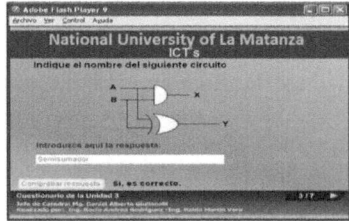

Fig. 6. Screen capture where it can be seen that the answer must be typed by the student using the keyboard

- Using the mouse to drag an element from a set to other set. This method is used to check several concepts. To answer correctly the question, it is necessary to join related concepts by dragging them with a mouse. Figure 7 shows an example of captured screens. The student's goal is to link the logic gate's name with its distinctive shape. It can be seen on the left screen the proposed question and on the right screen the answer selected by a student where each name has been dragged over a logic gate.

Fig. 7. Proposed question where it is necessary to drag the logic gate's name over its distinctive shape

When a student has answered a question he or she has two options: "restore" which means to erase the answer and return to the question's initial screen, or the second option "check the answer" (see Figure 7). When this option's button is selected, a message appears by the button saying if it is a correct or wrong answer (see right Figure 7). Each time an answer is checked, the next question is available and displayed. Once the student has finished all the questions paper, a new screen informs him or her how many questions had been answer correctly, and how many were wrong. Also, the percentage of correct answers is shown (Figure 8).

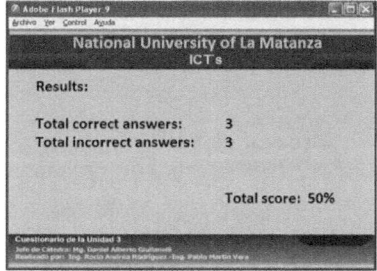

Fig. 8. Question paper's results

7 Research Results

In order to evaluate the proposal's effectiveness, an anonymous survey was circulated to the distance learning students that took the courses at the end of 2009. A list of the more relevant questions is shown and the results are displayed. Figure 9, shows the obtained results corresponding to the following question: "Understanding the themes through virtual classes has been..."

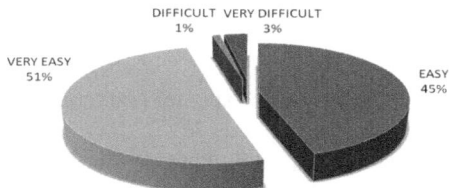

Fig. 9. Difficulty level of understanding virtual lesson themes

On the other hand, one of this proposal's advantages is that the student is able to see, hear and repeat the class and its didactic content the quantity of times that he wishes and needs. Figure 10 shows the results of asking the students the following question: Which was the highest number of times that you needed to repeat a part of a virtual class?

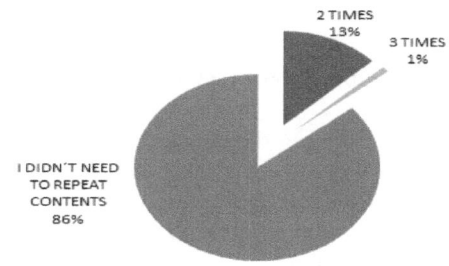

Fig. 10. Necessity of repeating some contents of the virtual classes

Figure 11 shows the obtained percentages when asking: "Did you need to consult the tutor about virtual classes' contents?"

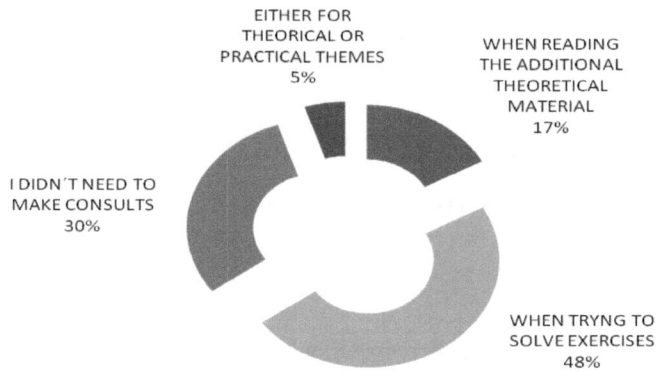

Fig. 11. Difficulty of understanding the virtual lessons' level

8 Conclusion and Future Works

Distance learning requires a good tutor who achieves the goal of building a strong link with his or her students. It also requires special pedagogic materials for this way of learning. For content with a higher difficulty level, these materials must not be just simple text, on the contrary, all the technological resources provided by technology must be used to build the materials. Undoubtedly this kind of material will be more attractive for students. Logically, the effort of building multimedia material is higher than writing a textual explanatory guide. In spite of this, we believe that the effort is worth making.

The results obtained through the anonymous polls presented to students who participated in this methodology show that only 4% of them considered that it is difficult or very difficult to understand the practice issues virtually and 96% considered it to be easy or very easy to understand them. These results widely exceeded our expectations. Virtual classes provide the possibility of taking a course as many times as it is necessary. This applies also for a single theme, unit or several themes or units within a course.

From 2007 to 2009 a huge effort has been made to include more didactic content, especially regarding those practice topics that are difficult to understand by reading a plain text.

This research showed, according to the research team criteria, that it is possible to explain practical topics, regardless of their difficulty level, in a virtual way. By preparing a clear set of examples and enriching the questions and answers interchange among students and tutors, it will be possible to achieve a fundamental tool as a proposal for future technological learning.

References

1. Barbera, E., Badia, A., Margarit, A.M.B.I., Mominó, J.M.: La Incógnita de la Educación a Distancia. Horsori, Barcelona (2001)
2. García Peñalvo, F.J., García Carrasco, J.: Los espacios virtuales educativos en el ámbito de Internet: un refuerzo a la formación tradicional. Ediciones Universidad de Salamanca, Salamanca (2002)
3. Godoy, M.M., Almeijde, M.D.: La construcción de la propuesta didáctica en formatos virtuales. In: Potencialidades y Desafíos. Universidad Nacional de Tucumán, Tucumán (2006)
4. Ahn, S.H.: Design and Implementation of E-Learning Contents for Scholarship Recognition of the Adult Learners. In: Koeran Educational Development Institute, In Proceedings of World Conference on Educational Multimedia Hypermedia and Telecommunications. EDMEDIA 2010, Toronto, pp. 1890–1906 (2010)

Copyright for Interactive Systems: Stratagems for Tourism and Cultural Heritage Promotion

Francisco V. Cipolla-Ficarra[1,2], Miguel Cipolla-Ficarra[2], and Valeria M. Ficarra[2]

HCI Lab. – F&F Multimedia Communic@tions Corp.
[1] ALAIPO: Asociación Latina de Interacción Persona-Ordenador
[2] AINCI: Asociación Internacional de la Comunicación Interactiva
Via Pascoli, S. 15 – CP 7, 24121 Bergamo, Italy
ficarra@alaipo.com, {ficarra,info}@ainci.com

Abstract. We present a series of strategies followed from the interactive design for the realization of a hypermedia system aimed at promoting in an original, simple and universal way the cultural and tourism heritage of a wide rural area in two Italian regions: Emilia Romagna and Lombardy. Besides, the main stratagems followed are disclosed to overcome the existing hurdles when it comes to copyright for the free diffusion of the tourism view of the area, such as can be photography or video, for instance. Finally, we present the first vade-mecum to be considered before making on-line and off-line interactive systems in Italy.

Keywords: Interactive Systems, Copyright, Globalization, Design, Photography, Tourism, Cultural Heritage, Human Factors.

1 Introduction

Without any doubt, one of the main problems deriving from the current era of expansion of communicability is the information copyright, whether it is in an analogical media or in a digital one. These problems have their origins in the first hand-made copies of the great works of art, such as can be painting, until the introduction of the Xerox machine. In the following figure 1 we can see how two professors of the XXI century have totally photocopied computer science handbooks, in front of the Law and Economics faculties, for instance. The inexistence of the tutelage of the copyright in the face of a law college inside the alleged European economic engine, such as the Lombardy (Italy).

An example of this kind renders meaningless all those associations who claim to tutor the copyright and intellectual property in Europe. In contrast to this reality we have some curators of castles, parks, gardens, etc., who claim to be the owners of the images and cash in for the rights of photographing buildings, streets, squares, statues, rivers, plants, etc. Between both there is the on-line and/or off-line hypermedia systems designer, who without economic resources or local, provincial, regional, state, European, etc. subventions intends to carry on with creative solutions to spread internationally the cultural and/or natural heritage of some regions of the Old World [1–4].

F.V. Cipolla Ficarra et al. (Eds.): HCITOCH 2010, LNCS 6529, pp. 136–147, 2011.
© Springer-Verlag Berlin Heidelberg 2011

Fig. 1. Professors of the XXI century have totally photocopied computer science handbooks, in front of the Law and Economics faculties in Bergamo city

Therefore, before designing the interactive system a long bureaucratic process must start to determine whether the images, music, etc., that he has available can be used in the multimedia project. Once all these permits have been obtained and the copyright has been paid, the work of elaborating the interactive process may begin. Now it is advisable that a beta version of the system is always made and it is deposited in the offices to tutor the authorship of the work being made. The reason why the massive production of the interactive systems is not advisable is that sometimes these permits lack validity in some places in Europe. They have to be collated and approved for another or umpteenth time by the competent authorities of the territory, for instance, the city hall, the province, the region, etc. Territorial bodies that little by little wish to take up power in cultural heritage matters with profit purposes, through the payment of rights and taxes. In other words, the greater the territorial division of the competence in the cultural heritage, the lesser the possibility of carrying out quickly an interactive system and, furthermore, the costs are so high that the projects are given up, and everything that is left is just a sketch. In contrast, a lesser division of the territory in regard to cultural heritage may generate binary situations, that is, a quick negative answer, without the possibility of appealing to higher instances, or also the quick approval, after having paid for these permits. Moreover, since there is no complete catalogue of the European cultural heritage in a free access database, for instance, one doesn't know beforehand whether the illustration material to be used has copyright or not.

At the start of the boom of the hypermedia systems in the Iberian Peninsula the approval of the heirs, owners or chief curators of the museums and cultural institutions was enough to set in motion the project. The designer's main problem was to create an original solution in each one of his/her interactive systems in regard to the volume of the dynamic and static images, sounds, music, texts locution, etc. With the momentum of the internet, the copyright problem has grown in an exponential way [5–8].

2   The Globalization of Copying and Pasting

In the 90s many Spanish artists, for instance, quickly developed an interest for the multimedia, specially the possibility of combining static or animated images, sounds, architecture, etc. One of them is Javier Mariscal author of the Barcelona Olympic

Games mascot) with a style of his own and which prompted interest in some Asian countries because of the richness of its colours or the curves of its figures. For centuries, the Dutch merchants settled down in the natural seaport of Japan, Nagasaki. In that same place, the denizens decided to set up a copycat replica of a Dutch village. "Nagasaki Holland Village". It was in this way that a park for children entertainment was created, an aquatic labyrinth called "Aquarinto" [9]. In this park there was a central character named Nina (a kind of Dutch relative of Cobi), which moved in a 2D and 3D animation environment (figure 2).

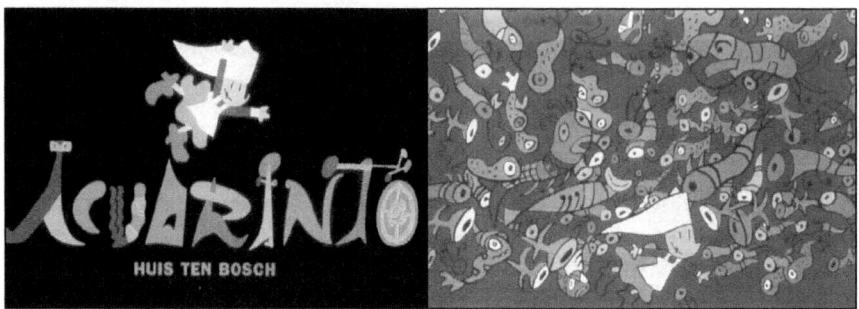

Fig. 2. Acuarinto (Javier Mariscal): 2D and 3D computer animation

The characters were animated in 2D, following the traditional canons of draughtsmanship in order not to lose their expressivity. The 3D was used to make the backgrounds, objects, textures, lightening and the camera movement. Besides, plants and shapes were made in bronze statues, so that they could be taken to the computer with a scanner. Now that work published in a specialized magazine of limited circulation [9] may serve to those designers, university professors and other professionals of multimedia communication who devote themselves to copying and pasting, as if it were something natural. Nowadays these very same shapes and style created for Acuarinto are to be found in many shops in the Balearic Islands. As a rule, the love of plagiarism may be part of the associations which protect copyright and it will even be tutored through the copyright of a part of these figures, such as can be creating cyclopean characters (figures 3 and 4), but instead of using a circle, resorts to a ellipsis, divided by a vertical line and two dots as eyes inside the big eye.

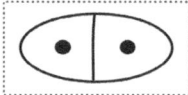

Fig. 3. Cyclops or thief's mask

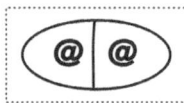

Fig. 4. Updated version and not legally registered in the case of a robot on-line

In this description we have the copying and pasting of the style, without the need of resorting to last generation software, because computer animations originate from the storyboard, made in paper sketches and using a simple pencil. Besides, it is the case of copying previously existing designs. Evidently, these issues in the context of painting, sculpture, architecture, etc. require specialists in art history to understand when something is original or not. Now the Web 2.0 with practically all the information from the users on-line, may automatically generate the cloning of people [10]. This is a usual practice in some university education centres of the Mediterranean. As a rule, in order to quickly promote inside the group some people just arrived to the professors team, the areas of knowledge, interest and even of research of those people who are going to leave said education centres are photocopied. This is very simple for them, since they have the financial resources and they can carry out the same heuristic research on the use of the computer in their leisure time, even in the incorrectly de-fined virtual spaces because of using such applications as Facebook. If the outgoing professor worked with his/her students and volunteers inside a multimedia publishing and communication lab, sometimes transformed into a usability or communicability lab, the plagiarizing professor can widen the universe of study to a province, region or even a state [10] [11] [12]. That is, the subjects are always the same as those of the professor to be plagiarized or imitated; multimedia communication, usability, quality, heuristics, descriptive statistics, etc. Evidently, these works are mere strategies that the dynamic persuader (specialist in copying and pasting, for instance [10]) has to draw the attention to himself and/or his/her collaborators in the work they make. Moreover, it is a way to justify the huge money sums that are invested from the universities. Instead of generating techniques and/or methodologies that allow saving money. From the point of view of the presentation in the audiovisual media, these experts in "copying and pasting" have a kind of isotopy in their look. Schematically, we can depict both situations in the following way:

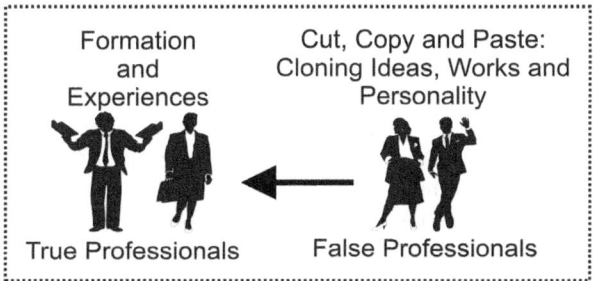

Fig. 5. New technologies –cloning professionals

Some isotopies that disclose and imply the presence of dynamic persuaders, such as can be the use of glasses with thick black frames, in the professor of mathematics, phisics or astronomy style. The interested reader may look up the following bibliography to go deeper into the dynamic persuaders and their negative influence in the development of the internet [10] [13].

In the figure 2 we see how the "copying and pasting" references the design of the computer animations but whose economical consequences are huge with the passing of time since the plagiarizer settles down in the institutions that allegedly tutor copyright. In the figure 6, the copying and pasting of a CV of a professional in new technologies does not only generate a cloning of the plagiarism, but it slows down in decades the progress of the community that consents and admits that modus operandi in issues of the new technologies related to the safeguard and promotion of the cultural and natural heritage as it is the case of our study. The above mentioned examples clearly show the harm that may be caused with fake professionals of multimedia communication in the tourism issues, especially in the economically developed countries. In the promotion of the heritage of the small localities, when the available economical resources are few, sometimes the original ideas in tourism subjects can be quickly imitated by those localities which, among themselves, keep a continuous competition loop to attract tourists. In other occasions the limitations derive from those who hold the copyright ownership, because they have gone through the registration and patents office asking heavy money sums to use images in small logos or labels of artisan products. Fortunately, the digitalization of the information allows that instead of a copyright drawing you can use the frame of a film, as it happens when there are no agreements between the interested parties. Another alternative may even be the 2D and/or 3D reconstruction of the characters of the film. Evidently, the costs may be higher because of the production time, instead of using a frame or a drawing. However, sometimes this may be the only possible solution.

3   Digital Photography versus Copyright

One of the advantages of digital photography is the speed with which one can create several guided tours [14] or scene reconstruction [15] inside an interactive system by presenting several alternatives to the users at the moment of the interaction, that is, with the purposes of tourism information, pastime, etc.

In our case we have joined several towns and villages from inside the regions Emilia-Romagna and Lombardia, following the texts by the writer Guareschi, in a special way in the creation of the portal "Little World of Guareschi" (www.mondopiccologuareschi.com). Once the legal permit from his inheritors for the project was obtained, the wide area of the north-centre of Italy was photographed, during springtime, which entailed touring those places for two years in a row until getting a sufficiently wide images bank (around 5.000 including indoors and outdoors) to pick those that had to go in the different formats of the on-line and off-line hypermedia systems: web portal, CD and DVD. Aside from being a writer, Guareschi was a draftsman, and he himself illustrated his texts. Therefore, these photographs had to be accompanied by a selection of those illustrations (300 approximately), after a self-edition of said photos because of the sorry conservation state. The self-edition of these illustrations entailed generating images in vector and bitmap formats. Later on, the damp stains were wiped out, paper folds, the yellowish colour, the author's jottings or by the typographers at the moment of making the print tests, etc. A work that implied almost three months of post-production, until obtaining an excellent quality of those images in the vector and bitmap formats. Consequently, the main idea was to balance the author's illustrations with the current images of the rural landscape, mainly. However, the authorization obtained later on for the reproduction in off-line format did not cover the whole bank of images on which it had been worked, but rather a small sample of it which did not reach 5%. Obviously, an unthinkable situation in the Spain of the 90s, with the boom of the multimedia systems in CD-ROM media to promote the works of Dali, Goya, Picasso, etc. or museums such as Orsay, National Gallery, State Hermitage, etc. As a stratagem in this case it was decided to place the illustrations on the on-line portal and that the same were the bait to draw the attention of the potential users to the title "Little World: Virtual Postcards". This was the first hurdle to be overcome and theoretically a written authorization was available before setting in motion the interactive project.

The other legal hurdle to be overcome was the issue of the monuments, castles, etc. which were located in small villages. These brick constructions –mainly– and stone, which reveal the strong Spanish presence in that area have been very well kept in some cases through the centuries and in others not so well, because the bricks have been used for other constructions after the Second World War. Besides, it is a kind of cultural heritage that is usually private. Consequently, the outdoor pictures do not require special permits. In contrast, the indoors pictures, including the vegetation in the shape of gardens or artificial lakes, etc., need an authorization. In the case of indoors whose ownership is held by the public authorities, it is necessary to request the permit to the public bodies who tutor that heritage. In the museums managed or under the tutelage of the associations named "Pro Loco", which fulfil an important mission of safeguarding and promoting the Italian territory, there were practically no problems to get the necessary permits to take the pictures. Many of these museums constitute the real engine of tourism (figure 6) as compared with the scarce activity that is carried out in castles —Little World area— which have works of an extremely high artistic value such as can be the frescos, hangings, sculptures, etc.

Fig. 6. Peppone and Don Camillo: Museum & logo

As months went by, the legal details concerning the copyright and royalties were better known. Valid or logical in some cases, while in others the transparency in these issues was equal to nil, even in those animations that had the necessary permits available. All of this had a direct repercussion on the dynamic and static means that would be used for the final project, since the initial plan for the contents of the several on-line and off-line interactive systems was being modified. For instance, one of the consequences of this continuous to-and-fro between the use or not of the images implied that the texts of the interactive works would be totally unpublished before (six languages: Italian,

German, Portuguese, French, Spanish and English) and clearly aimed at the cultural and natural heritage, excluding the writer's literary aspect, for instance.

In the case of the cartography of the past centuries and which is currently stored in the museums, the pertinent permits were requested to photograph the maps. Here it was also necessary to carry out a self-edition work of the images. These images, joined to the illustrations of the writer, were the only ones that existed previous to the project we are describing. All the rest if a long process of photographing the territory with its natural and cultural resources, always in the same time of the year. Although the digital camera, the software and the hardware, for instance, are of low economic cost. The financial resources available to carry out the hypermedia project such as can be trips, lodging facilities, etc. were equal to zero. The financial resources and time available are very important for the local and global turism promotion [16]. Here is the main reason why the strategies in the design of the interactive systems, whether from the point of view of communicability [17] and usability [18], are important.

4   Communicability and Interactive Design

Applying the notions, quality attributes and communicability metrics excellent results can be got in short time. Communicability is present in each one of the interactive design areas, regardless of the hardware platform and the software that is used in the creation of the on-line and off-line interactive systems [17]. In the following graphic we can see how communicability is the core of the intersections area:

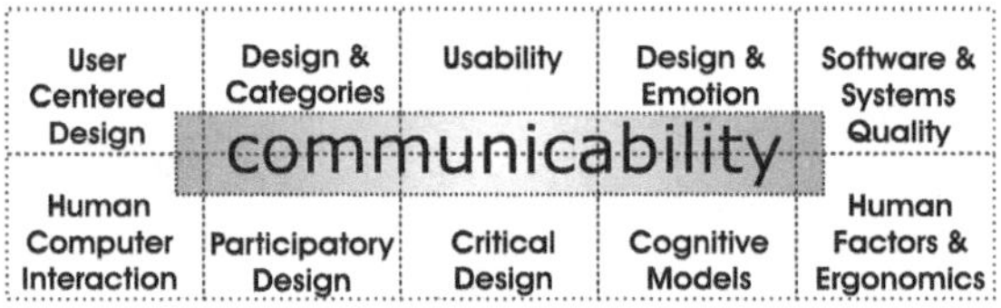

User Centered Design	Design & Categories	Usability	Design & Emotion	Software & Systems Quality
communicability				
Human Computer Interaction	Participatory Design	Critical Design	Cognitive Models	Human Factors & Ergonomics

Fig. 7. Communicability in the interactive design

In the case of the "Little World: Virtual Postcard" interactive systems [14] and the difficulties presented from the point of view of the necessary adjustments to the changes of the contents of those systems in a fast and accurate way, without causing strains inside the work team. The strategy followed was to split the contents into several modules and medias in relation to the potential users and following two central axes: universality and simplicity. In the beta version of the CD-ROM it was decided to create a virtual postalcards of "Little World" in six languages and with 300 photographies (figure 8). This product would be marketed in two formats: one to be sent by mail in a carboard envelope and inside it the CD and the other in the classical format with a plastic case of CD-DVD for collection.

Fig. 8. Home page Little World

The interactive system had to be aimed at all those people who had read some of the works by the author or watched the films of the "Don Camillo" series and who wished to make first a virtual updated tour of the area described in those landscapes, characters, etc. through the photography. Consequently, the potential user was supposed not to have physical impairments for accessibility to the contents and 6 languages were set up, leaving for a second stage other languages such as Chinese, Japanese and Russian. Once the pictures were chosen, the texts made, playing applications, etc., the first version or beta of the product was finally made in Portugal.

The content of the off-line interactive system is split into three great collections: guided tours, Little World and game –puzzle (figure 9). In the first collection of links each one of the villages is visited (alphabetically ordered) with their matching explanations. In the second, an interactive map allows direct access to the locality they wish to visualize. Finally, a puzzle was inserted as pastime. The readers interested in other details of the design of "Little World: Virtual Postcards" can look up the following bibliography [19] [20].

Fig. 9. Communicability in the interactive design

Simultaneously, the DVD was designed where there were indoors pictures of the main constructions visited inside these regions and which entailed a significant consumption of time for getting the permits, outdoors pictures as in the case of the CD but with a greater wealth of details. Besides, special studies had been made for the implementation of special algorithms in the panoramic view of the halls and the open spaces, with possibilities of increasing the sunlight, or switching off the enlightening, changing the colour of the constructions, etc. Also the drafts were made to animate in 3D the central characters of the writer's works Peppone and Don Camillo (www.mondoguareschi.com) and the reconstruction of the virtual stages where the author's illustrations, the photographs, the films and some texts of the literary works would be combined. Because of economic reasons of the copyright and royalties and last minute human factors this could not be implemented.

In the on-line version the portals were created with the combination of the CD images and of the eventual DVD, where the author's illustrations were included. All of them in high resolution. The same was made in Flash and as the Internet broadband expands, the time of access of the users to these images decreases.

One of the main reasons why usability may decrease with the passing of time is the impossibility of keeping the portals on-line updated because of the cost this entails from the point of view of the webmaster, webdesign, webcontent, etc. However, it has been seen how portals made at the beginning of the new millennium where the main principles of communicability were applied still draw the attention of thousands of users of the whole world, as is the case of "Mondo Guareschi" website (www.mondoguareschi.com). Obviously a website belonging to the Web 1.0 but which demonstrates once again the importance of the contents in the diverse dynamic and static means.

5 Vademecum

The current vademecum is the result of a series of practical experiences for the execution of a multimedia project where it was intended to elaborate several interactive systems. Some of these systems had to include mobile phones or the PDA, for instance. It serves for the stage design of the on-line and off-line interactive systems divided into three sections: copyright, design and strategy. The contents are related to tourism, cultural and natural heritage the elaboration of E-learning training courses, whose goal is the design and/or study in Italy and the design of interactive systems. This vademecum or set of guidelines for design can be used as a binary heuristic evaluation tablet. Its successive step is to define a set of quality attributes and metrics in the on-line interactive systems to detect the presence of stratagems in the promotion of cultural heritage for copyright reasons. Next the first listing, whose content is presented in alphabetical order (C=Copyright, S=Stratagem D=Design):

- To request in writing the authorization of the heirs of the copyright of the works (paintings, books, films, music, etc.) on which the interactive design will be made (C).
- To establish the number of authorized copies for the off-line multimedia supports, including paper, for instance, books, leaflets, magazines, etc. (C-S).
- To make a beta version and register it with the proper authorities to obtain a registration number or intellectual property (C-S).
- Submit this beta version to the final approval of the inheritors of the copyright (S).

- To establish financial damage clauses in the case that the multimedia project was suspended once the beta version was made or the process of massive production of the interactive systems started (S).
- To request in writing the authorization of the local authorities to photograph, film, record sounds, etc., inside museums, castles, workshops, rooms and/or houses of historical characters , etc., and also the nature that is to be found in those places, artificial lakes, forests, rivers, etc. (C-S).
- Verify that these authorizations are true and issued by the competent authorities in the tutoring of the cultural heritage. (C).
- To create analogical or digital models of those architectural areas for which no authorization has been obtained, for instance, the façade of a building, the vault of a church, the frescos of a castle, etc. (S-D).
- To generate with computer graphics 2D, 3D and/or computer animations all those elements for which there is no authorization and which can be made with a computer on the basis of pictures, drawings, sketches, etc. such as the objects of the inside parts of the buildings and constructions, the characters from the films, books, etc. (D).
- To activate the collaboration with the local bodies which foster tourism, especially those known as "Pro Loco" (S).
- To compile the greatest possible information in the local and state files on the territory from the cartographic point of view, the customs, the traditions, etc. since they can help identify the potential users with the digital characters or environments recreated through the computer (S-D).
- To carry out all the necessary operations for the transformation to the digital support of those works in analogical support and their matching corrections such as can be a self-editing process of the scanned images (S-D).
- To establish the role of each one of the members of the realization team of the interactive system, bearing in mind the advices received from the person responsible for the management of the copyrights and royalties. (C-S)
- To use the principles of communicability in the work team. (a common language of the members of the design categories, a set of quality attributes, inference of the potential users, etc.) to cheapen the costs in the case last minute changes had to be made because of authorization motives. (S-C-D)

6 Conclusion

The promotion of cultural heritage in certain areas of the EU is not easy, even if the latest technological breakthroughs in the ICT context are available (Information and Communication Technology). The main problem is that there is no complete catalogue of cultural and natural heritage in Europe. At the same time, there are in some member states laws and regulations still in force since the beginning of the last century in copyright and royalties issues. If we add to this state of the art the human factors and their deviations generated inside the main institutions which should tutor copyright, such as certain European universities, the future does not look very promising for the tourism sector. An analysis which excludes the overall situation from the current economic point of view. In order to let the interactive systems spread easily in this adverse context it is necessary that the communicability specialist has the necessary knowledge in legal technical matters for the circulation of the cultural and natural heritage in on-line and/or off-line in interactive systems, or that he is guided or advised by experts in these legal issues. However, constantly resorting to the communicability principles can spare production costs in the multimedia systems, since there is a set of strategies in interactive design which allow to solve quickly the changes deriving from the copyright sector or intellectual ownership. The strategies that make up the first presented vademecum are the fruit of a long preparation process for the realization of several interactive systems that were supposed to go with the evolutions deriving from the dynamic, static means and multimedia telecommunications. Consequently, not having reached all the goals scheduled in the original project of the multimedia systems does not mean a failure. Quite the opposite, it has been an enriching experience to know the reasons why the diffusion of cultural heritage and tourism are continuously slowed down inside a country in the European basin of the Mediterranean sea, with a cultural equivalent which is tantamount to a third of the whole now existing in the world.

Acknowledgments

A special thanks to City Council and inhabitants of Brescello, Luis Garcia (Universidad Nacional de La Pampa) for their helps and collaboration.

References

1. Witte, R.: Converting a Historial Architecture Encyclopedia into a Semantic Knowledge Base. IEEE Intelligent Systems 25(1), 59–66 (2010)
2. Anokwa, Y., et al.: Open Source Data Collection in the Developing World. IEEE. Computer 42(10), 97–99 (2009)
3. Bederson, B.: Experiencing the International Children's Digital Library. Interactions 15(6), 50–54 (2008)
4. Liesaputra, V., Witten, I., Bainbridge, D.: Creating and Reading Realistic Electronic Books. IEEE Computer 42(2), 72–81 (2009)
5. Nord, G., McCubbins, T., Nord, J.: E-Monotoring in the Workplace: Privacy, Legislation, and Surveillace Software. Communications of the ACM 49(8), 73–77 (2006)
6. Dempsey, J., Rubinstein, I.: Lawyers and Technologists: Joined at the Hip. IEEE Security & Privacy 4(3), 15–19 (2006)
7. White, J.: Intellectual Property in the Age of Universal Access. ACM Press, New York (1999)
8. Boyle, J.: What Intellectual Property Law Should Learn from Software. Communications of the ACM 52(2), 71–76 (2009)
9. Cipolla-Ficarra, F.: Metamorfosis aplicada a la vida artificial. Imaging 6(6), 12–18 (1993)
10. Cipolla-Ficarra, F.: Persuasion On-Line and Communicability: The Destruction of Credibility in the Virtual Community and Cognitive Models. Nova Science Publishers, New York (2010)
11. Bishop, M., Frincke, D.: Plagiarism, Education, and Information Security. IEEE Security and Privacy 5(5), 62–65 (2007)
12. Collberg, C., Kobourov, S.: Self-Plagiarism in Computer Science. Communications of the ACM 48(4), 88–94 (2005)

13. Cipolla-Ficarra, F., Nicol, E., Cipolla-Ficarra, M.: Strategies for a Creative Future with Computer Science, Quality Design and Communicability. In: Proc. First International Workshop HCITOCH 2010. Springer, Berlin (2010)
14. Cipolla-Ficarra, F.: Guided Tour for International User Interfaces: Multimedia Design in Ecological and Rural Regions. In: CD Proc. Applied Human Factors and Ergonomics, AHFE, Las Vegas (2008)
15. Goesele, M., et al.: Scene Reconstruction from Communicty Photo Collections. IEEE Computer 443(6), 48–53 (2010)
16. Cheverst, K., Mitchell, K., Davies, N.: The Role of Adaptive Hypermedia in a Context-Aware Tourist Guide. Communications of the ACM 45(5), 47–51 (2002)
17. Cipolla-Ficarra, F.: Quality and Communicability for Interactive Hypermedia Systems: Concepts and Practices for Design. IGI Global, Hershey (2010)
18. Nielsen, J., Pernice, K.: Eyetracking Web Usability. New Riders, Berkeley (2009)
19. Cipolla-Ficarra, F.: Tourism Promotion in Rural Areas: Tools for Quality Design. In: Proceedings of the CollECTeR, pp. 83–91. UNC, Córdoba (2007)
20. Cipolla-Ficarra, F., Cipolla-Ficarra, M.: Multimedia, User-Centered Design and Tourism: Simplicity, Originality and Universality. In: New Directions in Intelligent Interactive Multimedia, pp. 461–470. Springer, Heidelberg (2008)

Content Management System for Developing a Virtual Platform for Association of Women's Aid with Lack of Resources

Beatriz Sainz de Abajo[1], Alberto Flores García[1], Enrique García Salcines[2],
F. Javier Burón Fernández[2], Miguel López Coronado[1], and Carlos de Castro Lozano[2]

[1] Telecommunications Technical School (ETSIT), University of Valladolid,
Campus Miguel Delibes, Paseo de Belén n° 15, 47011 Valladolid, Spain
{beasai,miglop}@tel.uva.es, aflores248@gmail.com
[2] EATCO Research Group, University of Cordoba,
Edificio Leonardo da Vinci, Campus de Rabanales, 14071 Córdoba, Spain
{egsalcines,jburon,ma1caloc}@uco.es

Abstract. In this paper we show a Virtual Platform for an Association of Women's Aid called Centro Integral de Ayuda a la Mujer (CIAM). After analyzing different Content Management Systems (CMS) and the benefits that its use would contribute to the development of the Virtual Platform, taking into account the needs and requirements set by CIAM, we have opted for the use of Joomla!. This free CMS, for its characteristics, is the most benefits provided us. The virtual platform design has been developed following customer specifications, to have understood the simplicity and easy handling of the resulting platform. This platform will be integrated into the Web portal that has the Amarex Association and it will be able to be administrates from the CIAM without specific knowledge of programming languages. If new services were necessary, they would be easily implemented, adding new modules and components to perform these services.

Keywords: Content Management System (CMS), Virtual Platform, Joomla!, XAMPP, PHP, MySQL.

1 Introduction

In this paper we show a Virtual Platform for Centro Integral de Ayuda a la Mujer (CIAM), it is about a dynamic Platform in order to come near to more people, it will report and help it users in an easy ways allowing then to interact securely and easily. This platform will complete the web of Amarex Association and it will be able to be administrates from the CIAM without specific knowledge which was one of the handicaps for the development of the virtual platform. The simple interaction between different people with easy handling is vital. All users do not possess knowledge and it's necessary to create an environment which is as simple as possible.

We must decide the most suitable Content Management System. We depart from the study of the different Content Management System of market and evaluate its

F.V. Cipolla Ficarra et al. (Eds.): HCITOCH 2010, LNCS 6529, pp. 148–156, 2011.

convenience. Because of the economic limitations that the project imposes on us, we focus on the use of those systems that offer open source and free software. After the development of the platform we need to check by testing the seaworthiness of its use in other web browsers.

In the development of this project is justified the reason for the choice of this management system selected. If new services were necessary, they would be easily implemented, adding new modules and components to perform these services. And finally, there will be able to include new submenus that allow to modify some contents or to establish other sections.

2   Background

There are many Content Management Systems (CMS) [1]. *Mambo, Zope* and *PHP-Nuke*, despite of being well known in the past, actually they are very obsolete for this development, so we can refuse them. We analyzed other Content Management Systems to quantify their options of use and evaluate the advantages that we provide.

Moodle is a content management system, principally for teaching and learning. It allows us to store information easily and uploading and adding content by the administrator. Other users can access to this information, and contact the administrator to express their views. This CMS is aimed to contents. It does not have many more features than the download and display some contents, so it is not the best suited one for the platform that we want to implement as we give it dynamism.

eZ Publish is a dual content management system, which means that you have some free modules and other modules require an advance payment for use it. Despite this, it is a very complete CMS. *eZ Publish* enables you to create online content types and also has several categories for permissions to users. It is based on PHP, and its dual nature means we can not access the CMS in its totality, which makes hard its choice for use it in our virtual platform.

Infoglue and *OpenCms* are Content Management Systems that uses Java. Their data bases are built with Oracle. Both are CMS open source, but *OpenCms* is more complete than *Infoglue*, because *OpenCms* could be used with Perl or even Python or PHP. *OpenCms* includes a back-end, like the latest version of *Infoglue*. The difficulty of its use is limited to knowledge that takes in the use of Java and Oracle.

Jahia also uses Java language, noting that contains many features, bus has other disadvantages as it is aimed to WebPages, or its low standard in their access levels, because each module has different possibilities.

2.1   Needs or Requirements

Any Web site, whether intranet or Internet, should be administered by an interactive manner, so it must provide an interface to allow those responsible to define new pages, new options, as well as updating and reorganization of information beyond the needs of the platform. To reach these objectives in a simple management, we use a *Content Management System* (CMS) [1].

In our project, we give priority to a virtual platform aimed to contents, because if we aimed it on pages the use of our platform would be restricted. By focusing on content, we can base our platform on contents having access to these from different points of the virtual platform. *Typo3* is aimed to contents. It is also a very sophisticated and high quality CMS but is too difficult for people who are not expert users, so *Typo3* was refused.

SPIP has a great restriction, since it does not distinguish between users giving all the same permissions. It is not helpful since we do not want that everyone can see certain components of the virtual platform. Therefore rule out a *SPIP*.

Drupal and *Joomla*! CMS are very similar. Both are aimed to content and they have different levels of access. The contents are organized into different groups (though *Drupal* has the ability to multi-location). They have very similar components, and they have received several awards in the past year due to its easy handling and administration. This factor, ease of administration, is a key point in the development of the platform, because people whose will manage this platform, have not enough advanced computer knowledge, but they would want to manage on their own.

After analyzing the characteristics of different CMS, we chose *Joomla*! because has more extensions than *Drupal* and these extensions are very easy to install and manage.

The following table highlights some key factors relevant to choose the most suitable CMS for the development of our platform.

Table 1. Comparison of key factors between different CMS

CMS	SPIP	Joomla!	Typo3	Drupal
Aimed to...	Contents	Contents	Web pages	Contents
Contents division	Sections	Sections & categories	---	Categories & multi-location
Templates Language	HTML/PHP	PHP	HTML	PHP
User's levels	None	3 (8)	Adaptable	2
Could Import Content?	Yes	Yes	Yes	Yes
Search Engine	Trivial	Full	Full	Full

In table 1, we can see, principal for us, the four content management systems we have analyzed. They all have in common the PHP programming language and MySQL databases.

3 Targets

Among the objectives required from the CIAM for the creation of the Virtual Platform include the following:

- Easy handling as a user.
- Easy administration for non-experts in programming languages.
- Potential for expansion of their contents easily to users.
- Potential for expansion of the virtual platform in the future with extensions easily.
- Content to be included among sections to download documents, laws, articles, which an administrator can upload easily.
- Photo Gallery content.
- Inclusion of a calendar.
- Include the logos of the association that will manage the platform.

This should be on the platform in a provision clearly and colourful, with a template that fits the taste of our client.

4 Development

For this project we have studied different CMS. After a detailed analysis has been chosen *Joomla!* as the best choice. For the evaluation of this and other content management systems, we used a virtual server: XAMPP.

4.1 XAMPP

XAMPP is an easy to install Apache distribution containing MySQL, PHP and Perl. XAMPP is really very easy to install and to use - just download, extract and start. At the moment there are four XAMPP distributions: Windows, Mac OS X, Linux and Solaris [2]. The name comes from the acronym 'X' (for different Operating Systems), 'A' of *Apache*, 'M' of *MySQL*, 'P' of *PHP* and 'P' of *Perl*. The program is released and acts as a free Web server, easy to use and is able of serving dynamic pages. XAMPP only requires downloading and running the archive. With a small configuration may use its components.

Once installed, this program will get a door to a server. This, added Internet connection, will allow us to run the databases created by the virtual platform and view its contents.

4.2 Programming Languages

In order to use Joomla! We must know about different programming languages. Programming languages are words keys which we built each programme. These programmes are what give rise to the different Contents Managements Systems [3]:

- *PHP* (recursive acronym for *PHP: Hypertext Preprocessor*) is a widely-used open source general-purpose scripting language that is especially suited for web development and can be embedded into HTML what distinguishes PHP from something like client-side JavaScript is that the code is executed on the server, generating HTML which is then sent to the client. The client would receive the results of running that script, but would not know what the underlying code was [4]. You can even configure your web server to process all your HTML files with PHP, and then there's really no way that users can tell what you have up your sleeve.

- The *MySQL* software delivers a very fast, multi-threaded, multi-user, and robust SQL (Structured Query Language) database server. MySQL Server is intended for mission-critical, heavy-load production systems as well as for embedding into mass-deployed software. Oracle is a registered trademark of Oracle Corporation and/or its affiliates. MySQL is a trademark of Oracle Corporation and/or its affiliates, and shall not be used by Customer without Oracle's express written authorization [5]. The MySQL software is Dual Licensed. Users can choose to use the MySQL software as an Open Source product under the terms of the GNU General Public License or can purchase a standard commercial license from Sun Microsystems, Inc. [6].
- The *Apache* web Server is, according to several studies, the main web server in the world. Apache is not rigid, and has a modular built over a small core, which is adapted to the specific needs of each user [7].

4.3 Joomla!

Joomla! is a content management system open source and completely free. It is based on the use of templates, on which we can program or install modules, giving access to different components or plugins for running our virtual platform, and convert it in a more accessible and to give certain features that are useful to users [8]. In this way we can get a quick response from the virtual platform to send data from a user.

Joomla! does not use frameworks but it has a system of interlocking modules with content extensions or plugins required for its works. This CMS is aimed to content, so you can store the contents and be viewed from different components or sections, just as when we show an article on the home page.

Joomla! is organized in two levels of management (user and administrator). Within these levels, the user category is subdivided into: registered, author, editor and supervisor. Similarly, the level of manager is subdivided into three sub-levels: manager, administrator and super-administrator.

Joomla! uses templates in PHP that are fully inserted into PHP content, also can use HTML content (enabling easy use), such as style sheets or CSS. This Content Management System can import content from other web platforms as news managers by RSS. The URL links to these other platforms and are easy to administer by non-expert user.

5 Results

The choice of Joomla! for the development of our platform has been the most appropriate after an initial analysis. The main objective is the development of a platform for easy management by people untrained in programming languages that have basic knowledge of internet usage. This condition has been essential in the design, looking for simplify the use of the platform and providing access to all menus and submenus. When the contents were determined between the two parties, there have been settled the various modules and components in main menu, as we can see on figure 1.

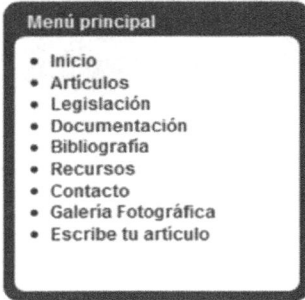

Fig. 1. Main menu

Among the various components have been installed modules developed by others, such as the photo gallery or file download manager.

In Joomla!, we use the templates as holes to fill with different modules. By placing the modules in the templates give an overview of the content of the platform in a clear and concrete way. The modules are sorted in templates.

Featured content among Joomla! we can find search engines, chat, text editors, photo galleries, download managers, etc. For the interaction between users, is useful to write comments about news or pictures to express views in a forum and issue ratings of articles. This debate is encouraged when we disagree, and in turn the support of other users on important issues, offering our help in certain cases.

5.1 User's Session

In the user session we have development a main menu and some sub-components (Fig.2 shows an example):

- Home.
- Articles: newspaper articles and articles written by users.
- Legislation: Spanish legislation and Castilla y León legislation.
- Documentation.
- Downloads: guides, training books, applications and books, by *Phoca download* [9].
- Links.
- Contact.
- Photo gallery, by *Joom:: Gallery* [10].
- Write your article.

At the same time there are other modules like image in the header, route and the search engine (At the top of the platform). On the left stands the main menu, the module of survey, the association's logo as a banner, and a module with most visited articles. On the right side, under search engine, stands out the registration form, the banner of *Amarex* (main association), the timing and magnitude of recent articles written.

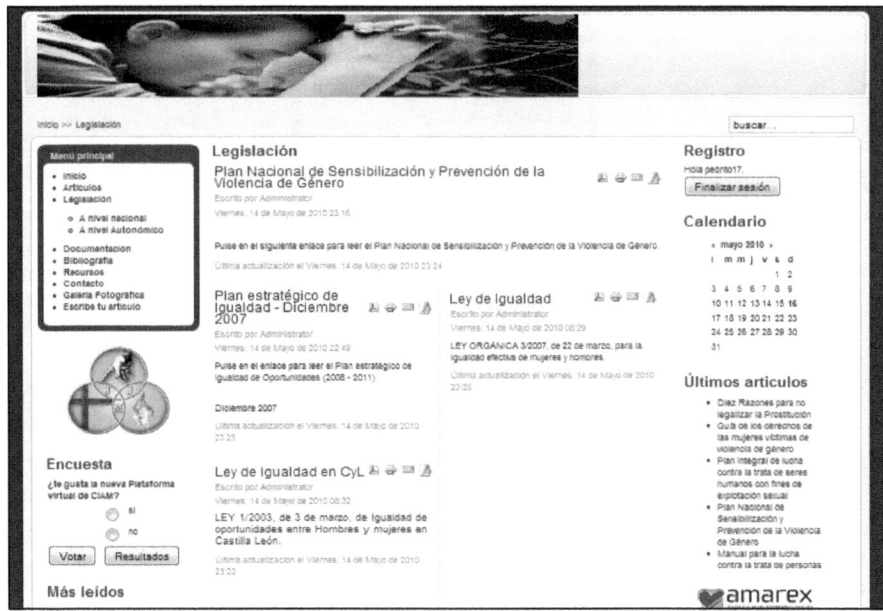

Fig. 2. Virtual Platform from CIAM (User's session)

5.2 Administrator's Session

In the administrator's menu, we manage all the contents of our virtual platform. As show in Figure 3, in the orange part, onto the control panel, we have:

- User manager: where you can manage privileges for each user.
- Articles manager: we can manage and sort articles written.
- Section manages: the sections are the libraries where items ordered.
- Categories manager: an article is stored in these categories and these categories into sections.
- Main menu manager: where manage the content visible on the homepage.

Within the components, in the yellow box, we can find these managers and administrators as well as components:

- *Joomla! Image Gallery Manager*: if has a control panel similar to the administrator from the images and we climbed administer.
- *Download system Manager*: all downloaded files are managed under a control panel, as the photo gallery and its contents.

The red box and blue box show us information about front-end of our virtual platform, like number of users connecting or who are those users.

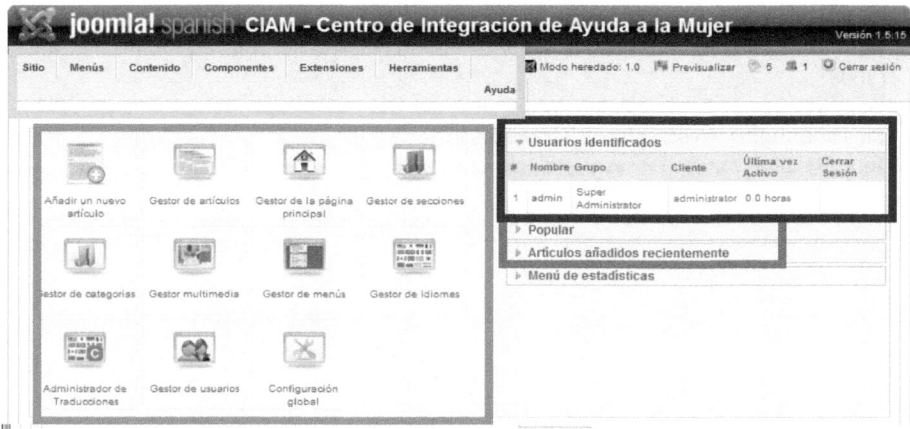

Fig. 3. Virtual Platform CIAM (administrator's setting center)

6 Conclusions

After analyzing different content management systems and the benefits that its use would contribute to the development of the virtual platform, taking into account the needs and requirements set by CIAM, we have opted for the use of *Joomla!*. Due to its characteristics, this free CMS is the most benefits provided us.

PHP and MySQL have been used for a better use of the CMS. It was necessary to modify the code and managing the fields of databases created.

The virtual platform design has been developed following customer specifications, to have understood the simplicity and easy handling of the resulting platform, a basic requirement given the lack of training with which users have managed from the now, and still vital adequate and simple interaction between the user and the same.

Acknowledgments. Thanks to Amarex Association (http://www.casanazareth.es/index.php?option=com_content&task=view&id=26&Itemid=47) for which we have developed the Virtual Platform that we present in this conference, for providing the logo of the Association.

References

1. Boiko, B.: Content Management bible, 2nd edn. Wiley Publishing, Indianapolis (2005)
2. Apache friends Website, http://www.apachefriends.org/en/xampp.html
3. Boronczyk, T., et al.: Desarrollo Web con PHP 6, Apache y MySQL. Anaya Multimedia, Madrid (2004)
4. Official webpage PHP, http://es.php.net/
5. Elmasri, R., Navathe, S.B.: Fundamentals of Database Systems. Addison-Wesley, New York (2006)

6. Official web page MySQL, http://dev.mysql.com/doc/
7. Kew, N.: Desarrollo de módulos y aplicaciones con Apache. Anaya Multimedia, Madrid (2008)
8. Derr, M., Symes, T.: Joomla!: Visual QuickStart Guide. Peachpit Press, Berkeley (2008)
9. Phoca: Building Web, http://www.phoca.cz/
10. Joom : Gallery, http://www.joomgallery.net/

Usable Interface Design for Everyone

Carlos de Castro Lozano[1], Enrique García Salcines[1], Beatriz Sainz de Abajo[2],
F. Javier Burón Fernández[1], José Miguel Ramírez[1], José Gabriel Zato Recellado[3],
Rafael Sanchez Montoya[4], John Bell[1], and Francisco Alcantud Marin[5]

[1] EATCO Research Group, University of Cordoba,
Edificio Leonardo da Vinci, Campus de Rabanales, 14071 Córdoba, Spain
{malcaloc,egsalcines,jburon}@uco.es,
{jmiguelramirez,jbellworks}@gmail.com
[2] Telecommunications Technical School (ETSIT), University of Valladolid,
Campus Miguel Delibes, Paseo de Belén n° 15, 47011 Valladolid, Spain
beasai@tel.uva.es
[3] Telecommunications Politechnical School (EUP), University of Madrid, C.E.U.
Department of Applied Intelligent Systems, Madrid, Spain
jzato@eui.upm.es
[4] EUEJE Campus Bahia de Algeciras University of Cadiz,
rsanchez@arrakis.es
[5] ACCESS Research Unit, University of Valencia
francisco.alcantud@uv.es

Abstract. When designing "interfaces for everyone" for interactive systems, it is important to consider factors such as cost, the intended market, the state of the environment, etc. User interfaces are fundamental for the developmental process in any application, and its design must be contemplated from the start. Of the distinct parts of a system (hardware and software), it is the interface that permits the user access to computer resources. The seven principles of "Universal Design" or "Design for Everyone" focus on a universal usable design, but at the same time acknowledge the influences of internal and external factors. Structural changes in social and health services could provide an increase in the well-being of a country's citizens through the use of self-care programming and proactive management/prevention of disease. Automated home platforms can act as an accessibility instrument which permits users to avoid, compensate, mitigate, or neutralize the deficiencies and dependencies caused by living alone.

Keywords: Person-to-computer interaction, Interface, Flexible, Dependence, Usability.

1 Introduction

To successfully, coherently and cognitively focus on person-to-computer interaction, as shown in the following figure, one must understand that both humans and computers process information. If the basic mechanisms which underly human cognition and computer systems are the same, it is possible to use the same methods and concepts to analyze both. From this information, one can compose a general theory which

F.V. Cipolla Ficarra et al. (Eds.): HCITOCH 2010, LNCS 6529, pp. 157–172, 2011.
© Springer-Verlag Berlin Heidelberg 2011

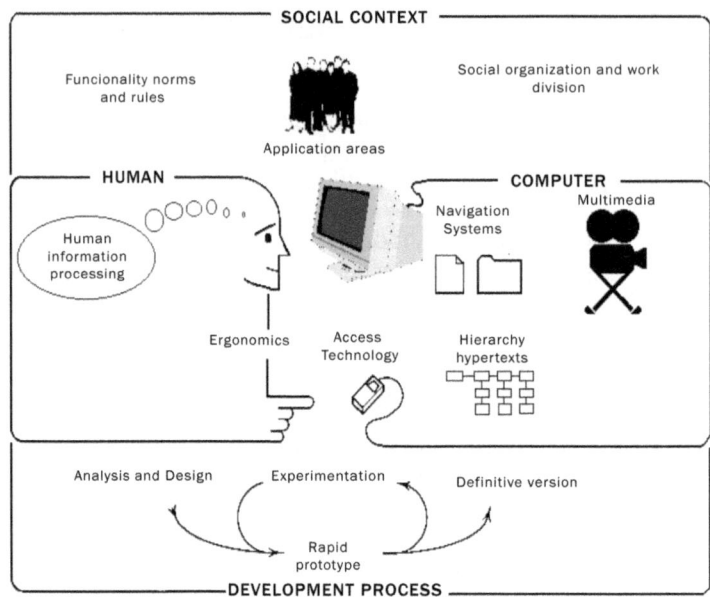

Fig. 1. Person-to-computer interaction layout (modified from Preece et al. [5])

explains the functionality of high level systems devised by computers and people [1]. Numerous studies have been made about this topic [2-4].

Interfaces which are more realistic and are adapted to user characteristics have lead to the creation of new applications. Virtual reality systems serve as an example of this, where the user interface permits an interactive exploration in such a way that the perception of a realistic environment is amplified. There are sophisticated systems which heighten the sensation of immersion: virtual reality, augmented reality, glasses, sensory gloves, curved screens, etc. Virtual scenes can be made interactive, with virtual images that are developed through special processes and accompanied by non-visual elements such as tactile and audio systems. The purpose of these elements is to convince the user to integrate into a synthetic but real environment.

The success of interactive systems is characterized by an emphasis on user participation. User interfaces are fundamental for the developmental process in any application, and its design must be contemplated from the start. Of the distinct parts of a system (hardware and software), it is **the interface** that permits the user access to computer resources. Thimbleby [6] suggests that the interface determines a user´s perception and impression of an application. Users are not interested in the internal structures of an application, only in how to use them. The seven principles of "Universal Design" or "Design for Everyone" focus on a universal usable design, but at the same time acknowledge the influences of internal and external factors. When designing "interfaces for everyone" for interactive systems, it is important to consider aspects such as cost, the intended market, the state of the environment, etc. Preece establishes the following directives for creating an interface design that is accessible and adaptable for everyone [7]:

- Know who is going to use the interface.
- Reduce the cognitive load.
- Error engineering: take measures to avoid possible user errors.
- Maintain clarity and consistency. Help create and maintain system mental models for users.
- Understand the (psychological, ergonomic, organization, and social) factors that determine how people work and use computers. By implementing this knowledge in tool and technical development, designers create ideal systems for activities - as well as efficient, cogent, and effective interaction on a user and group level.

"An interactive system design should satisfy the demands of those users who are going to use it." The computer is a tool which performs a determined job or activity. For a computer to be a good tool, it must be adequate, comfortable, and efficient in carrying out a task. A good design is achieved through a thorough analysis of the contexts where these assignments occur [8]. For this, user characteristics, activities, and environments must be analyzed. All of these factors define which system design requirements should be met.

A fundamental characteristic in interactive system development - with universal user interfaces - is the constant evaluation of its usability among people with disabilities. Through this method, it is fairly simple to try out different technical interface elements or components while developing a final prototype, and make modifications at each stage. For interface designers and Human Computer Interaction (HCI) researchers, the need for usability evaluation during the development process is evident [7, 9-12].

"Usability" can be defined as the level at which a product adapts to user needs, and can be used to reach objectives with effectivity, efficiency, and satisfaction [13]. This concept of "usability," because of its focus on user satisfaction, can be implemented to establish user interface evaluation standards. As it is difficult to measure usability directly, the best way to assess it is through indirect means or by the attributes which make up the concept of "usability." According to Alcantud usability is the inclusion, on a large or small scale, of [14]:

- *Effectivity:* any interface should have clear and reachable objectives.
- *Efficiency:* this characteristic depends on the user´s ability and the capabilities of the software. To analyze this correctly, one must perform a study on the different types of users.
- *Learnability:* the system has to be easy to learn so that a user can rapidly start working with it.
- *Memorability:* the different aspects and functionalities of the system must be memorable to the point where a user has no problems using it after extended periods of time.
- *Retainability:* control over the system and user errors.
- *Satisfaction:* the subjective state where a user has successfully performed a task without difficulties.

An application cannot reach a user without evaluating every interface component first, and without evidence that the application produces significantly better results in comparison to the existing conventional systems.

2 Usability Laboratory

Traditional scientific experimentation is performed in a controlled environment, resulting in maximum accuracy. Unfortunately, on occasion, the results of a controlled experiment can conflict with those of reality.

In the case of interface prototype evaluations, users must work with the computer or device in the exact setting for which the interface is intended. Usability laboratories are a place where these tests can take place [15]. A usability laboratory is a physical space which emulates the habitual work environment. Among the instruments in the laboratory should be an automatic video or semi-automatic video recording system to register interactions and responses for posterior evaluation. There should be one-way mirrors (to avoid observer detection), audio recording systems, and screen-action registering systems as well. Nielsen [16] performed a study on a total of thirty laboratories and came to the conclusion that: the majority of the laboratories date from 1989, although there are some which are older. 92% of these laboratories have one-direction mirrors, only 46% have direct screen recording systems, and all have video camera recording systems with a medium of 2 cameras per laboratory.

The ACCESO group from the University of Valencia developed a laboratory through the help of the "HAMTutor: Instruction Design for tele-education and author tools with intelligent tutors for the disabled" project, financed by FEDER funds (European Funds for Regional Development), and with the collaboration of the EATCO group at the University of Cordoba. This laboratory provided interaction observation for: individual and group interaction (up to three people at a time); for standard and specific system interaction; for interaction with the disabled; and for the interface design of the iFreeTablet®.

The objective was to establish a usability evaluation system for computer interfaces and systems, to assess usability during software design processes, and to define which adaptation/accessibility systems people with disabilities can use in order to eliminate any barriers between them and computer access. For this motive, the laboratory had to be very flexible and adapt to a series of different situations.

Currently, data mining is being developed with an emphasis on genetic and evolutionary fields. Nonetheless, it is already being used to evaluate learning activities on the internet, and create assessable models based on user information. By analyzing this information one can determine associations between visited pages, analyze visited page sequences, and asses user types/classes and their preferences.

Parts of these evaluations are performed via nervous system measurements. A person under stress undergoes a series of changes in their nervous system which can be observed with the appropriate tools. When a person is relaxed, the fluctuations in the nervous system achieve baseline values [17].

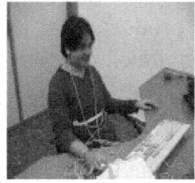 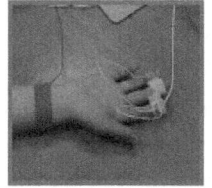 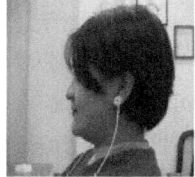

Fig. 2. Different electromyograph and polygraph electrode positions

The most frequently used devices to observe changes in the nervous system are: the electromyograph (EMG) which measures potential electric currents and muscle activity in muscular fiber; the electroencephalogram (EEG) which registers brain waves; the electrodermograph which measures the capacity of skin galvanic reactions (GSR) and shows modifications in its conductivity [18]; the thermograph (TP) which measures changes in skin temperature due to external vasoconstriction; and the pneumograph which observes thorax cavity expansion and consequentially the volume and frequency of respiration.

The different measurements tend to correlate when the subject is placed in a stressful or emotional situation – although there are external factors to consider [19]. When interpreting the results, one should keep in mind that the mechanisms which control internal temperature aren´t necessarily related to nervous system activities that control skin temperature. There are other influential factors, such as blood viscosity, the temperature of the surrounding environment, or biochemical factors such as the presence of lactic acid, carbon dioxide, nicotine, or alcohol in the blood. Psychological factors, like emotional tension, anxiety, and stimulation can influence results as well. The nervous system´s response to these different stimulants provoke changes in cardiac volume, arterial pressure, and external vasomotor activity [20].

3   Computer Interaction Devices and Systems for People in Situations of Dependency

3.1   Natural Language Recognition and Synthesis (Voice, Writing, Line Drawing, Signals, and Gestures)

The current use of Aid Technology (TA) is expanding the field of useful, interactive, and multi-sensorial devices for the development of communication and language abilities. Users who experience difficulties communicating find this technology to be psychologically comprehensible and flexible, and are able to overcome communication impediments fundamentally for two reasons:

- TA provides support for all symbolic systems (pictographs, morse, braille, etc). *People with communication disabilities normally feel limited by traditional systems.*

- Characters and images in Aid Technology are not static information symbols, but rather are the final representations of products and processes. These "representations" provide a more fluid communication experience.

The ALDICT project (Access for Persons with Intellectual Disability to Information and Communication), which produced the software "Writing with Symbols 2000," made web information sharing for people with communication and learning difficulties easier. The project developed a friendly interface based on the PCS, Rebus, and PIC symbol systems – allowing a wide range of communication techniques possible. This interface permitted the user to express both basic and advanced cognitive requirements, and provided simultaneous translation services between local and online users. This experience was evaluated very positively by more than 130 selected users from French, German, Portugal, and United Kingdom organizations (Inclusion for Europe, 2001). The results of these assessments confirm that the human eye is capable of simultaneously understanding diverse forms of information. As a result the creation of an effective graphic language with semantic fields that correspond to visible physical realities, and that encourage learning and communication, is a possibility. The use of microphones, which convert the speech acoustic parameters into interactive graphics, are reinforced by digitalized auditive synchronized repetitions. These visual animated effects permit speech therapists to motivate their patients and define parameters with notable clarity.

Interaction with a symbolic system is flexible and multi-sensorial. In only a few years, microelectronic development has increasingly prompted the production of devices which can connect to the computer. Currently, apart from the senses of smell and taste, it is possible to interact with all human senses.

Users which suffer from disorders can find new technologies which provide communication aids and alternatives in order to improve linguistic aptitudes. Among the newly developed technologies which offer interesting possibilities are wearable computers, and tablet PCs. Erwine Middle School (Ohio, USA) uses these devices and has achieved excellent results among people with autism and cerebral paralysis. As they are easy to use and transport, these devices become elements which a person can easily incorporate into their lives – much like glasses or a cane.

The project "Multisensory Environments: the use of interactive technology," from the London Institute of Education and University of Birmingham, demonstrates how multi-sensorial simulation (SME) can be considered as a way to perfect multimedia resources. Sounds, smells, lights, tactile surfaces, and system technology provide means to which students with severe communication and learning difficulties can improve motor and perceptive activities. The use of SME technologies can improve their integral and harmonic development [21].

The systems that do not have these kinds of aids have the advantage of being more dynamic, autonomous, economic, and easier to use - as communication is performed using the body. At the same time, however, they are more demanding in terms of cognitive aptitude and in short term memory, and do not last permanently on the market.

3.2   Learning through Augmentative Communication Systems and Speech Accessories

People with auditive deficiencies and deafness have difficulties coping in a society that uses the spoken and written word as the main communication medium. With this context in mind, Communication and Information Technologies (TIC) provide an opportunity which can eliminate communication difficulties, be integrated into the daily routine, and provide better chances for employment, education, and social welfare.

The most promising software for people who suffer from deafness or auditive deficiency helps users by reeducating them in speech (Speechviewer, Metavox, Visha, etc.), providing augmentative systems and communication alternatives (Sistema Bimodal´2000, Signos, La Palabra Completada, SIMICOLE, etc.), and teaching linguistic strategies.

Fluent Animated Speech, which was developed by the company Sensory (www.sensoryinc.com), is a computer application which teaches speech to deaf children. Its engaging design attracts the child´s attention with a 3D virtual doll that vocalizes words in a clear and perceptible manner. Through this system, a child can begin to recognize mouth movement and the facial expressions of its new "companion." Dolls can be customized by picking distinct physical characteristics. This product has been very positively rated at the North American "Tucker Maxon school for deaf children."

Another group of investigators who are experts in virtual reality (three-dimensional computer images) - from the British business Televisual - are working on sign language interpretation for computers. This system allows the deaf to communicate with others without the presence of an interpreter. The base of this system is a combination of software which recognizes speech and the movements of an interpreter archived through the use of sensors placed on the face and hands of a specialist.

3.3   Information Sharing and Supported Knowledge in a Virtual Environment

Lower digital camera prices and increased internet connection quality/velocity is converting virtual environments (videoconferences, virtual reality, etc.) into something more habitual. Many disabled citizens can benefit from these inventions: deaf people

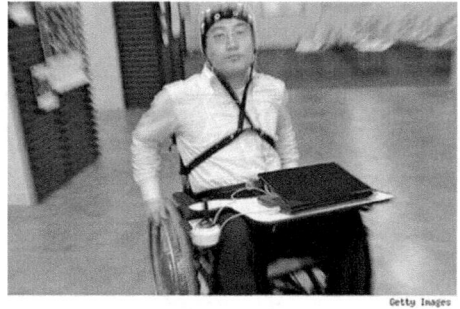

Fig. 3. Communication systems with physical aids

who communicate orally or with sign language, people with intellectual deficiencies who can use visual aids from a compute screen, and generally any professional who has problems commuting.

By using a PDA (Personal Digital Assistant), users - that need to use wheelchairs or have difficulties gaining access to a computer - can easily verify and obtain data, receive emails, send faxes, make telephone calls, or connect to their computer. These tasks can also be performed through devices such as the iFreeTablet.

3.4 Language and Communication Improvement with the Help of Software and Electronic Devices

Clearly, people who suffer from blindness or visual deficiency find interacting with a computer difficult, as they cannot perceive multiple visual cues that a computer screen or printer provides. While these users can manipulate a keyboard to quickly introduce data (in the case of pigmentary retinosis – simple, high contrast, adhesive tags ease keyboard character identification), screen information interpretation and manipulation is not easy.

"Portable-braille" is becoming more common, and permits users to introduce data in computers through the use of the 8 point braille system (which includes the highest number of standard braille characters). This device incorporates a voice synthesizer that reproduces information that is being written in any given moment, or information that is stored. Connection ports for communication with other devices are also included.

How information is presented on the screen is important. The adaptive technology for people who have visual deficiencies is different, and in some cases auxiliary. These technologies/devices aid users through:

SIGHT - the purpose of screen magnifiers, which act as magnifying glasses, is to make information larger. Accessibility properties offer users the chance to change contrast ratios, color combinations, mouse pointers, etc. The iFreeTablet is a good example of a device that enhances sight, as it uses the Guadalinex system´s magnifying glass.

SOUND – voice synthesis systems read the texts that appear on computer monitors out loud. This is possible through the activation of a reader program or screen revisor (Orca, Jaws, Hal, Simple Talker, Winvision, etc). In the last few years, advances have been outstanding in terms of quality and potential. There are even "speaking" web navigators in development such as Festival, IBM Home Page, Reader, Simply Web, Connect Outloud Browser, etc.

Fig. 4. Braille keyboard

TOUCH – braille lines allow blind people to read information that appears on computer screens. This is possible through the use of a device with a wide surface which reproduces braille in relief via electromechanical cells. Configuration menus and audible aids ease braille/user adaptation.

3.5   Learning How to Use Augmentative and Alternative Communication Systems with Multimedia Aids

Learning how to use Augmentative and Alternative Communication Systems (SCAA), with pictograph system supports, can serve as a benefit for people who have difficulties speaking, reading, or writing. The most common causes for these problems are intellectual, motor, or sensorial disabilities that serve as obstacles for speech and writing ability development. Traumas or sickness can also interrupt growth, and in turn cause these problems. Augmentative and Alternative Communication Systems are used generally by people with cerebral paralysis, autistic traits, blindness, deafness, and users which need non-vocal code communication.

Fig. 5. Sign language through video conference

4   Future Tendencies in New Interface Development

For as long as computers have existed, there have been barriers that have impeded human interaction. Until now, the most common devices that have provided access to the computer have been the mouse and keyboard. Although voice interaction will have a place in computer development, it is unlikely that it will become the preferred form. Rather, a combination of various systems (visual, position, gesture, voice recognition, touch, etc.) is the most probable solution to the evolution of the traditional person-to-computer interface. Of the systems, the ubiquitous multimodal systems and the adaptive and intelligent hypermedia systems stand out among the future tendencies in interface development.

4.1   Ubiquitous Multimodal Systems

According to Dürsteler, "human and computer interfaces still suffer from many shortcomings. The multimodal systems, which use multibiometric elements, multimodal interfaces and multisensorial systems are beginning to resolve many of these [insufficiencies]". As a result of human-computer problems, a new generation of multimodal systems is in development to find solutions. This new generation is based on: multibiometric systems that combine diverse biometric techniques which reduce error margins; multimodal interfaces that convert objects in a given environment into digital interaction elements; and multisensor systems that support the various synergetic multimodal and multibiometric combinations [22].

A simple example of a bimodal application is NISChart, which was developed by Natural Interaction Systems. This system permits doctors to combine voice recognition with normal writing on paper using the digital pen Anoto, which acts as a normal pen and detects movement at the same time. These gestures are captured thanks to a series of special printed marks on the paper, so any movement is communicated to the computer.

The development of current multimodal interfaces should evolve to the point where a user can interact with a system (via telephone, computer, television, electronic agendas, etc.) in a comfortable manner which is adaptable, robust, and error tolerant. By incorporating different modes of communication into an interface, the barriers which deny people in situations of dependency access to technology shall be removed. Voice interfaces, for example, are easier to use and require/demand less attention from a normal user. Using this reasoning, one can initiate a line of investigation which has the potential to provide people who have disabilities with access to this type of technology. This norm was applied during the design of SieSta, the operating system of the iFreeTablet, in such a way that the functions, organization, and concepts of the system follow a certain philosophy. For this particular system, there are six numerated pushable zones that are associated with six colors. The end result is that any given scenario is simplified to the point where there are no more than six actions a user can perform, which can be activated through touch, or through voice, gestures, or movement.

The development of computers that can think and act like people has been studied for years. These investigations have lead to the creation of machines that are sensitive to emotions thanks to the participation of experts from psychological, communicative, image process, computer science, philological, sign process, computer graphic, and artificial intelligence fields (amongst others). Humaine is a project that hopes to achieve exactly this, with the help of 160 investigators from 27 European institutions. This 4 year project - with a 10 million euro budget – is focused on multimodal interfaces that allow computers to understand the user´s habits and needs, and respond adequately to them. Professor and project coordinator Roddy Cowie, from the psychological department at Queen´s University, remarks that: "The computers that respond to human emotions seem like science fiction today, but they will exist. At this moment computers are limited to the keyboard and screen. If we could talk to them through a microphone, the difference would be enormous. But emotions are part of speech, and experience shows that the majority of people dislike talking to a machine. For this reason, if we were to make more intuitive, expressive, and easy to use computers there would be more people who would take advantage of them."

Natural spoken language or written investigations for the blind and deaf play a significant role in multimodal interface development. These investigations are important (as well) for the creation of computerized dialogue systems which model natural language communication mechanisms that imitate human behavior. Since 1984, the

Spanish Society for Natural Language Processing (SEPLN) has been a non-profit association formed by a variety of partners and institutions with the hopes of encouraging both national and international teaching, investigation, and development activities which focus on natural language processing.

Indisys (Intelligent Dialogue Systems) is a "spin-off" of the Julieta computational linguistic investigation group from the University of Seville. This group is dedicated to the creation of intelligent dialogue systems, or natural language voice interfaces which ease communication between a human user and a computer system. The idea is to provide the system with the ability to speak and understand natural/spoken languages without the user having to train previously or memorize commands. Indisys initially chose to work with two fields: automated environments, and telephonic autoservice. In the first case the user is provided with a virtual butler that can be accessed from any interior part of the house, via telephone or internet, and which controls all of the automated system devices (lights, heat, alarms, doors, blinds, etc.). In the second case the user can access a virtual telephone operator without having to deal with a series of predetermined menus. In both cases the system uses a dialogue manager, LOCUAZ, that provides a conversation-intelligence which follows and interprets the context of the dialogue in order to decide what to do: ask for more information, answer a question, perform a task, etc.

The quantity of applications which could offer this technology are unimaginable. In determined fields it would be easy to create systems which teach users in order to encourage the use of certain materials. One of the more interesting possibilities is an application which provides the disabled, the elderly, and those in situations of dependency with the ability to dominate their environment in a natural way, without having to train and with the added plus of a system that can monitor their needs.

Third and fourth generation telephones (3G and 4G) provide advantages in relation to interface analysis. Apart from being telephones, these devices serve as videocameras, personal computers, digitalized music players, and remote controls. For the construction of Voice-based User Interfaces there is currently a web standard called VoiceXML, which was conceived for human-computer dialogue and permits the development of services in response of interactive voice (IVR). If VoiceXML were paired with the variety of services that modern telephones offer, one could develop a universal remote control with an integrated voice navigator. This remote control would consist of a VoiceXML homepage and a list of URLS linked to any available devices. Through use of the remote control, VoiceXML would interpret menu choices, and retrieve the menu options of a chosen device.

Another future tendency has to do with interface design on a molecular level, which is to say the use of nanotechnology. Nanotechnology applications are becoming a reality, especially in the optoelectronic industry. Highly sensitive magnetic and compact-disc laser readers are the first devices with nanostructure materials to reach the market. Industrial and social impact from nanotechnology will go even farther in the future.

The most recent advances in ubiquitous computation have brought about the concept of "environmental intelligence" and new intelligent interaction possibilities between people and machines. In terms of practicality, environmental intelligence consists in the creation of a series of objects which are used daily and whose interactive

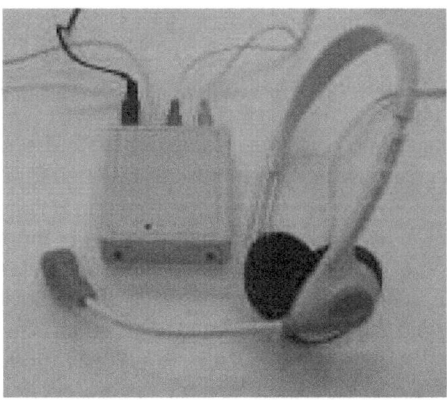

Fig. 6. Mouse system emulator with voice recognition

qualities are "smooth" and non-intrusive. The current systems based on environmental intelligence provide intuitive/intelligent interfaces for: furniture, clothing, vehicles, roads, and even paintings and cloths. All of these objects are capable of detecting human presence, personalities and needs - and respond in discontinuous, discreet, and frequently invisible ways.

Ubiquity, transparency, and intelligence are the three basic environmental intelligence properties. Ubiquity for identifying where the user is, transparency for being unnoticed, and intelligence for adapting to the preferences of each individual. "The ability to maintain itself," says López Villegas, "is one of the most significant aspects that devices have. For this reason we have to find efficient methodologies, which is to say, materials and systems that can fully take advantage of the available energy and reduce emission/reception unity consumption to a minimum".

To summarize the general future tendencies, technological investigation is moving towards the integration of different technical applications for those habitual environments in which people find themselves. Places such as the home, office, entertainment centers, etc. "will understand" likes and preferences as soon as a user enters. Environmental Intelligence is the new TIC paradigm in which people interact within a digital setting that is conscious of human presence, and the given general context of the situation. This intelligence in turn responds to the needs, habits, and emotions of the user.

4.2   Adaptive and Intelligent Hypermedia Systems

The first web adaptive and intelligent hypermedia systems (AIHS) date back to the 1990s. During this time, systems began to appear whose origins can be attributed to two interactive multimedia system areas. The first of these was the ITS area – which emphasized extending traditional user models and adaptation approximations with hypermedia components [23-26]. The other was Adaptive Hypermedia Systems (AHS) which attempted to adapt to individual users [27-30]. However, it was only from 1996 that the investigative community began to take interest in this type of system. This is due primarily to two factors: the accumulation and consolidation of investigatory experience in the field and, more importantly, the rapid growth of the World Wide Web. Because of this, there was a demand for systems with a high grade of adaptation to satisfy the variable nature of the intended audiences. So while the majority of the adaptive systems developed before 1996 used classic hypertexts and hypermedia, after 1996 all of the systems were AIHS. Some of the earliest systems were ELM-ART [31], InterBook [32], PT [33], y 2L670 [27]. Pioneer systems which influenced the creation of the posterior systems were: Medtec [34], AST [35], ADI [36], Hy-SOM [37], MetaLinks [38], CHEOPS [39], RATH [40], ACE [41], TANGOW [42], CAMELEON [43], KBS-Hyperbook [44], AHA! [45], SKILL [46], Multibook [47], ART-Web/NetCoach [48] y AHM [49].

Adaptation is one of the principal AIHS characteristics. There are various adaptation technologies that the ITS adopted such as user solution intelligent analysis, presentation adaptation, navigation adaptation, and interactive problem solution support based on examples and other technologies, all of which came from AIHS.

5 Conclusions

Recent published social protection and dependency reports emphasize the objective benefits, both physical and emotional, for the elderly - or for those in a situation of dependency or with disabilities - who continue residing in their own home with family assistance. In Spain, currently 8 out of 10 of the elderly or people in a situation of dependency live in their own home. As a consequence, 76% of families who are faced with this responsibility need some form of aid in order to perform all of the necessary daily tasks. As a further consequence, associations for people with disabilities not only report a lack of adequate aid services, but a lack of direct-family assistance as well. It is necessary, therefore, for an "evolution" or overhaul amongst the social and health service provision systems. The elderly, people in situations of dependency, or people with disabilities should be provided with enough resources and aids to allow them to decide their own future.

Structural changes in social and health services could provide an increase in the well-being of a country´s citizens through the use of self-care programming and pro-active management/prevention of disease. Automated home platforms can act as an accessibility instrument which permits users to avoid, compensate, mitigate, or neutralize the deficiencies and dependencies caused by living alone. At the same time it can improve the quality of the user´s life by easing domestic device activation and external assistance resource availability. An automated home platform could improve the quality of services given to citizens, as well as optimize resource consumption. At this time, however, automated platforms present some limitations: reduced functionality, insufficient technological infrastructure support, high installation and management cost, lack of privacy, complexity, etc.

Home technologies are becoming more and more orientated towards Environmental Intelligence systems. They consist of a combination of computation technologies and intelligent interfaces which provide an ideal setting for developing adaptive systems. These systems are based on user information and automatically change functionalities and interaction aspects in order to accommodate the preferences and requirements of different people. They can reorganize themselves through independent agents which react according to changes in their environment, or make decisions proactively before those changes occur. This concept has revolutionized the idea of the digital home.

References

1. Kaptelinin, V.: Activity theory: Implications for human-computer interaction. In: Nardo, B. (ed.) Contexts and consciousness. Activity theory and human-computer interaction, pp. 103–114. The MIT Press, Cambridge (1996)
2. Jones, M.G., Farquhar, J.D., Surry, D.W.: Using Metacognitive Theories to Design User Interfaces for Computer-based Learning. Educational Technology 35, 12–22 (1995)
3. Jones, M.G., Okey, J.R.: Interface Design for Computer-based Learning Environments (1995)
4. Jones, M.G.: Guidelines for screen design and user-interface design in computer-based learning environments. The University of Georgia. Dissertation Abstracts International 54(9), 308a–309a (1993)
5. Preece, J., Rogers, Y., Sharp, H., Benyon, D., Holland, S., Carey, T.: Human-Computer Interaction. Addison-Wesley, Wokingham (1994)
6. Thimbleby, H.: User interface design. In: (Principles for principles). ch. 10, pp. 197–226. ACM Press, New York (1990)
7. Preece, J. (ed.): Human-Computer Interaction. Addison-Wesley Publishing, New York (1994)
8. Hackos, J., Redish, J.: User and Task Analysis for Interface Design. Wiley, Chichester (1998)
9. Hartson, H.R.: Advances in Human-Computer Interaction, vol. 1. ABLEX Publishing Corporation, New Jersey (1988)
10. Hartson, H.R., Hix, D.: Advances in Human-Computer Interaction, vol. II. ABLEX Publishing Corporation, New Jersey (1988)
11. Hartson, H.R., Hix, D.: Advances in Human-Computer Interaction, vol. III. ABLEX Publishing Corporation, New Jersey (1992)
12. Carroll, J.M.: Interfacing Thought: Cognitive Aspects of Human-Computer Interaction. Bradford Book. MIT Press, Cambridge (1989)
13. Nielsen, J.: Usability Engineering. Academic Press, Boston (1993)
14. Alcantud, F.: Nuevas Tecnologías, Viejas Esperanzas. In: VVAA. Nuevas Tecnologías, Viejas Esperanzas: las nuevas tecnologías en el ámbito de la discapacidad y las necesidades educativas especiales, Consejería de Educación y Universidades, Murcia (2000)
15. Dumas, J.S., Redish, J.C.: A practical guide to usability testing. Ablex Publishing Corporation, Norwood (1993)
16. Nielsen, J.: Usability Inspection Methods. In: CHI Tutorials, pp. 413–414. ACM, New York (1994)
17. Naveteur, J., Freixa i Baque, E.: Individual differences in electrodermal activity as a function of subjects anxiety. Personality and Individual Differences 5, 615–626 (1987)
18. Boucsein, W.: Electrodermal activity. Plenum Press, New York (1992)
19. Katkin, E.S.: Electrodermal lability: A Psychophysiological analysis of individual differences in response to stress. In: Sarason, J.G., Spielberger, C.D. (eds.) Stress and Anxiety. Hemisphere Publishing, CO (1975)
20. Spielberger, C.D., Sarason, I.G., Kulcsar, Z., Van Heck, G.L. (eds.): Stress and Emotion. Series in Stress and Emotion: Anxiety, Anger, and Curiosity, vol. 14. Taylor & Francis, Abington (1991)

21. Sánchez, R.: Tecnologías estimuladoras de las inteligencias (2004),
    `http://www.aldeaeducativa.com/aldea/articulo.asp?which1=2146`
22. Dursteler, J.C.: Sistemas multimodales. Revista digital de InfoVis.net (2004),
    `http://www.infovis.net/printMag.php?num=139&lang=1`
23. Beaumont, I.: User modeling in the interactive anatomy tutoring system ANATOM-TUTOR.
    User Modeling and User-Adapted Interaction 4(1), 21–46 (1994)
24. Brusilovsky, P., Pesin, L., Zyryanov, M.: Towards an adaptive hypermedia component for
    an intelligent learning environment. In: Bass, L.J., Unger, C., Gornostaev, J. (eds.)
    EWHCI 1993. LNCS, vol. 753, pp. 348–358. Springer, Heidelberg (1993)
25. Gonschorek, M., Herzog, C.: Using hypertext for an adaptive helpsystem in an intelligent
    tutoring system. In: 7 th World Conference on Artificial Intelligence in Education, pp.
    274–281. AACE, Washington (1995)
26. Pérez, T.A., Gutiérrez, J., López, R., González, A., Vadillo, J.A.: Hipermedia, adaptación,
    constructivismo e instructivismo. Revista Iberoamericana de Inteligencia Artificial 2,
    29–38 (2001)
27. De Bra, P.: Teaching Hypertext and Hypermedia through the Web. Journal of universal
    computer science 2(12), 797–804 (1996)
28. De La Passardiere, B., Dufresne, A.: Adaptive navigational tools for educational hypermedia.
    In: Tomek, I. (ed.) ICCAL 1992. LNCS, vol. 602, pp. 555–567. Springer, Heidelberg (1992)
29. Hohl, H., Böcker, D., Gunzenhäuser, R.: Hypadapter: An adaptive hypertext system for
    exploratory learning and programming. User Models and User Adapted Interaction 6 (1996)
30. Kay, J., Kummerfeld, R.J.: An individualized course for the C programming language. In:
    Proceedings of Second International WWW Conference, Chicago, IL, pp. 17–20 (1994)
31. Brusilovsky, P., Schwarz, E., Weber, G.: ELM-ART: An intelligent tutoring system on
    World Wide Web. In: Lesgold, A.M., Frasson, C., Gauthier, G. (eds.) ITS 1996. LNCS,
    vol. 1086, pp. 261–269. Springer, Heidelberg (1996)
32. Brusilovsky, P., Schwarz, E., Weber, G.: A tool for developing adaptive electronic text-
    books on WWW. In: Maurer, H. (ed.) Proceedings of WebNet 1996, World Conference of
    the Web Society, San Francisco, CA, pp. 64–69. AACE, Boston (1996)
33. Kay, J., Kummerfeld, B.: User models for customized hypertext. In: Nicholas, C. (ed.)
    Intelligent Hypertext. LNCS, vol. 1326, Springer, Heidelberg (1997)
34. Eliot, C., Neiman, D., Lamar, M.: Medtec: A Web-based intelligent tutor for basic
    anatomy. In: Lobodzinski, S., Tomek, I. (eds.) Proceedings of WebNet 1997, World
    Conference of the WWW, Internet and Intranet, pp. 161–165. AACE, Toronto (1997)
35. Specht, M., Weber, G., Heitmeyer, S., Schöch, V.: AST: Adaptive WWWCourseware for
    Statistics. In: Brusilovsky, P., Fink, J., Kay, J. (eds.) Proceedings of Workshop "Adaptive
    Systems and User Modeling on the World Wide Web", at 6th International Conference on
    User Modeling, UM 1997, Chia Laguna, Sardinia, Italy, pp. 91–95 (1997)
36. Schöch, V., Specht, M., Weber, G.: ADI - an empirical evaluation of a tutorial agent. In:
    Ottmann, T., Tomek, I. (eds.) Proceedings of ED-MEDIA/ED-TELECOM 1998 - 10th
    World Conference on Educational Multimedia and Hypermedia and World Conference on
    Educational Telecommunications, pp. 1242–1247. AACE, Freiburg (1998)
37. Kayama, M., Okamoto, T.: Hy-SOM: The semantic map framework applied on an exam-
    ple case of navigation. In: Cumming, G., Okamoto, T., Gomez, L. (eds.) Advanced Re-
    search in Computers and Communications in Education. Frontiers ub Artificial Intelli-
    gence and Applications., pp. 252–259. IOS Press, Chiba (1999)
38. Murray, T., Condit, C., Haugsjaa, E.: MetaLinks: A preliminary framework for concept-
    based adaptive hypermedia. In: Goettl, B.P., Halff, H.M., Redfield, C.L., Shute, V.J. (eds.)
    ITS 1998. LNCS, vol. 1452, Springer, Heidelberg (1998)

39. Negro, A., Scarano, V., Simari, R.: User adaptivity on WWW through CHEOPS. In: Brusilovsky, P., De Bra, P. (eds.) Proceedings of Second Adaptive Hypertext and Hypermedia Workshop at the Ninth ACM International Hypertext Conference Hypertext 1998, Published as Computing Science Reports, Pittsburgh, PA, June 20, vol. 98/12, pp. 57–62. Eindhoven University of Technology, Eindhoven (1998)

40. Hockemeyer, C., Held, T., Albert, D.: RATH - A relational adaptive tutoring hypertext WWW-environment based on knowledge space theory. In: Alvegård, C. (ed.) Proceedings of CALISCE 1998, 4th International conference on Computer Aided Learning and Instruction in Science and Engineering, Göteborg, Sweden, pp. 417–423 (1998)

41. Specht, M., Oppermann, R.: ACE - Adaptive Courseware Environment. In: Brusilovsky, P., Milosavljevic, M. (eds.) The New Review of Hypermedia and Multimedia, Special Issue on Adaptivity and user modeling in hypermedia systems, vol. 4, pp. 141–161 (1998)

42. Carro, R.M., Pulido, E., Rodrígues, P.: TANGOW: Task-based Adaptive learNer Guidance on the WWW. In: Brusilovsky, P., De Bra, P. (eds.) Proceedings of Second Workshop on Adaptive Systems and User Modeling on the World Wide Web, Toronto, Banff, Canada, May 11-June 23-24, vol. 99–07, pp. 49–57. Eindhoven University of Technology, Eindhoven (1999) Published as Computer Science Report

43. Laroussi, M., Benahmed, M.: Providing an adaptive learning through the Web case of CAMELEON: Computer Aided MEdium for LEarning on Networks. In: Alvegård, C. (ed.) Proceedings of CALISCE 1998, 4th International conference on Computer Aided Learning and Instruction in Science and Engineering, Göteborg, Sweden, pp. 411–416 (1998)

44. Henze, N., Nejdl, W.: Adaptivity in the KBS Hyperbook System. In: Brusilovsky, P., De Bra, P. & Kobsa, A. (eds.). Proceedings of Second Workshop on Adaptive Systems and User Modeling on the World Wide Web, Toronto and Banff, Canada. No. 99-07, Eindhoven University of Technology, Eindhoven, pp. 67–74 (1999) Published as Computer Science Report

45. De Bra, P., Calvi, L.: AHA! An open Adaptive Hypermedia Architecture. In: Brusilovsky, P., Milosavljevic, M. (eds.) The New Review of Hypermedia and Multimedia, vol. 4, pp. 115–139 (1998) Special Issue on Adaptivity and user modeling in hypermedia systems

46. Neumann, G., Zirvas, J.: SKILL: A Scalable Internet-Based Teaching and Learning System. In: Maurer, H., Olson, R.G. (eds.) Proceedings of WebNet 1998, World Conference of the WWW, Internet, and Intranet, pp. 688–693. AACE, Orlando (1998)

47. Steinacker, A., Seeberg, C., Rechenberger, K., Fischer, S., Steinmetz, R.: Dynamically generated tables of contents as guided tours in adaptive hypermedia systems. In: Proceedings of ED-MEDIA/ED-TELECOM 1999 - 11th World Conference on Educational Multimedia and Hypermedia and World Conference on Educational Telecommunications. AACE, Seattle (1999)

48. Weber, G., Kuhl, H.-C., Weibelzahl, S.: Developing adaptive internet based courses with the authoring system NetCoach. In: De Bra, P., Brusilovsky, P., Kobsa, A. (eds.) Proceedings of Third workshop on Adaptive Hypertext and Hypermedia, Sonthofen, Germany, Technical University Eindhoven, pp. 35–48 (2001)

49. Pilar da Silva, D., Durm, R.V., Duval, E., Olivié, H.: Concepts and documents for adaptive educational hypermedia: a model and a prototype. In: Brusilovsky, P., De Bra, P. (eds.) Proceedings of Second Adaptive Hypertext and Hypermedia Workshop at the Ninth ACM International Hypertext Conference Hypertext 1998, Pittsburgh, PA, vol. 98/12, pp. 35–43. Eindhoven University of Technology, Eindhoven (1998) Published as Computing Science Reports

SIeSTA: From Concept Board to Concept Desktop

Carlos de Castro Lozano[1], Enrique García Salcines[1], Beatriz Sainz de Abajo[2],
F. Javier Burón Fernández[1], José Miguel Ramírez[1], José Gabriel Zato Recellado[3],
Rafael Sanchez Montoya[4], John Bell[1], and Francisco Alcantud Marin[5]

[1] EATCO Research Group, University of Cordoba,
Edificio Leonardo da Vinci, Campus de Rabanales, 14071 Córdoba, Spain
{malcaloc,egsalcines,jburon}@uco.es,
{jmiguelramirez,jbellworks}@gmail.com
[2] Telecommunications Technical School (ETSIT), University of Valladolid,
Campus Miguel Delibes, Paseo de Belén nº 15, 47011 Valladolid, Spain
beasai@tel.uva.es
[3] Telecommunications Politechnical School (EUP), University of Madrid, C.E.U.
Department of Applied Intelligent Systems, Madrid, Spain
jzato@eui.upm.es
[4] EUEJE Campus Bahia de Algeciras University of Cadiz
rsanchez@arrakis.es
[5] ACCESS Research Unit, University of Valencia
francisco.alcantud@uv.es

Abstract. Recently published social protection and dependence reports reaffirm that the elderly, the disabled, or those in situations of dependency objectively benefit from continuing to live at home with the assistance from direct family. Currently in Spain - amongst the elderly, or people in a situation of dependency - 8 out of every 10 people stay at home. The end result is that the direct family relations have the responsibility of performing 76% of the tasks during the daily routine where aid is needed. Associations for people with disabilities, however, not only report a lack of adequate aid services, but a lack of direct-family assistance as well. It is necessary, therefore, for an "evolution" or overhaul amongst the social and health service provision systems. The elderly, people in situations of dependency, or people with disabilities should be provided with enough resources and aids to allow them to decide their own future.

Keywords: HCI, Accessibility, iTV.

1 Introduction

Recently published social protection and dependence reports reaffirm that the elderly, the disabled, or those in situations of dependency objectively benefit from continuing to live at home with the assistance from direct family. Currently in Spain - amongst the elderly, or people in a situation of dependency - 8 out of every 10 people stay at home. The end result is that the direct family relations have the responsibility of performing 76% of the tasks during the daily routine where aid is needed. Associations for people with disabilities, however, not only report a lack of adequate aid services,

F.V. Cipolla Ficarra et al. (Eds.): HCITOCH 2010, LNCS 6529, pp. 173–183, 2011.
© Springer-Verlag Berlin Heidelberg 2011

but a lack of direct-family assistance as well. It is necessary, therefore, for an "evolution" or overhaul amongst the social and health service provision systems. The elderly, people in situations of dependency, or people with disabilities should be provided with enough resources and aids to allow them to decide their own future [1, 2].

2 Home Control and Support Programs – Providing Health and Social Services

Structural changes in social and health services could potentially provide an increase in the well-being of a country´s citizens through the use of self-care programming and proactive management/prevention of disease [3]. Automated home platforms can act as an accessibility instrument which permits users to avoid, compensate, mitigate, or neutralize the deficiencies and dependencies caused by living alone [4]. At the same time it can improve the quality of the user´s life by easing domestic device activation and external assistance resource availability. An automated home platform could improve the quality of services given to citizens, as well as optimize resource consumption. At this time, however, automated platforms present some limitations: reduced functionality, insufficient technological infrastructure support, high installation and management cost, lack of privacy, complexity, etc.

Home technologies are becoming the paradigm of Environmental Intelligence systems. They consist of a combination of computation technologies and intelligent interfaces which provide an ideal setting for developing adaptive systems [5, 6]. These systems are based on user information and automatically change functionalities and interaction aspects in order to accommodate the preferences and requirements of different people. They can reorganize themselves through independent agents which react according to changes in their environment, or make decisions proactively before those changes occur [7]. This concept is revolutionizing the idea of the digital home.

3 SIeSTA: The Adaptive, Usable, and Accessible User Interface

SIeSTA is a new user interface concept which endeavors to achieve the same objectives defined by Human Computer Interaction. The iFreeTablet is the combination of different physical devices (tablet-PC, remote control, web-camera, communication devices, home electronics, digital medical systems, and generally any element which can be integrated or connected to a PC) and logic devices (applications) created for SIeSTA (Aid Technology and e-Service Integrated System).

The iFreeTablet incorporates all assistive technologies and new person-to-computer interface tendencies, such as the multimodal ubiquitous systems and the adaptive and intelligent hypermedia systems.

SIeSTA was designed in order to integrate computer sciences, the most recent "environmental intelligence" ubiquitous computation advances, and the newest user-machine intelligent interaction concepts into a human setting [8]. Environmental intelligence consists in the creation of a series of objects which are used daily and whose interactive qualities are "smooth" and non-intrusive. The ability of a person to

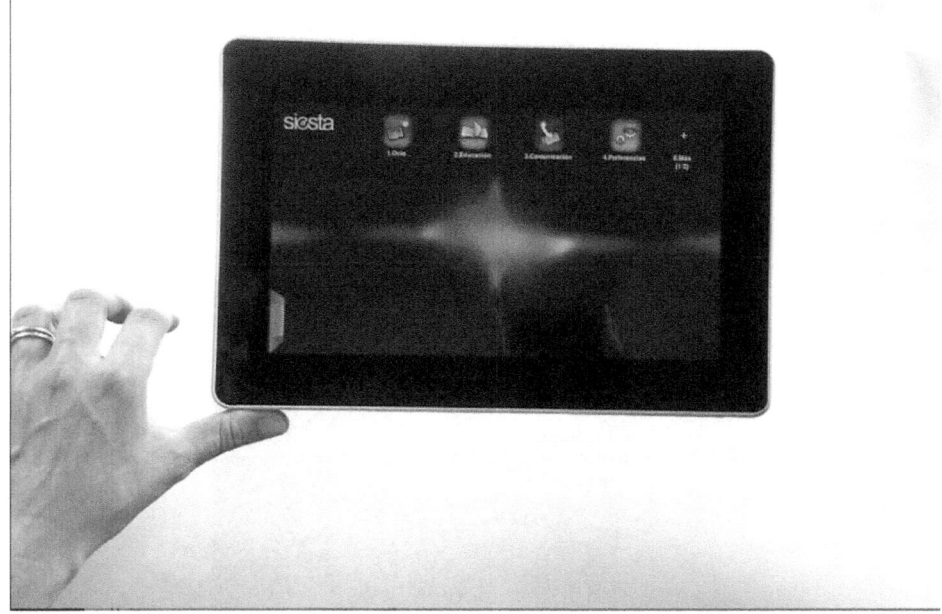

Fig. 1. iFreeTablet

communicate with the surrounding environment provides a range of possibilities for assistance in daily tasks - especially in those areas related to services for people in a situation of dependency [9, 10].

SIeSTA is based on software (operating systems, web platforms, authoring tools and applications) from the Concept and function Amplifier System (Concept Board or Keyboard) which was patented by the EATCO investigation group in 1988. This project was financed by IMSERSO, as was the web platform user interface IPTVMunicipal which was developed in 2007-2008 by CPMTI S.L. in collaboration with EATCO, the RedEspecial foundation, and Plan Avanza Contenidos Digitales from the Ministry of Industry, Tourism, and Commerce.

Although it shares many of the characteristics (educational, professional, and entertainment tools) which are advertised by similar projects such as OLPC, Classmate, iPad, Google Tablet, etc., the iFreeTablet is "designed for everyone". This is to say that the iFreeTablet was developed to conform to the needs of people who typically don´t have access to technology: the disabled, the elderly, children, people in situations of dependency, women in rural zones, etc. This product was the result of investigations performed by usability laboratories in collaboration with the Access Unit at the University of Valencia, following all accessibility models in order to achieve the SIMPLIT certificate from the Bio-mechanic Institute of Valencia (IBV) and AENOR. SIMPLIT ES EL is the first certificate which ensures that a product is easy to use and designed for the elderly.

As a result, the needs and experience of distinct user-types provided the necessary framework to create a simple, consistent, accessible, usable, and adaptive interface that can be accessed via distinct means (multimodal), in any setting (ubiquitous), and

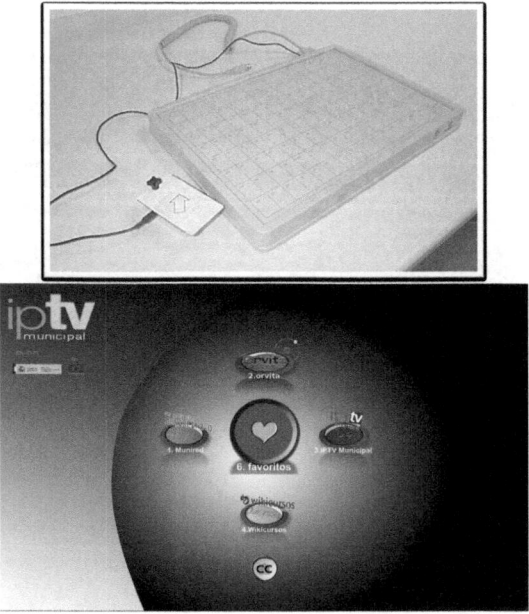

Fig. 2. Concept board and IPTVMunicipal main category menu

that uses Environmental Intelligence, Multi-agent intelligent systems, and semantic web as aid technologies in order to achieve its objectives [11, 12].

Human-to-computer interaction is possible through use of the iFreeTablet´s multi-touch screen, web camera, voice and movement recognition system, RFID system, or remote control (Natural Interaction System – iFreeSIN). Because of this, the barriers for people who have disabilities - which are created by high cost or limited access devices such as the keyboard, mouse, or special remote controls - are removed. The iFreeTablet has the functionality of a personal computer and the ergonomics and interface of a television. Internet, office applications, multimedia centers (music, movie, game, education, etc), and digital home and medical device controls are accessible through an integrated system of local applications and accessible web platform based on the Concept Desktop.

4 The Concept Desktop: A New Desktop Concept

The Internet Television Protocol (IPTV) is currently the most common television/video signal distribution system which uses broadband IP connections. IPTV represents an alternative mechanism for the distribution of live and stored content, all of which is available through computers via the internet. Currently, however, no standard exists for IP television interactive interface development. This is mainly due to the differences in human-to-device interface technology such as a larger screen with more resolution, and the majority of remote controls which have not been designed to deal with voice or movement recognition [13].

One of the components paired to work with the iFreeTablet is a colored remote control (the iFreeMando). This device was the culmination of usability studies that focused on the elderly, the disabled, and children. Pressing a button – depending on the context or scenario - works the same as pressing a keyboard key, keyboard combination, or mouse click. An application, in turn, detects whatever an action was taken and then performs that task.

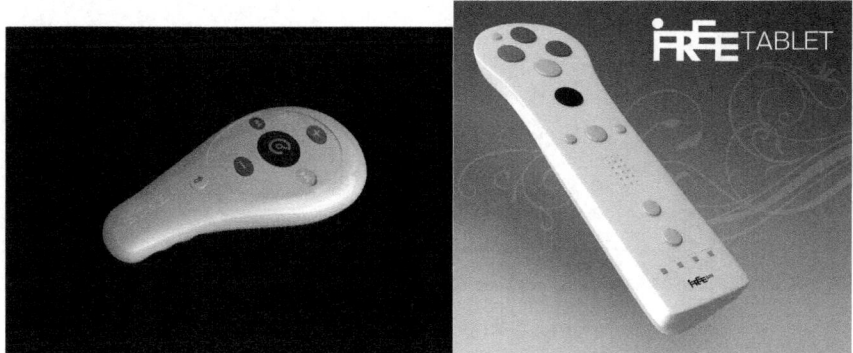

Fig. 3. Two iFreeMando models adapted with accelerometer and gyroscope

The Concept Desktop interface is designed in such a way that any system entity (category, application, scenario, etc.) can be accessed via a remote control with six colored buttons. This simplifies the system to the point where a user is only faced with six options at a time and activate any action or application with one movement, gesture, or voice.

The SIeSTA "white book" or interface guide clarifies the interface specifications which an application adapted for the Concept Desktop should meet. This guide was made in hopes of encouraging the development of free software (whether for GNU-Linux operating systems or web applications) which can be integrated into SIeSTA. Software which follows these guidelines would not only be accessible for any type of user – no matter whether they are disabled or not, but also could be compatible with a variety of different supports such as interactive IPTV, third generation mobile telephones, tablets, pads, UMPC, and computers.

The Concept Desktop, which is the SIeSTA operating system interface, is software designed to offer a user comfortable and friendly interaction. This interaction is achieved through a fully graphic interface consisting of icons, buttons, and tool bars that can be pushed, scrolled, and dragged. The purpose of the Concept Desktop is to achieve accessible, adaptable, and usable interaction between an operating system and people in a situation of dependency (the disabled, the elderly, etc) [14, 15, 16].

The distinct SIeSTA interface elements or concepts are classified as: ontologies, categories, scenarios, galleries, viewers, applications, resources, activities, content, metadata, semantic web, and intelligent multi-agents.

Ontology: in relation to computer sciences, ontology refers to the exhaustive and rigorous design of a conceptual scheme within one or various determined areas, with

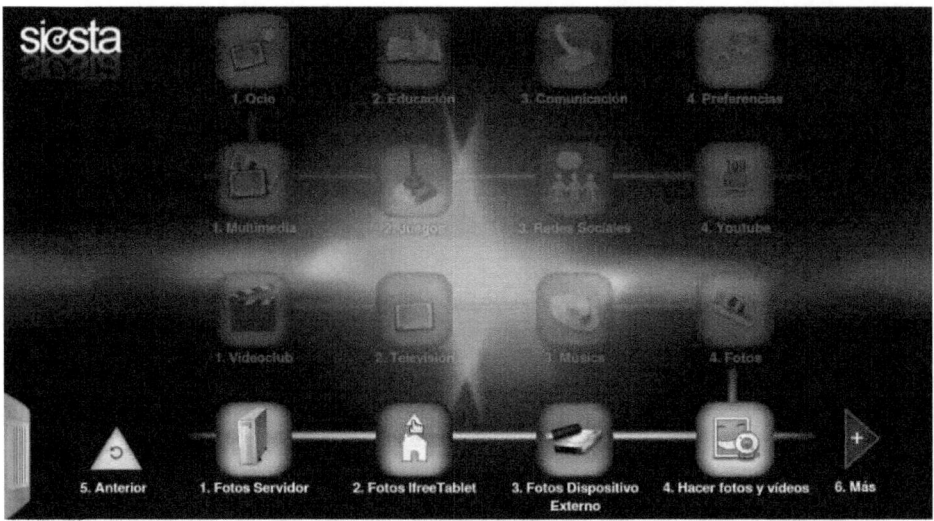

Fig. 4. SIeSTA category menu

the end result of easing information communication and sharing between different systems and entities.

Categories/subcategories: A category is one of the most abstract and general notions in which an entity can be recognized, differentiated, and classified into a hierarchy. Entities that are similar or have common characteristics form one category, and in turn those categories which share aspects can form a superior category.

The distinct Concept Desktop activities and contents are grouped (by default) in six categories which appear in the main configurable SIeSTA menu: 1. Leisure, 2. Home, 3. Health, 4. Education, 5. Communication, and 6. Preferences.

The category "leisure" can be subdivided into: **multimedia, games, social networks, YouTube,** and **web news.** The subcategory **multimedia** can be separated into: *video club, television, music, photos,* and *online radio. Video club* contains: online movies, iFreeTablet movies, and external device movies. *Television* contains: iFreeTablet channels, and TDT channels. *Music* contains: online music, iFreeTablet music, external device music, Spotify, and recorder. *Photos* contains: server photos, iFreeTablet photos, external device photos, take photos and videos (Cheese). The subcategory **games** can be separated into: *linux,* and *internet.* The subcategory **social networks** can be separated into: *iFreeSocial, Facebook, Tuenti,* and *Twitter.*

The category "education" can be subdivided into: **office, book reader** (FbReader), **Wiki-courses, PDF reader** (Evince), **paint, writer** (Xournal), **text editor** (Gedit), and **events.** The subcategory **office** can be separated into: *OpenOffice. OpenOffice* contains: "Writer" word processor, "Calc" spreadsheet, and "Impress" presentations.

The category "home" can be subdivided into: **lights, devices,** and **computers.** The category "health" can be subdivided into: **phonendoscope, tensiometer, measurements,** and **video-assistance.**

The category "communication" can be subdivided into: **internet navigation, video-chat, mail, calls, messenger,** and **RSS reader.** The subcategory **mail** can be separated into: *send mail, receive mail,* and *agenda.*

The category "preferences" can be subdivided into: **accessibility system, controls, connectivity, favorites, modify personal information, backend, internet connection, document explorer, remote control connection, VPN and connectivity.** The subcategory **accessibility system** can be separated into: *screen sweeper, auditive menu zoom, head-to- cursor gesture control, Orca, and menu sound system. Screen sweeper* contains: deactivate, activate, deactivate sound, and activate sound. The subcategory **controls** can be separated into: *connect to projector, sound control, brightness control,* and *connect to printer.* The subcategory **backend** can be separated into: *menu, health,* and *home.* The subcategory **connectivity** can be separated into: *iFreeMando,* and *Mobile telephone.* More categories, subcategories, applications, and content can be added through **iFreeMenu**, a web application designed to configure websites and web platforms.

Scenarios: Each SIeSTA interface concept is a composition of base information units called scenarios. A scenario is a template which contains the distinct interface types that determine interactivity and navigation. Several scenarios exist: Galleries, Viewers, and Interactive Objects.

Galleries: A way to present an organized collection of information elements (photos, videos, pdf, etc.) is through a content gallery.

Viewers: Once an element in a gallery is selected, it can be visualized through a viewer which provides options and more detail.

Applications: In computer sciences, an application is a type of program designed as a tool for carrying out certain tasks. There are two application types – local (OpenOffice writer, for example) and web (i.e. Wiki-courses). Local applications that have been integrated into SIeSTA still haven´t been adapted to the Concept Desktop. The majority of web applications integrated into SIeSTA have been personalized by CPMTI.

Content: Texts, images, photos, videos, learning objects, etc.

Metadata: In general, a metadata group refers to a group of data. This is analogous to the use of indexes in order to find information. Libraries, for example, use cards which specify authors, titles, editorial houses, and places to find books. Metadata works in this way as well.

Semantic web: Is based on the idea of adding semantic and ontological metadata to the World Wide Web. This additional information – which describes content, its significance, and its relation to other data – should be provided in a formal manner so that automatic machine process evaluation is possible. The objective is to improve the internet by increasing communication between systems using "intelligent agents."

Intelligent agents: Are computer programs, without human operators, which look for information.

Many Iber-american, European, and Spanish groups/centers have aided in the development of the iFreeTablet. Among these groups are ACCESO from the University of Valencia directed by Francisco Alcantud, the SIA group (Applied Intelligent Systems) from the Polytechnic University of Madrid directed by José Gabriel Zato, the Germán Ruiperez Philological Section Didactic Engineering laboratory, Antonio

Rodríguez de la Heras – director of the Technological and Cultural Institute at the University of Carlos III, the Information Society investigation group coordinated by Miguel Lopez Coronado, and the Virtual Teaching Center from the University of Huelva directed by Alfonso Infante Moro.

The iFreeTablet is ideal as an easy-to-understand educative computer for teaching children. The iFreeTablet integrates the e-Aprendo platform based on Moodle, with (Creative Commons License) free and open learning objects (interactive multimedia courses). The iFreeTablet bases its revolutionary technology on the following development premises:

- EATCO´s patented "Concept and Function Amplifier System"
- Usability, accessibility, and adaptability "for everyone"
- Compatibility with any system that has a linux kernel or FreeBSD
- Use of the Concept desktop as blueprint
- Interactive accessibility with the PC and digital TV
- Emphasis on natural and multimodal interaction

5   Physical Characteristics

The **physical characteristics** of the iFreeTablet - which is to say the actual device is the combination of a touch screen tablet-PC and remote control, paired with hardware support for various devices which permit interaction with other systems. The tablet-PC has a 10.2 inch screen with 1024x600 pixel resolution, a 1.6G Intel Atom Mobile N470 processor with the following components:

- 160G SATA HDD hard drive
- Ethernet connection, WLAN WiFi
- 1.3 Megapixel Camera
- 3 USB ports, 1 VGA port, 1 earphone jack, 1 microphone jack, 1 internal microphone, 1 RJ-45 LAN port, 1 DC-in jack, 1 four-inch card reader
- 1 DIMM slot, 2 mini PCI-E for WiFi, 802.11b / g 54Mb and 3G/3.5G HSDPA / WCDMA card
- 5 hour battery duration, 35W adaptor, thermic refrigeration system with intelligent ventilator
- Kensington Lock Security
- Dimensions: 28 x 18 cm, 2 cm thick
- Weight: 1.03 kg (including battery)

5.1   Nucleus

The nucleus of the iFreeTablet is the adaptation of Ubuntu GNU/Linux and the IPTVMunicipal Web platform to specific device characteristics and hardware components.

5.2   iFreeTablet Applications

5.2.1   For Leisure
This module - comprised of a multimedia center, games, educational courses, and interactive TV - serves as the base entertainment service.

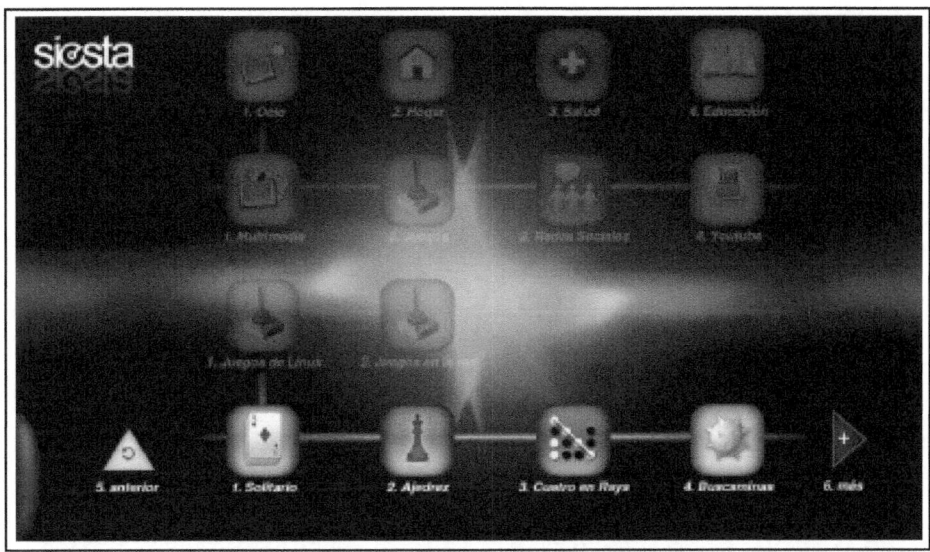

Fig. 5. SIeSTA Multimedia resources center menu

5.2.2   For Games
From the iFreeTablet, the user can access categorized Linux or web based games (sports, logic, arcade, etc.).

Fig. 6. Game menu

5.2.3 For Education

From the iFreeTablet, the user can access Guadalinex EDU applications, interactive multimedia courses such as the European Computer Driving License (ECDL), OpenOffice, Web browsers, Mozilla mail, and any FREE or Creative Common License application.

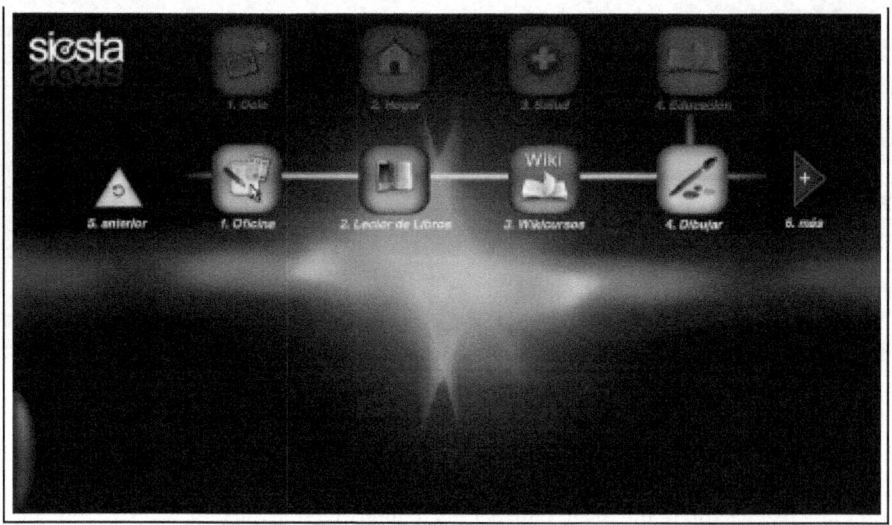

Fig. 7. Education menu

6 Conclusions

The design of the iFreeTablet interface focuses on person-to-computer interaction, using usability and accessibility as the main objectives. **Accessibility** consists in providing access to content without any limitation, avoiding any barriers that disabilities can provoke. The International Standardization Organization (ISO) refers to Usability, ISO/IEC 9126, as the "ability of software to be understood, learned, and utilized by the user and attract the user´s attention in specific use conditions." This definition stresses the internal and external product attributes which contribute to usability, functionality, and efficiency. Usability not only depends on the product, however, but also the user. For this reason, no product is intrinsically usable, but rather each product has the capacity to be used in a particular context by particular users. Usability cannot be evaluated through isolated study [17, 18].

By using the Concept Desktop as a standard; by simplifying the actions, providing a fully graphic interface, and creating multimodal interaction - the principal definitions of usability and accessibility are achieved.

References

1. Kaptelinin, V.: Activity theory: Implications for human-computer interaction. In: Nardo, B. (ed.) Contexts and consciousness. Activity theory and human-computer interaction, pp. 103–114. The MIT Press, Cambridge (1996)

2. Jones, M.G., Farquhar, J.D., Surry, D.W.: Using Metacognitive Theories to Design User Interfaces for Computer-based Learning. Educational Technology 35, 12–22 (1995)
3. Jones, M.G., Okey, J.R.: Interface Design for Computer-based Learning Environments (1995)
4. Jones, M.G.: Guidelines for screen design and user-interface design in computer-based learning environments. The University of Georgia. Dissertation Abstracts International 54(9), 308a–309a (1993)
5. Artiles, A., García, E., De Castro, C., et al.: Wiki tool for adaptive, accesibility, usability, colaborative hypermedia courses: wikicourse. Congress: Current developments in technology-assisted education 2, 84-690-2472-8, 1021–1024 (2006)
6. Burón, F., Artiles, A., García, E., De Castro, C., et al.: e-aprendo, virtual learning management based on moodle. Current Development in Technology-Assisted Education 1, 84-690-2471-X, 40–44 (2006)
7. Nielsen, J.: Usability Inspection Methods. In: CHI Tutorials, pp. 413–414. ACM, New York (1994)
8. Naveteur, J., Freixa i Baque, E.: Individual differences in electrodermal activity as a function of subjects anxiety. Personality and Individual Differences 5, 615–626 (1987)
9. Boucsein, W.: Electrodermal activity. Plenum Press, New York (1992)
10. Katkin, E.S.: Electrodermal lability: A Psychophysiological analysis of individual differences in response to stress. In: Sarason, J.G., Spielberger, C.D. (eds.) Stress and Anxiety. Hemisphere Publishing, CO (1975)
11. Spielberger, C.D., Sarason, I.G., Kulcsar, Z., Van Heck, G.L. (eds.): Stress and Emotion. Series in Stress and Emotion, Anxiety, Anger, and Curiosity, vol. 14. Taylor & Francis/Hemisphere, New York (1991)
12. Nielsen, J.: Usability Engineering. Academic Press, Boston (1993)
13. Alcantud, F.: Nuevas Tecnologías, Viejas Esperanzas. In: VVAA. Nuevas Tecnologías, Viejas Esperanzas: las nuevas tecnologías en el ámbito de la discapacidad y las necesidades educativas especiales. Consejería de Educación y Universidades, Murcia (2000)
14. Dumas, J.S., Redish, J.C.: A practical guide to usability testing. Ablex Publishing Corporation, Norwood (1993)
15. Naveteur, J., Freixa i Baque, E.: Individual differences in electrodermal activity as a function of subjects anxiety. Personality and Individual Differences 5, 615–626 (1987)
16. Boucsein, W.: Electrodermal activity. Plenum Press, New York (1992)
17. Katkin, E.S.: Electrodermal lability: A Psychophysiological analysis of individual differences in response to stress. In: Sarason, J.G., Spielberger, C.D. (eds.) Stress and Anxiety. Hemisphere Publishing, CO (1975)
18. Spielberger, C.D., Sarason, I.G., Kulcsar, Z., Van Heck, G.L. (eds.): Stress and Emotion. Series in Stress and Emotion: Anxiety, Anger, and Curiosity, vol. 14. Taylor & Francis/Hemisphere, New York (1991)

Web 1.0 to Web 3.0 Evolution: Reviewing the Impacts on Tourism Development and Opportunities

M. Hossein Eftekhari, Zeynab Barzegar, and M.T. Isaai

Computer Engineering Department and MBA Department,
Sharif University of Technology, Tehran, Iran
eftekhari@alum.sharif.edu, barzegar@ce.sharif.edu,
isaai@sharif.edu

Abstract. The most important event following the establishmenet of the Internet network was the Web introduced by Tim Berners-Lee. Websites give their owners features that allow sharing with which they can publish their content with users and visitors. In the last 5 years, we have seen some changes in the use of web. Users want to participate in content sharing and they like to interact with each other. This is known as Web 2.0. In the last year, Web 2.0 has reached maturity and now we need a smart web which will be accordingly be called Web 3.0. Web 3.0 is based on semantic web definition. Changing the way of using the web has had a clear impact on E-Tourism and its development and also on business models. In this paper, we review the definitions and describe the impacts of web evolution on E-Tourism.

Keywords: Web 1.0, Web 2.0, Web 3.0, Advertising, Marketing, E-Tourism.

1 Introduction

Web is the internet networ kwherein computers that are joined together via telecommunications infrastructure such as telephones, local networks, wireless networks, satellite, etc. These computers are online. It means that they can be available if it is necessary. When this kind of network is drawn on paper, it looks like a spider's web. So it has come to be known as the'*web*'.

By entering services like chat, users not only connect to each other but also they can interact with the site. So, interaction emerges. But the concept of 'social community' has not been entered in to the web yet. In other words, in communication with sites, the user cannot connect to the site's owner and the goal is up gradation of the internet communities. In communication with the other, users can not spread all the thoughts and therefore it is not possible to criticize each other. whereas, judging and analyzing the thoughts can increase the speed of creativity and invention of new ideas.

In traditional technologies, these kinds of communication did not exist. In Web 2.0 the protocols have been not changed but the use of the services has changed. Web 2.0 affects both the user level and the publisher level. It is just a new way of seeing the new and an existing technologies that helps toward advanced technologies. This results in an improvement in society where everyone knows everything.

F.V. Cipolla Ficarra et al. (Eds.): HCITOCH 2010, LNCS 6529, pp. 184–193, 2011.

Web 3.0 is an expression which points to the future. The word 'Web 2.0' has become common and popular for referring to the completed web, the word 'Web 3.0' has emerged to discuss upcoming Internet changes. Opinions about the next evolution of web are divided. Some theorists argue that emerging the semantic web technology will change the path of web and will lead to artificial intelligence. Other theorists believe that Web 3.0 will increase the speed of internet and web based applications and will improve computer graphics and will impress on web evolution.

Beside web evolutionary history, tourism is changed in some respects. One of the expressions which is used today is "E-Tourism". The result of combination of E-Tourism and Web 2.0 is known asTravel 2.0.

This paper begins by both introducing and explaining the revised generations of the web from Web 1.0 to Web 3.0. In the rest of the paper, the new business models in tourism are investigated and the effects of the web on these are studied. Finally, certain methods for prevalence of tourism via web evolution are presented.

2 Distinction between Web 1.0 and Web 2.0

In general procedure in the new web each service tries to appear as a suitable platform for web user activity [1]. For example, consider Yahoo as a symbol of the old web. The website of Yahoo tried to collect all the essential contents for everyone and gave them to its users. In new web, services do not give the ready contents to the user; users produced the contents themselves and gave them to others. The role of sites and services was just providing safe and suitable platforms.[4]

The figure below is the most important figure that our discussion is based on and we refer to this figure frequently in this paper. The figure is the result of studies of Brian Solis and his research partner. They had chosen 'the conversation prism' or 'the conversation map' as the name of this figure [2].

The figure's word by word analysis can be useful for many concepts of the web. We begin from the center of this picture. *The conversation* is the center and core of new web. This word is all that the structure of the web is analyzed on. Below this word we can see '*the art of listening, learning and sharing*'. Each of these words was arranged carefully. Maybe it seems that the word 'speaking' is missed out here. We believe that it shows the cleverness of Solis. He omitted speaking on purpose. He used art for the description of conversation: the art of listening, the art of learning and the art of sharing.

It is not important whether your material is text, film, video, image, idea, opinion, thought, emotion, etc. Everything is as material here and you are an artist who must enter these materials into the conversation [5]. One must learn how listen to different materials, how to learn through using them and how to share them with each other. In regard to regular changes and the dynamic nature of new web it is not possible to map Web 2.0 completely [3].

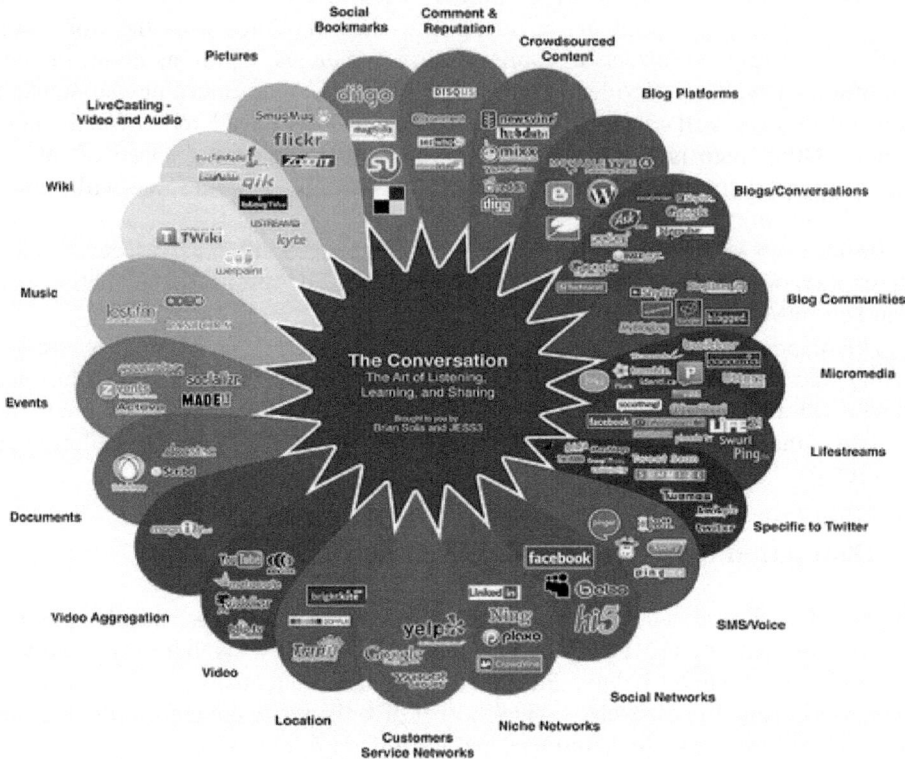

Fig. 1. The conversation prism or map in Web 2.0

3   What Is Web 3.0?

The comments of technologists about Web 3.0 are a sign of the future. Tim Berners-Lee, web inventor said: "people ask always *'what is the web?'* I think that when you huddle some books, it seems scaly and crackly. Web 2.0 and access to semantic web, integrate the huge volume of information. As a result, you can access to information sources unbelievably [6]".

Therefore, the word 'Web 3.0' is used by Berners-Lee firstly to attract attention to it. The World Wide Web innovator introduced the concept of Web 3.0 by writing a scientific paper in 2001. He described Web 3.0 as an environment in which machines and systems can read webpages like human beings [6].

There are many ideas about Web 3.0 in these days. But something that is common among the ideas is the idea of the *semantic*. If we want to show web evolution in a diagram, there is one model we agree on:

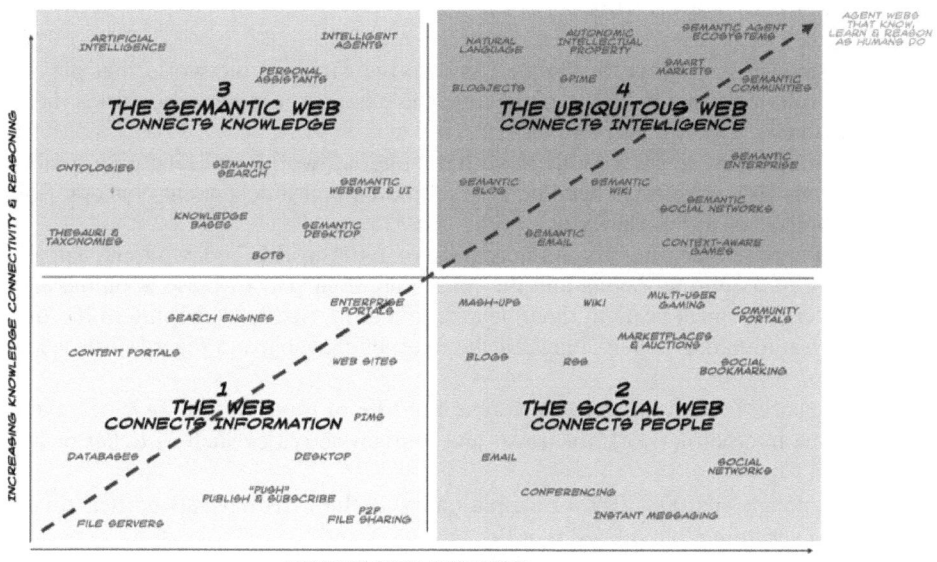

Fig. 2. Web evolution map [13]

As we can see in the diagram, Web 2.0 is more about social networks. But in Web 3.0, the social aspect is less than it was in Web 2.0 and we are going to have knowledge based communities and also the power of semantic technologies to know users and decide what they need.

3.1 A Suitable Model for Web 3.0

In the opinion of most experts, Web 3.0 has dealings with software and vertical domains. Public software similar to markets and vertical industries is going towards a vertical structure in which their general tendency is movement to be applied to the professional requirements [7].

In this way, the web analyzers believe that the social and service-oriented websites which have many users not only could not proceed to make software vertical but also the distance with the future generation of the world web was not decreased.

In their belief, Web 3.0 is defined with a specific formula that must be considered as a model for websites like Google [7].

$$Web\ 3.0 = 4C + P + VS$$

In this formula, 4C refers to content, commerce, community and concept. P means personalization and VS means vertical search in order to limit the search channels. In other words it distinguishes the fields of the search in detail.

With the above description, the Web 3.0 formula can imagine a proper model for a service-oriented website with a wide range of users.

4   Tourism in Electronic World

The tourism industry is one of the well known industries of the world that plays an important role in economy and commerce to the extent that in some countries the national income is largely based on tourism.

The joining of the tourism industry with the internet world could increase financial turnover thus E-Tourism has become an evolutional and independent concept. Some statistics will be of use to clarify this.

There are more than one billion internet users in the world. Today, online activities are thought of as normal habits and the most important part of these is online shopping. Travel is the best issue in three years ago that is used for shopping in the internet and it has remarkable percentage of the internet exchanges in regard of travel and tourism.

Websites are the first information source for 70% of travelers and 48% of travelers use only the internet network for travel and tourism activities such as ticket or hotel reservation [9].

Oddly enough, in 2008, 40% of people online in the USA have spent their time on travel and everything that related to it [9].

In terms of economy, more than 120 billion dollars was exchanged in E-Tourism industry (when?)[9].

All of these numbers show the growth of tourism through information technology and internet. In regard to the upward tendency to web and its evolution like Web 2.0 and Web 3.0 which are discussed about in previous section, in follow sale models in E-Tourism are revised and then the opportunities are presented that are perused in new web fields to extend tourism industry.

4.1   New Sale Models in E-Tourism

Common sales models that are used in e-tourism are described in what follows. All of these models are common in business(?). All models need to access the reservation source in real time in order to ensure website success.

Direct sale Model
In this model the user buys the services directly from supplier; such as reservations and purchases one room from a Hilton Hotel directly via its website.

Meta Search Model
In this model websites are searched using several suppliers and the comparison is possible for the user to choose the best choice and finalize it. 'Kayak.com' is a suitable sample in this model.

Tour Operators Model
These suppliers combine all the travel and tourism transactions(?) and present them in different formats.

Online Intermediary or OTAs Model
In this model, services act as an intermediate. Some services like Dynamic Packaging are presented in which the user can make a journey himself and use every service. The websites give these services in the package format. 'expedia.com' is a good sample for this model.

5   E-Tourism and Web Evolution

The current generation which is known as the digital generation has grown up with the evolution of access to the computer and internet. This generation is different from other previous generation. The individuals in this generation are arguably more intelligent. They search and read and write more than any previous generation. Some of the adolescents write more than 10000 words at online world [8].

This generation tends to pursue the truth and they have highly advanced visual and problem solving skills through gaming and challenging entertainment. They typically read 8 books, 2300 web pages and 1281 Facebook profiles each year. 64% of them never read newspapers. They use the internet more than they watch TV. They are connected to extensive and trusted networks of friends. They increasingly use their phones rather than their computers [8].

According to the above points, this generation follows out these important factors [8]:

- Freedom – Give me choice and the more the better
- Customization – Make it my own
- Scrutiny – I will check it out before I buy
- Integrity – Does this company deserve my money?
- Collaboration – Let me help you make it better
- Entertainment – Make it fun
- Speed – Serve me now
- Innovation – Give me the latest

Now the reason for the rapid improvement of new web – Web 2.0- is obvious. In some kind of industries that people work with system as a user, by use of concepts which exist in Web 2.0 ,communication with individuals and users is simply possible, in order to persuade them to surrender their affairs to the web. In result, the tourism industry can grow up by using Web 2.0 features in any business model for tourism because we are faced with a new generation that needs to have reason and also can read all the experiences of other users and participate to share their thoughts about any service in the tourism area.

5.1   Web 2.0 and E-Tourism

As will be mentioned later, users participate in the content provision of web 2.0. According to the growth of web 2.0 so far, it seems that 70% of web contents will produce within next three-two years and it shows that the websites which support UGC

(User Generated Content) are so user friendly e.g. weblogs, video/ image sharing centers, wikis, reviews, user profiles, and et [4]. on the other hand, when the basis of web content creation is user participation, and virtual marketing appears strongly then the reliance and word of mouth is taken effect on internet seriously.

The best environment for introduction, tourist attraction and also promotion is web 2.0 websites. Figure 3 and figure 4 in below show this fact better [11].

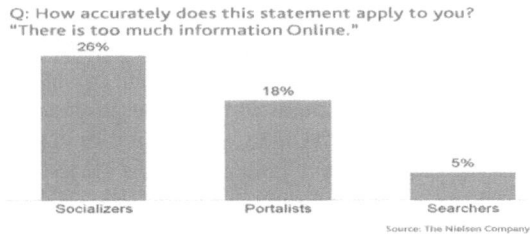

Fig. 3. Survey result in Nielsen

Socializers trust what their friends have to say and social media acts as an information filtration tool. This is key because Socializers gravitate towards and believe what is shared with friends and family. If your friend creates or links to the content, then you are more likely to believe it and like it. And this thought plays out in the data [11].

Fig. 4. Comparison of the survey result in Nielsen

So are social networks replacing portals or search engines? Perhaps. Regardless, if we don't understand and address people feeling increasingly alienated by the amount of information on the Internet, and the need for a human guide, yes, your favorite social network (or something like it) will become the next great content gateway.

In Figure 3 the most effective factors on decision making are recommendation and internet search. As it is mentioned, in UGC websites the contents are generated by the other users, so the role of web 2.0 becomes so clear here. The meaning of the last sentence is understood by the next figure [11].

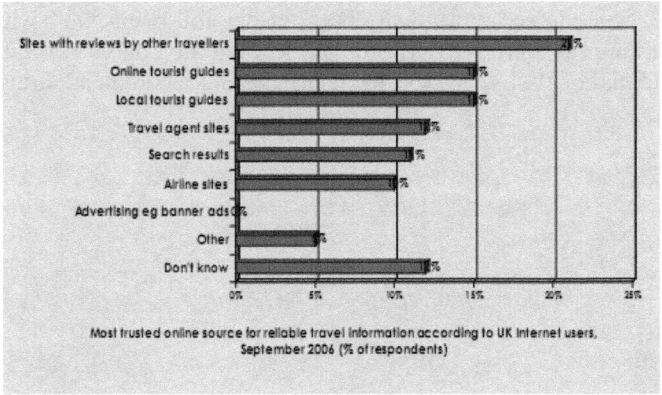

Fig. 5. Public opinion poll about traveling decision making in UK

In terms of reliance and confidence, as it shows in figure 5, 21% of travelers in UK have chosen the websites with others traveler's reviews as a reliable source for decision making. Also for the other 15%, the online tourist guide is a decision making source.

Therefore, the users search for their information via the internet and in regard of web 2.0 growth, the huge information resources have been collected by users themselves and they believe in these resource rather than others. In this case, TripAdvisor.com is the one of the most popular and most important references of tourism information sources in which exist 35 million comments related to all tourism affairs e.g. flights, hotels, tourism services and tourist attraction places [10]. In regard of issues about new generation of web and internet users, it is clear that the best choice for decision making in the field of tourism industry is such websites.

5.2 Example of the Web 2.0 Potential for Tourism Development

Figure 6 is released by two Canadian tourists. When the two tourists were shooting using a self timer on a camera they were faced with this:

Fig. 6. Picture taken by two tourists

Publication of this picture led to the popularity of the photo and created a profile available for this image in Twitter.

In figure 7, you can see more than 2000 persons following the Twitter page that could each be the next tourists to visit the place where that photo was taken. And this shows the potential of Web 2.0 for content sharing and recommendations.

Fig. 7. Example of Twitter page

Another example that can introduce potential tourist attractions is Youtube. *"The battle at the kruger"* a tourist video shot in South Africa has become one of the most popular videos on Youtube. It has been viewed 53,328,053 times and counting. The samples from popular Web 2.0 sites such as Facebook can also be found.

The goal of these samples is to show the potential of Web 2.0 to introduce tourist attractions and publish it directly between the potential tourists.

6   Conclusions

In consideration of the issues mentioned in this article, E-Tourism industry growth in the world has had extensive expansion and its operator is specifically web. The phase of the Web has been changed and Web 2.0 sites attract a large volume of users, the governments must consider the concepts of Web 2.0 in the current E-Tourism industry for tourism development, and also concentrate their marketing strategies in the Great Web 2.0 websites such as Twitter, YouTube, Facebook and other popular sites in this area. The examples given above, show the performance of these websites for empowering tourism market. It seems every business models in E-tourism services should consider about Web 2.0 features and let all users participate in their service, not only expect them to buy and pay money. The services should find a way to user acquisition by providing some feature for participation of users on it. They can get many users and these users are a potential customer for them. It is also important to say that now that Web 2.0 has reached maturity and Web 3.0 with the characteristics mentioned above is on the way. It is natural that the transition from Web 2.0 to Web 3.0 will suffer tourism developments again.

Although we could find the important aspect of Web 3.0, semantic technology, which can have great effects on E-Tourism business models but there are other aspects that no research has done about.

References

1. Orr. B.: Parsing the Meaning of Web 2.0, ABA Banking journal (2007),
   `http://www.ababj.com/`
2. Solis, B.: The Conversation Prism v1.0, http://www.theconversationprism.com (2008)
3. Cooke, M., Buckley, N.: Web 2.0 Social Networks and the Future of Market Research. International Journal of Market Research 50(2), 267–292 (2008)
4. Dearstyne, B.: Blogs, mashups & wikis. The Information Management journal (July 2007)
5. Barlow, T.: Web 2.0: Creating a Classroom without Walls. Teaching Science Magazine 54(1), 46–48 (2008)
6. Berners-Lee, T.: The Evolution of The Internet. Campaign Magazine (2008)
7. Walmesly, A.: The Whys and Wherefores of Web 3.0. Marketing Magazine (2008)
8. Tapscott, D.: Grown up digital: How the net generation is changing your world. McGraw-Hill, New York (2009)
9. Office of Travel and Tourism Industries, US Travel and Tourism Industries: A Year in A Review, US Department of Commerce, International Trade Administration (2009)
10. Trip Advisor (2010), `http://www.tripadvisor.com`
11. Nielsen, J.: Social Media: the next great gateway for content discovery (2009),
    `http://blog.nielsen.com/nielsenwire/online_mobile/social-media-the-next-great-gateway-for-content-discovery/`

Author Index